ENDORSEMENTS

This book is a refreshing reminder of God at work in the world today. We are encouraged to reflect and develop a missional understanding of church that appreciates the roles of the church in the global West and global South, recognizing that the Christian church is the most diverse and inclusive community on earth. The contributors challenge us not to think of "church and mission" as if they were two separate aspects of church but rather the "church in Mission." Its rootedness in Scripture and reflections of "missions praxis" around the world is enriching, and encourages local church leaders to see "mission" as the work and responsibility of each church member wherever they may find themselves.

Esme Bowers, minister of religion at Calvary Sanctuary Full Gospel Church and secretary of the board of directors of the Lausanne Movement

This book is a feast for anyone who is passionately mission minded. With the biblical and theological foundations for missions by the church, the contemporary missiological issues and the case studies on the church in mission, this book is a delight. It addresses the key themes and issues for a strong reflection on the church and mission. Another thing I like about this book is that it is really global in its scope: geographically-wise, gender-wise and generation-wise. All the contributors are not only great commission global leaders, but also passionate and reflective practitioners. Do you want to deepen your ecclesiological and missiological reflections? This a very good place to be. Any reflective practitioner on mission by the church will like this book. It is a must read for any church and missional leader. I am expecting to see it become a book of reference in the mission world.

Younoussa Djao, Africa director, Cityteam International

It is a joy for me to welcome once again a publication from the WEA Mission Commission. Like previous publications, this is a valuable collection of evangelical reflection on practice. Authors come from a rich variety of situations and in some cases from decades of missionary experience in five continents. They engage in theological dialogue with both classic and contemporary theologians, and they also offer us fresh approaches to the understanding of Scripture with questions forged in missionary practice in places as diverse as Brazil, Singapore, Poland, or the USA. This book is evidence that evangelical missionary commitment continues to be alive around the world, but also that practitioners are engaged in a critical reflection about their practice.

Dr. Samuel Escobar, professor emeritus of missiology, Palmer Theological Seminary, presently teaching in the Facultad Protestante de Teología UEBE, Madrid, Spain

Like the Book of Acts, *The Church in Mission: Foundations and Global Case Studies* captures and conveys the acts of the Holy Spirit as he leads the global church in carrying out the mission of God at a time when mission has become multifaceted, multidirectional, multilateral and multifarious, involving multiple players from multiple backgrounds with multiple roles. However, unlike the Book of Acts which was authored by one individual, Luke the physician-missionary, the multiple authors of *The Church in Mission* from multiple mission-contexts and trans-generational scope, make *The Church in Mission* enlightening and enriching for any serious minded believer who wants to understand and key into the last age of mission.

Reading through the pages of the *The Church in Mission: Foundations and Global Case Studies* has helped me to appreciate the fact that the mission of the church is the same as it has been in the past because it is led and directed by the same Holy Spirit whom the Lord of the Harvest has sent to drive this mission of God throughout the ages. I therefore commend this book to all who are waiting for the return of the King, while we are occupying till he comes back!

Dr. Reuben Ezemadu, international director, Christian Missionary Foundation (CMF) and continental coordinator, Movement for African National Initiatives (MANI)

The theme "the church in mission" remains one of the most critical subjects for today's global mission. This book weaves together solid biblical theological reflections, contemporary missiological issues and real-life case studies from scholars and practitioners of different continents on the subject of church in mission. Similar to other books published by WEA, this book once again carries deep level scholarly reflection as well as relevant contemporary applications for anyone committed to global mission. I highly recommend this book to you.

Dr. Patrick Fung, OMF International

We live in the age where the churches are connected on a global scale. Therefore, this encounter of various understandings of the church and mission across the globe is invaluable and came at a propitious time. This book yields a wonderful insight into global churches' understanding on the church and its mission based on its comprehensive collection.

Chulho Han, director, Mission Partners Korea

This book is indeed a treasure chest, not just for evangelicals, but for all who are eager to bring together church, gospel, and mission. We sorely need the theological and practical dialogue between ecclesiology and missiology lest we end up with a missionless church or a churchless mission. The strength of this volume is that it is scripturally based and includes solid critical analysis. And then, of course, it includes the manifold case studies from all corners of the world. These cases make the book a genuine treasure chest.

Dr. Knud Jørgensen, PhD, adjunct professor at MF Norwegian School of Theology, one of the editors of the Regnum Edinburgh Centenary Series

The twenty-first century provides the global church with incredible and tremendous opportunity for the advancement of the gospel in human history. The world is indeed flat and human advancement in all respects and divine interventions have created an opportune moment for the church and heightened the hope to finish the awesome task of spreading the good news to the ends of the earth.

Every generation is called upon to reflect on its past, reassess its present and reimagine the future as impacted by the church. And then, redesign strategies with the view of realigning them with God's revealed truth and God's heart for the nations.

This incredible work undertaken by WEA-MC could not have come at the better time! It unequivocally locates the church as God's missional instrument and a conduit in the fulfillment of one the greatest tasks ever conceived by the Godhead—that of Christ reconciling the alienated world to himself through the power of the Spirit, who convicts humanity of sin, judgement, and convinces them of the better promise of life eternal. It also reaffirms the church as a movement that defies every conceived human barrier seeking to confine, limit, and render it ineffective and irrelevant.

Church in Mission does not shy away from the basics, and yet with freshness, it restates the foundational principles and provides practical ways of engaging our culture with the view of transforming our communities. I highly commend this resource with the hope that it will help create a "missional revolution" in our lifetime.

Ndaba Mazabane, chairman of the International Council of the World Evangelical Alliance

One of the realities of the state of the church in mission is that it must include global case studies. Once we talked of the global church as if it were a visible reality. Today we ignore that reality at our own peril. God is moving across the world and continuing to call the church in mission. God's mission has a church and that church is missional. This new volume provides contemporary evidence of that inextricable link. The writers represent some of the more dynamic perspectives in missions today. This volume represents a compelling reason to support the World Evangelical Alliance Mission Commission. Collaboration in work and reporting are essential for adequately discerning God's work in the world. Thankfully in these pages is yet another confirmation that God's mission has a church!

Dr. Doug McConnell, provost, Fuller Seminary

This timely book on "The Church in Mission" displays once more the WEA Mission Commission's commitment to remain biblically based, globally diverse, and creative in producing relevant materials to help the global church measure up to her mission to reach the world with the gospel of Jesus Christ and address new missiological challenges in contemporary religious, sociological, and economic issues in various contexts. Mission practitioners, professors, students, as well as global church leaders will be compelled through the reading and study of this book to remain rooted in the biblical and theological foundations which firmly establish the raison d'être of the church in Mission today and always.

Dr. Abel Ndjerareou, former president of Bangui Evangelical School of Theology (FATEB)

Church in Mission: Foundations and Global Case Studies offers readers an impressive collage of international perspectives on key missiological issues. Essays addressing theological foundations and current issues are complimented by case studies that illustrate how the church lives out its mission in a diversity of settings. Church in Mission makes a welcome contribution to the ongoing global conversation on theology and mission.

Dr. Craig Ott, professor of mission and intercultural studies, Trinity Evangelical Divinity School

The church, the people called out by God and the followers of Jesus Christ, is going through many stages of understanding to make sure that communities of people worship, live godly and missionally-minded as the called-out people of God. To understand this the articles establish the theology of Ecclesia, helping the readers to understand the "church" beyond the denominational, colonial, and regional models. The question of church-based mission or mission-based church has been lurking for the past 2000 years! Once we have solved the complimentary effects of "church and mission organizations," we then move on to different models of churches which impact different sectors of the world in different societies and show how God works in different ways. May you enjoy reading these articles to strengthen your views of church in mission. I strongly recommend the book.

Dr. K. Rajendran, associate director for Strategic Thinking, Leadership Development and Global Roundtables, World Evangelical Alliance Mission Commission, based in Bangalore India

If historians write about early twenty-first century Christians, what will they say? If our lives (individually and collectively) are, by God's grace and our hard work, shaped by the thinking of this book, they will describe an authentic, vibrant, relevant, faithful, united, Spirit-filled and mission-shaped church

We're indebted to the WEA Mission Commission for asking various authors, all "reflective practitioners," to help us struggle with various biblical tensions, including those between perceived "faithfulness" and "relevance" (the Bible's own tension, in its own contextualization).

Our prayer is that their helpful writings will stimulate the building of healthy missional communities, at a time of bewilderingly rapid global change—so that His Kingdom might come, His will might be done on earth, as it is in heaven.

Gordon Showell-Rogers, associate secretary general, World Evangelical Alliance

This book is an amazing gift to the global body of Christ. It sets in perspective the mission mandate of the church and gives great insights into diverse approaches to bringing the gospel of the Kingdom to hundreds of millions around the world. Every pastor, mission leader and theological student should read this book. We applaud Bertil and his team for doing such a splendid job in producing this most relevant book for our time.

Peter Tarantal, associate international director: OM International and chairman of the WEA Mission Commission

My passion is the church, with a particular focus on the local assembly of believers, in whatever form or context or language or stage of development. I am very grateful to God for this new resource produced by our Mission Commission. It was conceived and birthed with a keen eye on the global church of Jesus Christ in all of its manifestations. It is comprehensive on its biblical and theological reflections, deals with contemporary issues on church and mission, and provides contextual case studies of different expressions of the church. The worldwide church is richer because of this publication.

Bishop Efraim Tendero, secretary general of the World Evangelical Alliance

The Church in Mission: Foundations and Global Case Studies reaches the purpose expressed in its title, which is to be theologically and biblically well-rooted. While the gospel, the church, and mission have the Bible and its conviction as reference, this is taken into consideration in the light and experiences of thirty-one well-experienced writers. Together they relate mission-based convictions to the world around us, which is diverse in culture and language contexts. In other words, what is the gospel, the church, and mission to a world full of real people? I recommend this book highly.

Silas Tostes, director of the Antioch Mission, Brazil and executive director of the Brazilian Evangelical Alliance

Don't just dip into this book. But take my advice and don't try to read it all the way through from the start. There is a lot of excellent food to digest. Go and whet your appetite with Part Three first. That way you will not only appreciate the rich teaching of what the Bible's gospel says the church in mission should be about (Part One), nor only wrestle with what some fine missiologists think the church in mission should (or should not) be doing (Part Two), you will already be excited by a fascinating range of individuals and churches and what they actually are doing in mission. Or rather, what God has done and is doing through them, which seems rather more important.

Dr. Christopher J. H. Wright, Langham Partnership, author of The Mission of God

THE CHURCH IN MISSION

THE CHURCH IN MISSION

Foundations and Global Case Studies

Bertil Ekström, editor

Foreword by William D. Taylor

WILLIAM CAREY
LIBRARY

Published by William Carey Library
1605 E. Elizabeth St.
Pasadena, CA 91104 | www.missionbooks.org

Koe Pahlka, editor and graphic design
Julia Evans, cover design
Koe Pahlka, indexer

William Carey Library is a ministry of
Frontier Ventures | www.frontierventures.org

Printed in the United States of America
20 19 18 17 16   5 4 3 2 1 BP1500

Library of Congress Cataloging-in-Publication Data
Names: Ekström, Bertil (Executive Director) editor.
Title: The church in mission : foundations and global case studies / Bertil
   Ekström, editor ; foreword by William D. Taylor.
Description: Pasadena, CA : William Carey Library, 2016. | Series:
   Globalization of mission series | Includes bibliographical references and
   index.
Identifiers: LCCN 2015042891| ISBN 9780878080533 (pbk.) | ISBN 0878080538
   (pbk.)
Subjects: LCSH: Church. | Missions. | Mission of the church.
Classification: LCC BV600.3 .C477 2016 | DDC 266--dc23 LC record available at http://lccn.loc.gov/2015042891

CONTENTS

PART THREE: CHURCH IN MISSION: CASE STUDIES

FOREWORD

William D. Taylor

I start with two analogies.

It is a delight to "fore-word" this book on the nature of the church in mission. It reminds me of two very different sensory metaphor-realities that require explanation. First, the Newton Circus food court I first visited one evening in Singapore back in 1986—the year I began serving with the WEA Mission Commission. It was an open-air culinary feast of all foods birthed out of South East Asia (and beyond), ready for you to make your succulent (and for some of us, first-ever) choices.

The book's table of contents reflects that menu-feast. It will nourish you, and perhaps challenge your missiological taste buds. It will also be a cross-cultural specialization. The thirty-one writers come from twenty-one nations, a distinctive of the WEA Mission Commission "Globalization of Mission" series of books (the full list is in the appendix). Our authors are women and men, younger and older, tested by the fires of cross-cultural ministry and ecclesiology. Some serve on the very cutting edge of the advancing church, and others in the context of the church in decline, burned over, desperately needing the fresh winds of the Spirit of God (i.e., Europe).

We invite you to engage here with the biblical and theological foundations of gospel, church, and mission; move on to some of the contemporary missiological issues; rejoice and grow as you evaluate the many case studies—from Europe to Ethiopia, from Japan to Brazil—and more. A contextualization banquet awaits you.

Second, this resource also recalls that fabled story of the five (or six or seven) Indian blind men trying to describe an elephant. Is the elephant a large hose, a spear, a fan, a wall, a tree, a snake, a brush, or something more? Why can't people agree on MY definition of church? Or of mission? Or even gospel? Good grief! Must we be globally confused?

What I appreciate about this book is its rootedness in Scripture, in a robust gospel, in global mission, in the cross-cultural advance of the church of Christ—universal and invisible. At the same time, those realities are worked out in the stuff of time and space, in our cultures and languages, in geographies and human lives.

The Genesis of an MC Publication

The publication emerges out of an Mission Commission (MC) process having to do with the issues of church on mission: it started with an interest group, which then morphed into a formal discussion under the leadership of its eventual editor, Dr. Bertil Ekström. That led to a face-to-face consultation in Glasgow with some of the key players, which in turn generated a global search for a potential table of contents and strategic writers. Then we begin the long process of writer commitment and chapter production by the deadline—always extended. Kudos to Bertil and team (especially Rose Dowsett), and to Koe Pahlka, our gifted editorial expert, with her flowing manuscript. The process then moved to William Carey Library with Jeff Minard and their leadership team.

The long conception and gestation process finally leads to the birth of a new MC Globalization of Mission book , which you have in your hands.

Personal Challenges

But this book has forced me to reflect again on the nature of the biblical term, "church." In my childhood in Latin America, the churches we were part of were physical places, individual congregations of God's gathered people. In my early childhood (back in the 1940s and 1950s), church was the only entertainment in town for the evangelical minority. And one thing was clear to all of us. We were NOT Roman Catholic. Thus our churches were negatively characterized by many things to ensure we could not be confused with the Roman Catholic world. The organization was simple, non-hierarchical, and many times led by lay pastors with deacons and elders; the architecture was boxy and functional without a hint of beauty; we had definitions for the church spectrum—from preaching point to informal congregation to organized church (in one country a "church" was defined as one with at least ten men (assumed that women were part of it but that men were counted), deacons, elders, and some kind of pastor leading the church. That's what I grew up with. Contextualization and importation of models, structure, and organization were not items of consideration. Our hymnbook was a translation of the Christian and Missionary Alliance USA hymnbook. The back inside cover even had a suggested order of service for us low-church folk.

Of course, we now know that the failures of uncontextualized ministry are not the shortcomings of just those servants from the global North. Brazilians, Nigerians, Koreans, and so many today are committing the same mistakes, and hopefully are learning from them.

Thank God for his patient Holy Spirit, for there was hope even for many of us, locked in history but yet seeking new patterns and models and ways of being and doing church.

Over my seventy-five years of life and fifty years of cross-cultural ministry, the ecclesiastical pilgrimage has taken my wife and me through various streams of the church: from Presbyterian to independent, to Guatemalan denomination, to Evangelical Free Church, to a more Plymouth Brethren sample, to the Bible church, to the charismatic church, and ending up in the Anglican stream. At times I smile when I think of this church journey, and that now I would be a confirmed Anglican—a radical departure from my roots. Perhaps it helps that our church is woven together by three strands: Scripture (evangelical), Spirit (charismatic), Sacrament (formalized, historic liturgy). Some of my older friends wonder where next.

I could take the time to engage the issues of "gospel" and "mission," but let me focus on just one, "church." How do we define "church" in this book? Well, get ready for a variety of working definitions and perhaps no shared-by-all version. Yet there will be shared values that produce a complex theology and practice of the church.

Our colleague, Dr. Kent Parks, veteran Asia-based servant, coleader of the global Ethné network and president of Act Beyond, has shared some of the "church" definitions and descriptions that they work with in Asia—and it is really a process of development. They move from unbelievers to baptized believers to a group to a church. In a sense this is a version of evolving ground zero ecclesiology. More or less in Kent's words:

> *Discovery groups:* The starting ground of nonbelievers moving toward (we pray and believe) to being ekklesia (church). As seen in Luke 10 and Acts 10, etc., a person of peace who is hungry for spiritual relationship has gathered/opened his/her group to learn together of God. The group meets regularly to be discipled to faith by seeking to obey what they discover in Scripture.

> *Baptized believers:* People who show public commitment to follow Jesus through public baptism. Like in the book of Acts where all but three people come to faith in groups, most people are baptized with their "oikos" (household/social unit). Existing social groups being baptized together is occurring globally.

> *Group:* A regular meeting of persons being discipled to faith and/or followers of Christ to learn to obey the commands of Jesus. DBS (Discovery Bible Studies) and T4T (Training for Teachers) formats typical of the group meeting process.

> *"Ekklesia" ("out-called") or Church:* An ekklesia is a "loving and obeying Jesus" group of baptized believers who are feeding the poor, helping widows, healing the sick, sharing the good news, discipling other groups to become ekklesia, casting out demons, etc. These distinctives are because of the focus on obedience-based discipleship rather than merely knowledge-based discipleship. They carry out ekklesia functions such as summarized in Acts 2:37–47, (e.g., recognized leaders, gathering together, and self-identity as an ekklesia). In some areas these movements do not call it an ekklesia until the group has started another ekklesia.

> Another distinctive of the church—because of the focus on obedience-based discipleship and inherent in Acts 2 and other Bible passages on church—is that if they are not feeding the poor, healing the sick, and helping the widow, they are not fulfilling the Acts 2 descriptions.

So when does a group become a church? That's a mystical issue, and only in the heart of God will it ever be fully sorted out. My wife and I in Guatemala City, circa 1971, helped start a Discovery Bible Study that grew into a group and then, about two years later, became a church. So what happened? It was the group consensus that they wanted to become a church and not just be a group that met regularly to worship, build community, learn from Scripture, reach those without Christ. It was after that change of identity that we began to baptize new believers. We might have celebrated the Lord's Supper before but I'm not sure.

What about my InterVarsity group back in university days. Was it a local church? As Christian students we gathered regularly on campus to build community, we engaged Scripture, we worshiped, we evangelized. But no, it was not a local church and did not have that sense of self-identification. Neither did it celebrate the sacraments of Holy Communion and baptism.

So can some of the "insider groups" be churches? Perhaps so and perhaps not. Only the Spirit really knows. But there must be a process to self-realization that they want to be something similar to those Christian communities of the book of Acts that became "churches."

These and many other issues swirl in and around these thirty-three chapters. Engage with this variegated community of evangelical, missional, global, and diverse writers, together reflecting the challenging edges of the global church on mission. This is an important book to all who grapple with these central issues of church, gospel, and integral mission. We are forced to think theologically, biblically, missiologically, practically. We are invited into that rich fellowship of the "reflective practioners," those women and men who in the midst of ministry praxis, take time to ask hard questions, all because they are anointed by the Spirit to exercise their gifts in the multifaceted global community of the church and in the churches.

Be nourished; be stretched; be encouraged; pass it on.

INTRODUCTION

Bertil Ekström

What does it mean today to be a church totally committed to the gospel and fully engaged in God's mission? What major religious and sociological trends in our world are affecting the role of the global church and local churches? How must we understand and be prepared to face these trends? How do we define "church" in the twenty-first century, being faithful to the Scriptures and at the same time relevant to a generation that does not believe in the institutional church anymore? What are some good models of missional churches in different regions of the world that will encourage and inspire those who long to see a church making difference in society and in the world?

These are some of the issues that the book you are holding in your hands addresses. There are certainly no final answers and magical forms; rather, we present a broad and deep discussion on how the gospel should be lived out by Jesus' followers in our time and through our communities. Questions are raised and analyzed both from the perspective of a local church as well as from a global and general understanding of the Christian church. Some of our examples will focus more on local realities, others more on global challenges.

Of course, many books have been written on ecclesiology and missiology. It is not uncommon that these two areas of theology are treated as completely separate and almost as competing realities. "Church" has been seen exclusively as the locally established community or the denominational structure. On the other hand, mission is seen as a mobile, non-static activity, done outside the church and many times far away from the sending church. In theological seminaries we train either pastors or missionaries, as if they were two completely different kinds of Christian workers.

Undoubtedly God calls people into different ministries and one's main focus varies from person to person. However, the dichotomy between church and mission has in many cases led to churches that are not mission-minded and to missionary work that is not church-minded. It has also created the false idea that missionary work and mission organizations are not "church" but something parallel to the church, often called parachurch movements. Fortunately we have many good exceptions and some of them you will find in this anthology.

The first part of the book is dedicated to a biblical and theological reflection on gospel, church, and mission. It includes Old and New Testament studies on the theological implications of being church, based on the biblical narrative.

The second part deals with a variety of contemporary missiological issues related to the broader theme of church and mission. Different perspectives from current discussions and dialogues around the globe are included, covering both ideological reflections and practical aspects of being a mission-shaped church.

The third part presents regional and national case studies that show the enormous creativity in church planting and engagement of local communities in their own societies. Models applied in the secularized Europe are contrasted to ways of functioning as church in fast growing congregations in the global South.

As in most of the books produced by the Mission Commission of the World Evangelical Alliance, this resource is marked by diversity of perspectives and of the geographical and denominational realities. Although we develop a common theme, no attempt has been made to force the chapters into a pre-established or uniform theology or ecclesiastic tradition. Each author is responsible for his or her own text. Nevertheless they are all evangelicals, leaders committed to the gospel and with a passion for the church of the Lord Jesus Christ, engaged in the mission of God.

The book has also another characteristic in common with other WEAMC books: it started with a reflection group out of the MC Global Missiology Task Force. It has been enriched with new texts over the period of several years. It is not an instant piece of work done in a hurry in order to compete with other literature but well-thought out and slowly matured material that we believe will be of blessing and help to many.

We are grateful to all who have contributed to this book and particularly to the team that has been responsible for leading the project. The members are Rose Dowsett (Scotland), David Ruiz (Guatemala), Tom Hayes (USA), Rita Rimkiene (Lithuania/UK), Paul Coulter (North Ireland), Paul Joshua (India), Richard Tiplady (UK/Scotland) and Bertil Ekström (Sweden/Brazil). All contributed key chapters.

A special word of thanks goes to Rose Dowsett who has done most of the language correction and to Koe Pahlka who has transformed the chapters into a well-formatted manuscript. I am thankful for my friend and colleague Dr. William Taylor, coordinator of the publication program of the MC, whose support and advice have been decisive for the production of this book. We are also grateful to William Carey Library that once again has agreed to publish one of our WEAMC books.

For me personally, it has been a significant and invaluable journey to work with these texts. Having served both as a pastor and as a mission executive involved in training leaders for the established church and for mission outreach, I have been forced to reflect in a much deeper way what it means to be a mission-shaped and missional church in our days. It is clear that a single model will not fit all in every place, but the challenge to offer today's generation of believers a stimulating place for worship, spiritual growth, diaconal ministry, true fellowship, and community service is really paramount. Our prayer is that this book will help us to take a new step in that direction.

Örebro, September 2015

Part One

BIBLICAL AND THEOLOGICAL FOUNDATIONS:

GOSPEL, CHURCH, AND MISSION

CHAPTER 1

THE GOOD LIFE?

Reflections on the Highest Goals of Human Life

Richard Tiplady

Riots and Reflections

During the summer of 2011, with the outbreak of rioting and looting that convulsed several English cities, I found myself unable to get away from the question of what is "the good life" and how do we define it in a society like the United Kingdom.

I found it interesting that much of what was looted from shops during that time were the symbols of our mainstream consumer culture: expensive trainer shoes, fashion clothing, smartphones and flat-screen televisions. Our culture aspires to such symbols, and those who looted seized the opportunity of acquiring these things free, even though some could clearly have afforded to buy them. Blackberry's Messenger service, BBM, was blamed for the coordination of the crowds who came to loot, so it wasn't being done by people who couldn't afford to buy such items.

Our politicians and media tried to occupy the moral high ground, but had no rights to do so: they themselves were caught up at the time in scandals over expense claims by some Members of Parliament (MPs) and phone-hacking by journalists. Some MPs had availed themselves of as much "free stuff" as the looters, just in different ways. Further, the economic stimulus actions of recent years have all been aimed at increasing consumerism, thus inflating the very bubble that led to the worldwide economic crash in the first place.

There is, therefore, a fairly clear idea of "the good life" circulating in my culture, shared across class and ethnicity, based on consuming, spending, and possessing.

I found myself wondering whether and how we as Christians really differ from those around us. True, some churches got involved in riot clean-up activities, but so did many other people. So it wasn't distinctively Christian, even if it was a good thing to do. Most of us Christians aspire to similar things as those around us: I live in a nice house, I drive a nice car, I have good quality clothes, a decent flat-screen television, a good laptop, a tablet computer, and a smartphone, and I take good holidays in warm places. So I'm not that different from those around me.

The thought also struck me that our current missional focus in the West is often aimed at demonstrating "community" to a lonely, disparate, "networked" society. But isn't that what gang culture offers to its members as well?

Augustine and the Good Life

Augustine's concept of the *Summom Bonum* came to mind and I dug out my old copy of *The City of God* and began to look at what that great theologian had to say about Christian hope and responsibility when one's society and culture appear to be on the verge of collapse.

Augustine addressed the question of the *Summom Bonum* (the Final, Ultimate, Sovereign or Highest Good) because it was a matter of great interest to the Greek philosophical traditions with which he was engaging. It is that "to which we refer all our actions, which we seek for its own sake, not for any ulterior end, and the attainment of which leaves us nothing more to seek for our happiness" (*City of God*, VIII.8). He goes on to observe that most Greek philosophers located it in the human mind, body, or a combination of both, and mostly they did not seek to locate it beyond man himself. The one exception to this was Plato, who located it in the enjoyment of God: "Plato defined the Sovereign Good as the life in accordance with virtue; and he declared that this was possible only for one who had the knowledge of God and who strove to imitate him; this was the sole condition of happiness" (VIII.8).

Augustine's approval of Platonism ensured that it became influential in Christian theology until the rediscovery of Aristotle by Thomas Aquinas and his scholastic contemporaries eight hundred years later. Augustine could write: "There are philosophers who have conceived of God, the supreme and true God, as the author of all created things, the light of knowledge, the truth of doctrine and the blessedness of life. They may be called, most suitably, Platonists; or they may give some other title to their school. ... Whoever they may have been, we rank such thinkers above all others and acknowledge them as representing the closest approximation to our Christian position" (VIII.9).

Augustine outlines the various possible alternatives of the Final Good as offered by Greek philosophers, many of which sound rather contemporary: "Men long for pleasure, which is a stimulation of the bodily senses that gives delight; or for repose, the state in which the person suffers no bodily distress; or for a combination of the two (which Epicurus lumps together under the one name of pleasure)" (XIX.1) or the Stoic "first things according to nature," being "the wholeness and health of the body's parts and the sound condition of the whole organism." He expands this to include not just a relaxed and healthy life but also involvement in one's community or with friends: "the first, without being slothful, is still a life of leisure passed in the consideration of truth or the quest for it; the second is busily engaged in the world's affairs" (XIX.2) and "this happy life is social, and for its own sake values the good of friends as its own, just as it wishes for them, for their own sake, what it wishes for itself" (XIX.3).

All of this sounds perfectly reasonable, but this was Augustine. *The City of God* was written primarily in response to the Visigoths' sack of Rome in 410, for which Catholic Christianity was blamed, and so he was in no way minded to affirm such aspirations. On the contrary, for Augustine the City of God is characterized by those who forget earthly pleasures in order to commit themselves to the eternal truths of the Christian faith, in contrast with the City of Man whose inhabitants immerse themselves in the cares and pleasures of this passing world.

The effect of Augustine's idea of the City of God was to develop the Christian idea of heaven as a spiritual place for which we long, and this world as a place through which we are simply passing. He describes the Christian view very simply—"eternal life is the Supreme Good"—and goes on to show the weakness and risks inherent in locating the *Summom Bonum* in the mind, the body, social or community life (XIX.4–9). He then repeats the Christian position (as he sees it), rather cleverly changing the meaning of the Bible passage he quotes to suit his purposes: "the name of the City [of God] itself has a mystical significance, for 'Jerusalem,' as I have already said, means 'vision of peace' [here alluding to Psalm 147:12–14]. But the word 'peace' is freely used in application to the events of this mortal state, where there is certainly no eternal life; and so I have preferred to use the term 'eternal life' instead of 'peace' in describing the end of this City, where its Ultimate Good will be found" (XIX.11). For Augustine, then, the Ultimate Good is eternal life, in conscious contradistinction to this life.

Augustine was clearly heavily influenced by the Platonism he admired, quoting as he does from a Greek comedy to illustrate his argument of the inadequacy of locating the *Summom Bonum* in social life: "I married a wife, and misery I found! Children were born, and they increased my cares" (XIX.5). This somewhat cynical and despairing quotation is far removed in tone and aspiration from the longings and ideals expressed in the Old Testament:

> I know that there is nothing better for people than to be happy and to do good while they live. That each of them may eat and drink, and find satisfaction in all their toil— this is the gift of God. (Eccl 3:12–13)

> This is what I have observed to be good: that it is appropriate for a person to eat, to drink and to find satisfaction in their toilsome labor under the sun during the few days of life God has given them—for this is their lot. Moreover, when God gives someone wealth and possessions, and the ability to enjoy them, to accept their lot and be happy in their toil—this is a gift of God. They seldom reflect on the days of their life, because God keeps them occupied with gladness of heart. (Eccl 5:18–20)

This last quotation from Ecclesiastes links us quite nicely back to the 2011 riots and looting in England, the question of what this tells us about the *Summom Bonum* of our contemporary Western culture, and what we as Christians might have to say in response to this. The looting of flat-screen televisions, smartphones, and fashion clothing tells us something about what these people value as the Ultimate Good. But before we get too condemnatory, we should recognize that all they were doing was "finding a way of joining the party," as one journalist noted:

Obscene inequalities of wealth have disfigured our civil society, so is it any wonder that the dispossessed stop playing by the rules? We have created a world in which human worth is measured by crude material gain—is it surprising then that those without decide to acquire it by whatever means?

Ecclesiastes seems to say more that connects with the *Summom Bonum* of contemporary Western society than does Augustine. For even today's "feral youth," when asked, say that what they really want are the things that most of us aspire to, that is, a job, a home, a husband or wife, and children. It is the perceived difficulty in attaining or sustaining such aspirations that drives them to frustration and anger. To give them Augustine's message—the pleasures of this world are passing, and what you should be longing for is heaven—might sound Christian, but is it really going to connect?

And is it really even that Christian? For, as I have suggested, Augustine was perhaps overly influenced by the Platonism to which he sought to respond. Is "heaven" or "eternal life" really the *Summom Bonum* for Christians? Or would it be better to say that our *Summom Bonum* is "resurrection"?

The Good Life: Living in the Light of the Resurrection

New Testament scholar Dominic Crossan asks a provocative question about the resurrection of Jesus: "If Jesus did rise from the dead, then so what? Very nice for him, but what's it got to do with anything else? Why should he be so specially favored? If God can pull off a stunt like that, why can't he intervene and do a lot more useful things like stopping genocide and earthquakes?"

German theologian Wolfhart Pannenburg gives a clear answer to this question in his book *Jesus: God and Man*, summarizing the implications of the resurrection of Jesus for his followers and his contemporaries: "In the historical context of first-century Palestine, the resurrection of Jesus from the dead did not need to be interpreted—it would automatically be understood as the beginning of the general resurrection of the dead, as the beginning of the last days."

The New Testament presents Jesus' resurrection as the foretaste, the "first fruits," of the resurrection of the dead that the Jews expected at the end of the age (1 Cor 15:20–23). As such it has brought the full saving work of God into human history. Resurrection takes as its basis the assumption that there is something fundamentally good about bodily life, that it was created by God and that it is not evil (in supposed contrast to the good "spiritual" life). The resurrection of Jesus affirms that this life is not meaningless, nor has it been abandoned by God.

If the last days have begun in the resurrection of Christ, then all the expectations of the Old Testament are fulfilled in Christ. Nicholas Wolterstorff notes, "Israel's religion was a religion of salvation, not of contemplation—that is what accounts for the mantra of the widows, the orphans, the aliens and the poor. (It is) not a religion of salvation from this earthly existence, but a religion of salvation from injustice in this earthly existence." In Jesus, the "first-born from the dead" (Col 1:18; Rev 1:5), God has broken into the world, establishing his reign of righteousness and justice, not just at the end of the age as the Jews expected, but in history itself. Creating a better future for this world is not an afterthought to the gospel, as if it were an extra, a mere add-on. It is part of it.

If this is what God did and is doing through the resurrection of Jesus, then how will he bring it about? Not by magic, but through the church, the people of God. This may sound like a bold claim to others, but it is unavoidable. Perhaps surprisingly, the church is also called the "first fruits" in the New Testament (2 Thess 2:13; Jas 1:18) and so we are part of this resurrection work of God. We are called by God to be his people, set apart for him, who will be a sign and an agent of his purposes that will ultimately be fulfilled and completed at the end (1 Cor 15:24). Before we get too carried away with this claim, we should note its sobering responsibility. God's resurrection work is not just to be served by the church, but to be exemplified by it and embodied in it. In many of his letters, Paul sees the church as the new humanity, Jew and Gentile united, no longer hostile and divided but one. For this reason he found Christian unity essential to our mission. Our disunity and conflict is a scandal, and something which rightly undermines the very claims we make about God.

At the very end of a very long exposition of the implications of Jesus' resurrection, Paul writes: "Always give yourselves fully to the work of the Lord, because you know that your labor in the Lord is not in vain." Because of Jesus' resurrection, our work is not in vain. Because of Jesus' resurrection, what we do matters. The resurrection of Christ demands a personal response to Christ, and a personal commitment to his cause. Evangelism is not just announcing the great fact of the resurrection of Jesus (Acts 17:18, 31–32) and inviting a response, it is also an invitation to join with the great cause of God.

The scope and impact of Jesus' resurrection is not just national, but global. An Old Testament expectation of God's work in the last days would be that all peoples would worship Israel's God (Isa 60:1–3). We should see the Spirit-led explosion of mission in Acts 8–11 as the first example of this. First Samaritans, then an Ethiopian, then Cornelius the Roman soldier, and finally Greeks in Antioch—all of them respond to the message of Jesus. Paul's mission from Antioch in Acts 13 is not the first Christian mission; it was just the next step in something that began with the resurrection of Jesus and the outpouring of the Spirit at Pentecost, and is something which has continued to this very day.

In the death and resurrection of Jesus, God has decisively and finally broken into human history, to bring his redemption and transformation to the whole of life. This fact demands a personal response—not just our allegiance, but our whole life, committed to God's purposes. If we understand "heaven" not as our final destination but as the "place" where the will of God is done (Matt 6:10), then perhaps one of the best descriptions of life in the light of Jesus' resurrection is "grabbing chunks of heaven and dragging them down to earth."

And if this is our calling and our purpose as Christians, then perhaps we have something concrete to say about an alternative *Summom Bonum*, one which leads to transformed lives today, lived for others and for God.

Questions for Reflection:

1. Describing Christians in the Western culture, Tiplady says that "most of us Christians aspire to similar things as those around us." Is that a true picture of believers also in other cultures? How does that notion of "good life" affect the church community today?

2. In light of the author's reflection on the Ultimate Good, how can the gospel be presented as a valid and relevant alternative to the current understanding of good life in our societies?

3. How could the church in your context be "grabbing chunks of heaven and dragging them down to earth"? Give some concrete examples.

Richard Tiplady is the Principal of the Scottish School of Christian Mission (previously known as International Christian College). He is passionate about finding ways to respond to the missionary challenge of the West, and has served in leadership roles in mission for many years. He has written extensively on the changing nature of world mission, and is keen to invest his energies in developing creative and innovative leaders in mission. He is married to Irene, who works in a mental health project in one of the most deprived council estates in Scotland, and they have one son, Jamie, who is a computer game designer.

CHAPTER 2

WHY GOD IS CALLING OUT A PEOPLE

Tom Hayes

The God of all creation, the one who spoke the world into existence, reveals himself and his purposes in his creation. God desires to be known and worshiped, so he created a world that would fully express his creativity and that would allow his creation to worship him. Within this world of his creation, God gave a special dispensation to only one portion of his creation—human beings. Humans, due to this unique gift, would then be the primary carriers of God and his glory. Humans could view themselves as God does—as his witnesses to those individuals who have not yet heard, received, and embraced God and his plan.

With this thought in mind, there are really only two questions to address: (1) How has God uniquely crafted humans to be his representatives? (2) Has God chosen specific people to be his representatives?

Uniquely Crafted

In Genesis 1:27 the Bible says that humans were made in the image of God. There is no other part of God's creation that has been given this honor. God has chosen humans to be his reflection and the representation of his image on earth. There are entire books written about all of the possible meanings of humans being made in the image of God. Christopher J.H. Wright helpfully sums up the principal idea in one paragraph:

> Much theological ink has been spilled on trying to pin down exactly what it is about human beings that can be identified as the essence of the image of God in us. Is it our rationality, our sense of responsibility to God? Even our upright posture and the expressiveness of the human face have been canvassed as the locus of the image of God in mankind. Since the Bible nowhere defines the term, it is probably futile to attempt to do so very precisely. In any case, we should not so much think of the image of God as an independent "thing" that we somehow possess. God did not give to human beings the image of God. Rather, it is a dimension of our very creation. The expression "in our image" is adverbial (that is, it describes the way God made us), not adjectival (that is, as if it simply described a quality we possess). The image of God is not so much something we possess, as what we are. To be human is to be

the image of God. It is not an extra feature added on to our species; it is definitive of what it means to be human.[1]

What then are the implications for these humans who have been made in the image of God? It is to join with God in revealing himself to his creation. Art Glasser says it this way:

> The Creation account is of such universal significance that one is pressed to conclude that it is the inalienable right of all people to know the God whose image they bear. Surely God desires that those who know him should share with those who do not know him the reality of God's existence and nature. The Great Commission explicitly expresses what the Creation account implies.[2]

Humans are to join with God in accomplishing what he has already begun. He is revealing himself to his creation, which responds by worshiping him. Humans have the special task of joining with God in that work.

The next question would be, "Are there certain humans through whom God will work primarily, or are all humans tasked with this assignment?" All humans are made in the image of God and bear this responsibility. However, not all humans have been faithful participants with God in this endeavor for various reasons. What cannot be argued though is that God has uniquely revealed himself to individuals and communities of believers throughout time, empowering them to serve as the people of God. These people of God have taken various forms through the generations, but all serve as witnesses to what God is doing in history. From a scriptural standpoint, these people could be called Israel in the Old Testament and the Church in the New Testament. However, their task remains the same: revealing the nature of God to those who do not yet know him. There are two passages of Scripture that bear examination to see how the mandate has been the same for the people of God in both Testaments.

The Old Testament

Exodus 19 comes at a unique point in history. The people that would one day be known as the Israelites have been freed from slavery in Egypt after experiencing multiple miracles performed by God for their benefit. Among the miracles seen during those previous two months were plagues, the Passover, the crossing of the Red Sea, and miraculous provision of food and water. Even though these people were prone to complain, they could not deny that God had displayed remarkable power for their wellbeing.

In the story found in Exodus 19, God meets with Moses on Mount Sinai and says:

> Give these instructions to the family of Jacob; announce it to the descendants of Israel: "You have seen what I did to the Egyptians. You know that I carried you on eagles' wings and brought you to myself. Now if you will obey me and keep my cov-

---

1   Christopher J.H. Wright, *Old Testament Ethics for the People of God* (Leicester: IVP/Downers Grove, Ill.:IVP, 2004), 11.

2   Arthur Glasser, *Announcing the Kingdom* (Grand Rapids, MI: Baker Academic, 2005), 36.

enant, you will be my own special treasure from among all the peoples on earth; for all the earth belongs to me. And you will be my kingdom of priests, my holy nation." This is the message you must give to the people of Israel. Exodus 19:3–6

It is not possible here to unpack fully this Mosaic covenant. However, note how God intended for Israel to understand its existence as the people of God. God did not choose Israel because they were special, as some argue. On the contrary, these people are shown to be complainers by nature, who were more often unfaithful than faithful to the covenant. The Bible repeatedly records the sin of the nation of Israel.

If God did not choose the nation of Israel because of its special nature, what was the basis for choosing them? God chose them because *he* is special. As a special, unique, and holy God, he wanted a people to represent him on the earth. As his representatives, chosen by him, they share in his purposes on this earth—revealing himself and receiving the worship that is due him alone.

Exodus 19:5–6 shows this to be true. God chose the nation of Israel to be his witnesses to all other nations, calling Israel his special treasure whose role was to serve as priests before all other nations. The *role* of the priest was to serve people before God. The *duties* of the priest were to present offerings on behalf of the people of Israel. Just as the individual priests served between the nation and God, so he intended that the nation of Israel collectively would serve between God and the nations. Charles Pfeiffer says, "As the priest is a mediator between God and man, so Israel is called to be the vehicle of the knowledge and salvation of God to the nations of the earth."[3] God did not choose the people of Israel to love them more or to bless them more, but he chose them to use them as his witnesses.

The New Testament
1 Peter 2:4–10 is a fascinating passage that reiterates much of what was said to the people of Israel in Exodus 19, but this time the audience is different.

> You are coming to Christ, who is the living cornerstone of God's temple. He was rejected by people, but he was chosen by God for great honor. And you are living stones that God is building into his spiritual temple. What's more, you are his holy priests. Through the mediation of Jesus Christ, you offer spiritual sacrifices that please God. As the Scriptures say, "I am placing a cornerstone in Jerusalem, chosen for great honor, and anyone who trusts in him will never be disgraced."

> Yes, you who trust him recognize the honor God has given him. But for those who reject him, "the stone that the builders rejected has now become the cornerstone" and "he is the stone that makes people stumble, the rock that makes them fall."

> They stumble because they do not obey God's word, and so they meet their fate that was planned for them. But you are not like that, for you are a chosen people. You are royal priests, a holy nation, God's very own possession. As a result, you can show oth-

---

3   Charles Pfeiffer, *The Wycliffe Bible Commentary*, (Chicago, IL: Moody Press, 1962;), 68.

ers the goodness of God, for he has called you out of the darkness into his wonderful light. "Once you had no identity as a people; now you are God's people. Once you received no mercy, now you have received God's mercy."

Echoing Exodus 19, in verse 5 the recipients of the letter are told that they are holy priests, offering spiritual sacrifices that please God. This indicates to the hearers and readers of the letter their role as participants with God in revealing himself to his creation. The task of serving as mediators or servants of God as he reveals himself is not a new one, but a continuation of what God has always intended for the people of God to represent. 1 Peter 2:9 is even closer to the Exodus text. Peter explicitly and distinctly ties the role of his present readers and hearers to those who first heard the message of Exodus 19. The people of God are wonderfully included in what God is accomplishing on earth!

Who were "God's chosen people" to whom Peter addresses his letter? They were both Jewish background believers, and Gentile believers, living throughout what is modern day Turkey. The language Peter uses would resonate with both groups of believers, uniting them as equal recipients of his letter. In fact, Peter goes to great lengths to include both Jewish background believers and Gentile believers, using phrases that strongly resonate with the former (e.g., the very term "God's chosen people") but making inclusion of Gentiles clear as well (e.g., the emphasis on salvation being through faith in Christ, not ethnicity).

In *The Classic Bible Commentary*, A.R. Faussett writes:

> The heading of 1 Peter 1:1 "to the elect strangers (spiritually *pilgrims*) of *the dispersion*" clearly marks the Christians of the *Jewish* dispersion as prominently addressed, but still including *Gentile* Christians as grafted into the Christian Jewish stock by adoption and faith, and so being part of the true Israel. 1 Peter 1:14, 2:9–10, 3:6 and 4:3 clearly prove this. Thus he, the apostle of the circumcision, sought to unite in one Christ, Jew and Gentile, promoting thereby the same work and doctrine as Paul the apostle of the uncircumcision.[4]

Scripture clearly presents the role of the people of God as participants with God to reveal him to the nations. This role is not tied to birthrights or country of origin, but instead tied to purposes and plans that God himself has established. God has not only established this plan, but through the work of Christ makes it possible for any and all individuals who receive the grace of Christ to participate with him.

Questions for Reflection:

1. What does the author mean by the humans being "uniquely crafted" and how does that relate to the mandate given by the Creator to join him in his work?

2. Compare Peter's description of the church in 1 Peter chapters 1 and 2 with the role God had given to the Jews in the Old Testament. How can and should the church in

---

4   A.R. Faussett, *The Classic Bible Commentary,* (Wheaton, IL: Crossway Books, 1999), 1485.

your specific context fulfill today the task of being "a chosen people, royal priests, a holy nation, God's very own possession"?

References

Glasser, Arthur. 2005. *Announcing the Kingdom.* Grand Rapids, MI: Baker Academic.

Pfeiffer, Charles. 1962. *The Wycliffe Bible Commentary.* Chicago, IL: Moody Press.

Wright, Christopher J.H. 2004. *Old Testament Ethics for the People of God.* Leicester: IVP/ Downers Grove, IL: IVP.

Tom Hayes serves as the Executive Vice President of International Ministries for Insight for Living Ministries. He has been involved in international ministry efforts for many years helping to equip the Western church to be involved globally, regularly traveling to and speaking in countries around the world. Tom and his wife Katie are blessed with two sons.

CHAPTER 3

THE GOSPEL IN THE GOSPELS

Andrew B. Spurgeon

The Old English word "gospel" is a translation of a Greek word *euangelion* that in ordinary circumstances meant *news* and in extraordinary circumstances meant *good-news*. The word "Gospel" (with the capital G) refers to any one of the first four books of the New Testament: Matthew, Mark, Luke, and John. Justin Martyr (c. AD 100–165) was the earliest known author to refer to the four apostolic biographies of Christ in this way.[1] So, this essay explores the question, "What is the *good-news* proclaimed in the four Gospels?"

John Stott says, "God's good news is about Jesus."[2] He reflects Paul's declaration, "Remember Jesus Christ, raised from the dead, descended from David. This is my gospel" (2 Timothy 2:8, Romans 1:1–4, 1 Corinthians 15:3–5). Since the Gospels elaborate on the life, actions, and speech of Jesus, they become primary sources of what the early Christians understood as the *gospel*.

There are various ways to explain the meaning of the *gospel*. For instance, Snodgrass explains it in terms of "the gospel [that] Jesus preached," in which four elements dominate: celebration, compassion, the role of Israel, and the kingdom of God. All other themes provide foundations for these four or become "windows through which the rest of Jesus' message may be understood."[3]

Dodd speaks of the gospel message in terms of *kerygma*, "that which is preached." He differentiates between teachings that are instructional for Christians and *kerygma* that is preaching for non-Christians. The essentials of the *kerygma* are: the prophecies are fulfilled and a new age has been inaugurated in the coming of Christ, Christ is born of the seed of David, he died according to the Scriptures to deliver his people from the present evil age,

---

1   A. Roberts, J. Donaldson and A.C. Coxe, eds., "First Apology Justin Martyr 66," in *The Apostolic Fathers with Justin Martyr and Irenaeus: The Ante-Nicene Fathers* (New York: Christian Literature Company, electronic edition of 1885 original).

2   John R.W. Stott, *The Message of Romans: God's Good News for the World* (Downers Grove, IL/Leicester: IVP; 1994), 49.

3   K. Snodgrass, "The Gospel of Jesus," in *The Written Gospel*, eds. M. Bockmuehl and D.A. Hagner (Cambridge: Cambridge University Press; 2005), 31–44.

he was buried, he rose on the third day, he is exalted to the right hand of God as the Son of God and Lord, and he will come again as judge and savior of humanity.[4]

Or again: Hooker examines the beginnings and the endings of the Gospels and concludes that the beginnings communicate that Jesus is the fulfillment of God's plan for his people and the endings are open-ended, implying that the stories of his people continue. The final chapters in the Gospels deal with resurrection, "which brings new life, not just for Jesus, but for all his followers."[5] Abogunrin sees a comprehensive picture: "The gospel is the good news of salvation, deliverance, and restoration for the whole of humanity, regardless of sex, race, or color. It is the story about what God accomplished for people through Jesus Christ. It is the good tidings of total liberation and forgiveness addressed to a world lost in sin."[6]

Each of these approaches is valid and gives a diverse and multifaceted understanding of the gospel as portrayed in the Gospels. This short essay examines yet another aspect: how the word *gospel* itself etymologically provides a powerful portrait of Jesus.

Etymology of the Gospel

Ancient people proclaimed three events as *good-news*: the birth of a king or emperor, the coronation of a king or emperor, and the victories of a king or emperor. For example, the birth and coronation of Caesar Augustus were announced as *good-news* in the Priene calendar inscription, c. AD 9; likewise, Vespasian's victory over Vitellius was proclaimed as *good-news*. In the same way, the Gospels proclaim the birth, victories, and coronation of King Jesus as *good-news*.

Matthew's Gospel

Matthew begins with the announcement: "This is the book of the generation of Jesus Christ, the son of David." To the ancient ears, that introduction would have sounded like a birth announcement of a king, the accepted formulation of *good-news*. David was a beloved king of the Jews. God had promised him an everlasting reign through an unending progeny (2 Sam 7:8–16). So the hearers would have heard, "a king is born, in the lineage of King David." The birth narrative of Jesus further authenticates his royalty: wise men (astronomers) from the east come to pay homage to him, ruling King Herod is alarmed by their visit and tries to eliminate his competition (although a baby), and upon seeing the baby the Magi bow down to pay homage as they would to a king. The experience of the infant Jesus—the plot to murder him, the escape to Egypt, and taking shelter in non-Jewish territory—echoes that of David, with Saul's plot to kill him, his escape, and exile in non-Judean territory, Gath (see 1 Sam chapters 19–21). Truly, a king in the in the lineage of David has come.

Matthew also speaks of victories of the king over his enemies. His enemies are satanic forces, earthly forces, and human infirmities. When Jesus defeats satanic forces by casting

---

4   C. H. Dodd, *The Apostolic Preaching and Its Development* (London: Hodder & Stoughton, 1936), 28.

5   M. Hooker, "Beginnings and Endings," in *The Written Gospel*, op cit; 184–202.

6   S.O. Abogunrin, "St Matthew: The Gospel for All Nations," in *Resourcing New Testament Studies: Literary, Historical and Theological Essays in Honour of David L. Dungan*, eds. A.J. McNicol, D.B. Peabody and J.S. Subramanian (New York: T&T Clark, 2009), 96–106.

out demons and the Jewish leaders accuse him of working in collaboration with Beelzebub, Jesus answers, "How can anyone enter a strong man's house and carry off his possessions unless he first ties up the strong man? Then he can rob his house" (Matt 12:29). Jesus chases away demons because he has already bound up Satan. He is victorious just as a king in a battle. He also conquers earthly forces such as winds and waves (14:22–23), plants and trees (he feeds bread without harvesting, 14:13–21; the fig tree withers at his word, 21:18–22), and earth and sky (the earth quakes and the sun hides at his death, 27:45, 51). He is also victorious over human infirmities. Lepers are cured (8:1–3), the blind see (9:27–31), the deaf hear (12:22–23), and the lame walk (15:30). The dead arise at his word (9:18–26) and at his death "the holy people who had died were raised to life" (27:52). Infirmities of humans and the ultimate enemy, death, are subject to him because he is victorious and reigns in glory.

Since he is victorious, he can proclaim a new decree, the beloved words of the *Beatitudes* (5:2–11). The poor in spirit (i.e., the frightened) are abused and overrun by the forceful and powerful, but in Jesus' reign they are blessed and receive his kingdom. Those who grieve in this world are blessed in Jesus' reign because he comforts them. The meek inherit the earth as their possession in Jesus' reign. The merciful receive mercy, the pure in heart see God, and the peacemakers are God's children. When disciples are persecuted for righteousness, Jesus offers them God's kingdom; when people insult, abuse, falsely accuse, and speak evil against them, Jesus rewards them in heaven. Truly they are blessed because he reigns victoriously.

Matthew also proclaims the *good-news* of Jesus' coronation. Twice the heavenly Father declares, "This is my Son, whom I love; with him I am well pleased" (Matt 3:17; 17:5). This parallels God calling David his son, a concept many of the Psalms affirm (e.g., Psalm 2:7; 2:12; 72:1; 132:11–12). Similarly, Jesus is Davidic and the Father's Son, the rightful heir to the throne of David. Another coronation proclamation boldly comes direct from the lips of Jesus himself after his resurrection: "All authority in heaven and on earth has been given to me" (Matt 28:18).

Mark

Mark's opening words are, "The beginning of the *gospel* about Jesus Christ, the Son of God" (Mark 1:1). Mark also emphasizes Jesus' kingship by the titles "Christ" and "the Son of God." *Christ* is the Greek translation of the Hebrew *Messiah*, which means "the anointed one." Since oil was poured on kings' heads as they were appointed to office (c.f. 1 Sam 15:1; 16:13), they were called "the anointed ones," or Messiah—Christ. Jews anticipated such a Jewish Christ to come and overthrow the Gentile rule. Mark sees Jesus as the anticipated Christ. He is also "the Son of God." In the ancient world, kings and emperors were considered as sons of the gods. They represented their gods on earth. For instance, Pharaoh was deemed to be the son of *Ra* or *Re*, and Caesar Augustus was thought of as the divine son (*divi filius*) of Julius Caesar. The Jews, too, thought of Davidic kings as God's sons (for example, Psalms 2:7, 72:1, 110:1). Jesus is both Messiah and Son of God, who has come to earth to rule.

Mark then portrays the *good-news* of Jesus' victories. Jesus heals people with unclean spirits (Mark 1:21–28; 5:1–20; 9:14–29), leprosy (1:40–45), paralysis (2:1–12), shriveled hands (3:1–6), uncontrollable menstrual flow (5:21–43), deafness (7:31–37), and blindness (8:22–26; 10:46–52). He even raises dying or dead children back to life (5:21–43; 7:24–30). His miracles are so numerous that Mark merely summarizes them: "Jesus healed many who had various diseases. He also drove out many demons" (1:34) and "wherever he went—into villages, towns or countryside—they placed the sick in the marketplaces. They begged him to let them touch even the edge of his cloak, and all who touched him were healed" (6:56).

Mark's *good-news* also includes the coronation of King Jesus. Two pivotal declarations crown his writing. The first occurs in a discussion between Jesus and his disciples. He begins asking, "Who do people say I am?" (Mark 8:27), and narrows his query saying, "Who do you say I am?" (8:29). Peter proclaims—as if announcing a coronation declaration—"You are the Christ." The second declaration comes from the mouth of a Roman centurion, who pays homage to no one except Caesar; at the foot of the cross, watching Jesus die, he declares, "Surely this man was the Son of God!" (15:39). Just as Mark begins his Gospel with the affirmation of Jesus as the Son of God, so he accentuates these events and declarations to state categorically that Jesus is the Christ, the Son of God.

Luke

Luke also begins with a proclamation. However, it is about Jesus' forerunner, John, whom we know as John the Baptist. The announcement of John's birth occurs in the Lord's temple with an angel of the Lord appearing to the priest, Zachariah. The angel declares, "I am Gabriel. I stand in the presence of God, and I have been sent to speak to you and to tell you this good news" (Luke 1:19). Later, the proclamation of *good-news* concerning Jesus' birth occurs when an angel appears to the shepherds in the field, announcing, "Do not be afraid. I bring you good news of great joy that will be for all people. Today in the town of David a Savior has been born to you; he is Christ the Lord" (2:10–11). Much later, both John (3:18) and Jesus (4:18) proclaim this *good-news*.

Luke narrates Jesus' victories, starting with Jesus' own bold assertion of his authority and identity. At the synagogue in Nazareth, he is given the scroll of Isaiah. He unrolls it and reads: "The Sprit of the Lord is on me, because he has anointed me, to preach good news to the poor. He has sent me to proclaim freedom for the prisoners and recovery of sight for the blind, to release the oppressed, to proclaim the year of the Lord's favor" (Luke 4:18–19). When everyone's eyes are on him, he boldly asserts, "Today this Scripture is fulfilled in your hearing" (4:22). He is the anointed one—the King—who would deliver them, as a conqueror, from all their oppressions. Howard Marshall writes, "He [Jesus} appears as the prophesied spokesman anointed by God to announce good news of deliverance and divine favor (Isaiah 61:1–2).... The proclamation brings into being what is announced, as when a powerful conqueror announces the overturning of the oppressive regime that previously existed."[7] Just as Jesus proclaims, the poor are fed (Luke 9:10–17), those imprisoned by demons are freed (4:31–41; 8:26–39), the blind receive sight (18:35–43), those oppressed

---

7   I. H. Marshall, *A Concise New Testament Theology* (Downers Grove, IL: IVP Academic, 2008), 46.

by illness and death are set free (e.g., 5:17–26; 5:12–16; 8:40–56; 17:1–4, etc.), and debts are cancelled as in the year of the Lord's favor (7:36–50; 19:1–10). When John's followers are sent to enquire if he is the one to come, Jesus replies, "Go back and report to John what you have seen and heard. The blind receive sight, the lame walk, those who have leprosy are cured, the deaf hear, the dead are raised, and the good news is preached to the poor" (7:22). The King has come in victory: surely, this is *good-news*!

Luke's coronation proclamation occurs early in Jesus' life. Simeon, a righteous and devout man, awaits the coming of the Lord's Christ (2:26). When he sees the nearly forty-day-old baby Jesus at the Temple, he blesses God saying, "Sovereign Lord, as you have promised, you now dismiss your servant in peace. For my eyes have seen your salvation, which you have prepared in the sight of all people, a light for revelation to the Gentiles and for glory to your people Israel" (2:29–32). The prophetess Anna echoes similar claims; "She gave thanks to God and spoke about the child to all who were looking forward to the redemption of Jerusalem" (2:38). God's Messiah, the redeemer of humanity, has come.

John

John takes this imagery of a kingly Jesus to a higher level: he is the *divine* king.[8] Since Jesus is divine, John does not talk about his birth; instead he talks about God-becoming-human or "the self-manifestation of God."[9] John states, "In the beginning was the Word, and the Word was with God, the Word was God … the Word became flesh and dwelt among us" (John 1:1, 14). Whereas the other Gospels speak of God reigning on earth through Jesus, John sees Jesus as the God who reigns.

John sees Jesus' triumph over enemies in a selective way, by recording only a few miracles; but each miracle is a sample of what the other Gospels affirm. He is victorious over the elements and the natural world (e.g., he provides food and drink, 2:1–11; 6:1–13). He is victorious over sickness and death (5:1–9; 9:1–7). He is victorious over satanic oppression (Satan enters the heart of Judas Iscariot in order to betray Jesus to death, but Jesus conquers death by his resurrection, 13:27; 21:14). A key victory is *putting things straight* between himself and others. Nicodemus, a learned Pharisee, knows Jesus is from God because of his actions. However, Jesus is neither from nobility nor from a priestly family, and he often feasts with the poor and sinful: how then could he be the Messiah? Nicodemus approaches Jesus and receives a powerful lesson on eternal life (3:1–21). A woman from Samaria encounters him by a well, only expecting rejection from him. Instead, he accepts her and speaks of the true essence of worship that eventually leads the whole village to God (4:4–41). When the disciples are puzzled by his saying that he is going away, Jesus comforts them with the assurance of another Comforter's constant presence; he is not leaving them as orphans (chapters 13–17). Peter, having denied Jesus, expects rebuke; instead he finds restoration and a commission to care for the sheep and lambs of God's flock (21:15–19). Jesus triumphs over

---

8   John's Gospel does not use either the noun "gospel" or the verb "to preach good news," but the concept of *good-news* is found within the Gospel.

9   A term used by Jey Kanagaraj in *The Gospel of John: A Commentary with Elements of Comparison to Indian Religious Thought and Cultural Practices* (Secunderabad, India: OM Books, 2005), 37.

those who fear rejection, and he restores them to friendship, love, and to mission: that's *good-news*!

His coronation declaration comes early from the mouth of the forerunner John the Baptist, who identified himself as "I am the voice of one calling in the desert, 'Make straight the way for the Lord'" (1:23). He vehemently denies that he is the Christ, Elijah, and *the* prophet. He further affirms that he is not even worthy as a servant to untie the sandals of the Messiah. Then, he utters the coronation proclamation: "Look, the Lamb of God, who takes away the sin of the world!" (1:29). That declaration was not his own; God had said to him that the one on whom the Holy Spirit descended would be the Lamb of God. So John declares again, "I have seen and I testify that this is the Son of God" (1:34). Others soon follow with similar proclamations. John's own disciples call Jesus "Rabbi" (1:38). Andrew calls him "Messiah" (1:41). Philip declares him the one Moses prophesied about (1:45; c.f. Deut 18:18). Nathanael, after a moment of doubt declares, "Rabbi, you are the Son of God; you are the King of Israel" (1:49). Jesus refers to himself as "the Son of Man" (1:51). After his death and resurrection, a great proclamation occurs. When Jesus appears to his disciples behind closed doors, Thomas—who had earlier doubted his resurrection—boldly utters his coronation declaration: "My Lord and my God!" (20:28).

Conclusion

The gospel in the Gospels is about Jesus—his birth, his victories, and his coronation. Even the ultimate enemy, death, could not conquer him; Jesus rose again to life. So the early church spoke of his birth-victories-death-burial-resurrection-coronation as the gospel (Acts 10:34–43). Peter, for example, says: "Let all Israel be assured of this: God has made this Jesus, whom you crucified, both Lord and Christ" (Acts 2:36). Paul likewise, "guided by what he knows of Jesus, and especially his cross and resurrection, pulls out one strand in particular, that of the coming king who would be God's son (2 Sam 7:14, and elsewhere). This is the 'good news': it has happened! God has done it! The king has come!"

Questions for Reflection:

1. What comes first to your mind when you think of the word gospel? In what way has the word been used in your specific context and how does that relate to the presentation of the gospel in the four gospels?

2. How can the gospel about Jesus the King be good news to our world? Think of practical areas where the gospel makes a difference in society today.

3. "The gospel in the Gospels is about Jesus," the author concludes. In what way does the church proclaim that gospel in our days?

References

Abogunrin, S.O. 2009. St. Matthew: The Gospel for All Nations. In *Resourcing New Testament Studies: Literary, Historical and Theological Essays in Honour of David L Dungan*, eds. A.J. McNicol, D.B. Peabody and J.S. Subramanian. New York: T&T Clark.

Dodd, C.H. 1936. *The Apostolic Preaching and Its Development.* London: Hodder & Stoughton; 1936.

Hooker, M. 2005. Beginnings and Endings. In *The Written Gospel,* eds. M. Bockmuehl and D.A. Hagner. Cambridge: Cambridge University Press.

Kanagaraj, Jey. 2005. *The Gospel of John: A Commentary with Elements of Comparison to Indian Religious Thought and Cultural Practices.* Secunderabad, India: OM Books.

Marshall, I. H. 2008. *A Concise New Testament Theology.* Downers Grove, IL: IVP Academic.

Roberts, A., J. Donaldson, and A.C. Coxe, eds. 1885. "First Apology Justin Martyr 66." In *The Apostolic Fathers with Justin Martyr and Irenaeus: The Ante-Nicene Fathers.* New York: Christian Literature Company (electronic edition of 1885 original).

Snodgrass, K. 2005. The Gospel of Jesus. In *The Written Gospel,* eds. M. Bockmuehl and D.A. Hagner. Cambridge: Cambridge University Press.

Stott, John R.W. 1994. *The Message of Romans: God's Good News for the World.* Downers Grove, IL/ Leicester: IVP.

Andrew B. Spurgeon (PhD in New Testament Studies) is a native of India and a missionary involved in theological education in Asia. He is the Publications Chairperson for Asia Theological Association. He and his wife Lori live in India.

CHAPTER 4

NEW TESTAMENT METAPHORS OF THE CHURCH

Eileen Poh

Introduction

Metaphor, *noun. Application of name or descriptive term to an object to which it is not literally applicable (e.g., "a glaring error")* (Concise Oxford Dictionary).

The New Testament uses many metaphors for the church.[1] This chapter will focus on selected metaphors in 1 Corinthians, Ephesians, and 1 Peter to examine the essence of church, in particular, its mission in proclaiming God's salvation to the world. A metaphor in Scripture is more than description or emotion; it highlights theological truth. To say that "the Lord is my shepherd" implies that God is like a shepherd in some ways but also unlike a shepherd in other ways. New Testament metaphors of the church are not simply word substitutes for "Christ" or "church," but enrich our theological understanding.

1 Corinthians

The church in Corinth was predominantly Gentile, though there were some Jews (Acts 18:1–17). Paul wrote to address the issue of divisions and quarrels in the church (1:11–12; 3:3–4), which arose out of factionalism and arrogance, and the way they exercised spiritual gifts (12:12–14:40).

Paul's use of field, building, and temple as metaphors for the church in 1 Corinthians 3 emphasizes the oneness of the church. As God's field, God's building, and God's temple, the church belongs to God. The church as God's field is expected to grow under his care. This metaphor excludes self-reliance, competition, and rivalry. As God's building, the church has Jesus Christ as its foundation. As God's temple, the church is where the Holy Spirit dwells. Since it is God's holy temple, no one can destroy the church with impunity (3:17). This is a warning to those who through their quarrels and schisms would damage the witness of the church. Holiness must be evident in the way Christians live their lives (2 Cor 6:16), for

---

1   Paul Minear examines ninety-six metaphors for church in the New Testament. See P. S. Minear, *Images of the Church in the New Testament* (Nashville, TN: Westminster John Knox Press, 1960).

God's temple is the community of Christians by whom people will be attracted to come to meet with God.[2]

The body metaphor in chapter 12—the body is one but made up of many parts—did not originate with Paul. Graeco-Roman writers used it to encourage cooperation and concord among people and to stress the oneness of the body.[3] It was also applied to the state to emphasize the responsibility of individual members for each other and for the whole state. Paul Christianized the body metaphor to address the issue of divisiveness in the Corinthian church, using it to stress the close relationship between Christ and his church and the corporate nature of the church, with its unity and diversity, its sense of oneness, and mutual care for and service to one another. When church members exercise spiritual gifts in a loving and orderly manner (13:1–14:40), this can even convict unbelievers in their midst and turn them to worship God (14:22–25).

Dunn suggests that "the church, whether local or universal, precisely by being designated the body of Christ, is probably being called upon to provide an alternative community and probably also to serve as a model of what true community should be."[4] If Dunn is right, then the church as the body of Christ would demonstrate to the pagan world that people from different ethnic groups (Jews or Greeks) and socioeconomic status (slave or free) can relate to one another in harmony and unity, bearing witness to what true community should be. Their quarrelling and divisiveness would only diminish or negate their impact as a community of God's people in Corinth.

Ephesians

The church in Ephesus was also predominantly Gentile. Paul addresses Gentile believers directly (Eph 2:11; 3:1), urging them to put off their old way of life (Eph 4:17–5:18).[5]

Paul uses the body metaphor in a different way from 1 Corinthians: here Christ is the head, and his body is the church. This head-body metaphor emphasizes the vital and intimate

---

2   In the Old Testament, the temple was where God chose to dwell, and where his people could meet with him and worship (1 Kings 6–7; 8:29). Jesus "took over its role and significance, as the person in whom God's presence is among his people (Immanuel), and as the person through whom people must now come to God in worship (John 4:2–26)": C. J. H. Wright, "The Church" in *The New Lion Handbook: Christian Belief*, ed. A. E. McGrath, (Oxford: Lion Hudson, 2006), 218–230. The church in Corinth is now God's temple.

3   M. V. Lee, *Paul: The Stoics and the Body of Christ* (Cambridge: CUP, 2006), 31–43 cites Dio's speech to promote concord among the Nicaeans: "When a city has concord, as many citizens as there are, so many are the eyes with which to see that city's interest, so many the ears with which to hear, so many the tongues to give advice, so many the minds concerned in its behalf … Conversely neither abundance of riches nor number of men nor any other element of strength is of advantage to those who are divided, but all these things are rather on the side of loss, and the more abundant they are, so much the greater and more grievous the loss. Just so too, methinks, it is with human bodies—that body which is in sound health finds advantage in its height and bulk, while the body which is diseased and in poor condition finds a physical state of that kind to be most perilous and productive of severest risk" (Chrysostom, Nicaean, 39.3–7).

4   James Dunn, "The Body of Christ in Paul" in *Worship, Theology and Ministry in the Early Church: Essays in Honour of Ralph P. Martin*, eds. M. J. Wilkins and T. Paige (Sheffield, UK: JSOT Press, 1992), 161.

5   The vehement opposition from the silversmiths and others in trades related to the worship of Artemis shows that many Gentiles had been converted (Acts 19:23–27). A number of believers brought out their magic scrolls and burned them publicly (Acts 19:19). These too would have come from a Gentile background.

union between Christ and the church in three ways. First, whatever God has accomplished in Christ is done also for the church (1:22–23). As Christ is "head-over-all-things," so the church is also above "all things."[6] The church as Christ's body expresses his fullness, being filled by him.[7] Second, Christ is the source and goal of the church's growth (4:11–16). From Christ the head, the body grows as every part contributes to the building process, which is characterized by love.

Third, the relationship between Christ the head and the church his body is characterized by Christ's self-sacrificial love for the church. In 5:22–33, Paul compares the husband-wife relationship to that between Christ and his church. He cites Genesis 2:24, stressing that the church is in intimate union with him, just as the man and his wife are one flesh.[8] Wives are to submit to their husbands, just as the church, the body of Christ, submits to Christ, the head.[9] Husbands are to love their wives, just as Christ loved the church and "gave himself up for her." This is "an act of complete, self-abandoning love."[10] His purpose is to make her holy in order to present her to himself as a radiant church, without any blemish. The church will find her full expression in the bride of Christ, clothed in fine linen, ready for the wedding of the Lamb at the culmination of God's redemption plan (Rev 19:6–8; 21:2).

Other metaphors for church are found in Ephesians 2:11–22; they emphasize the reconciliation and unity between Jewish and Gentile Christians. Gentiles had not been part of God's people in the Old Testament; they were called "uncircumcised" by the Jews; they were separate from Christ, excluded from citizenship in Israel, and foreigners to the covenants of the promise, without hope and without God in the world.

But Christ's death on the cross has destroyed the dividing wall of hostility between Jews and Gentiles.[11] By abolishing the laws that kept up the barrier between them, Jesus has

---

6   Frank Thielman, *Ephesians* (Grand Rapids, MI: Baker Academic, 2010), 107. These include the pagan gods, the Roman emperor, as well as local officials, provincial rulers, and governors.

7   John Stott, *The Message of Ephesians* (Nottingham, UK: IVP, 1979), 61–62.

8   This intimate union "was originally intended to prefigure and to illustrate the union that Christ now has with the church. This is something that could become clear only after Christ had died to create the church in its new, multiethnic form (2:14–15; 3:8–11) and this is why it is a mystery; a truth that could be known only through God's gracious revelation of it (1:9; 3:3–4; 6:19)" (Thielman 2010, 389).

9   Paul's injunction to wives to submit to their own husbands would not have been unusual for the women of his day, as seen in Plutarch's view on marriage: "If [women] subordinate themselves to their husbands, they are commended, but if they want to have control, they cut a sorrier figure than the subjects of their control. And control ought to be exercised by the man over the woman, not as the owner has control of a piece of property, but, as the soul controls the body, by entering into her feelings and being knit to her through good will. As, therefore, it is possible to exercise care over the body without being a slave to its pleasure and desire good will. As, therefore, it is possible to govern a wife, and at the same time to delight and gratify her": Conj. praec. 142e.

10.   Tom Wright, *Paul for Everyone: The Prison Letters: Ephesians, Philippians, Colossians and Philemon* (London: SPCK, 2002), 67.

11   In Paul's day, the Jew-Gentile divide was the most fundamental division between two groups of people. This was evident in the Jerusalem temple. Josephus in Antiquities XV. 11.5 describes the temple as "encompassed by a stone wall for a partition, with an inscription which forbade any foreigner to go in under pain of death." According to Josephus in Jewish Wars V.5.2, "a partition made of stone all round, whose height was three cubits. Its construction was very elegant; upon it stood pillars at equal distance from one another, declaring the law of purity, some in Greek and some in Roman letters, that "no foreigner should go within that sanctuary."

reconciled Jews and Gentiles, creating in himself one new man or humanity, and one body (2:14–16).[12] These two metaphors emphasise oneness or unity. If the Jew-Gentile divide is "a prototype of all divisions," then the church as one body displays a unity that transcends all barriers.[13] Not only is the church the place of reconciliation between Jews and Gentiles, it is also the place of reconciliation between humanity and God.

In Christ, Gentile Christians have become "fellow citizens with the saints" (2:19). They are no longer strangers and aliens, without legal rights as citizens. They are now members of God's household (2:19). They are God's sons and daughters by adoption through Christ (1:5), with access to the Father (2:18; 3:14). Paul also uses the metaphor of a holy temple, the foundation of which is the apostles and the prophets (2:20). Jesus himself is the chief cornerstone; he holds the rest of the building together.[14] The church is not a building but consists of the people themselves, who are the "place" where God dwells by his Spirit.

Paul sums up the status of Gentile believers in 3:6: they are now coheirs with Jewish believers of the full blessings of God's salvation, members together of one body, and cosharers in the promise. This is the mystery of Christ, kept hidden in God for ages past but now revealed. The purpose is to manifest the wisdom of God to the rulers and authorities in the heavenly realms (3:10–11). The church as one new humanity and one body, made up of Jews and Gentiles, men and women from every socioeconomic and cultural background, united through Christ's death "is the sign to the principalities and powers that their time is up … the church is constituted, and lives its life in public, in such a way as to confront the rulers of the world with the news that there is 'another king, this Jesus' (Acts 17:7)."[15] The church also displays the manifold wisdom of God to the principalities and powers of darkness in the heavenly realms.

Paul's use of the head-body metaphor stresses the intimate relationship between Christ and the church. The church as Christ's body is "over all things," and expresses Christ's fullness. The church is also a household, in which people from different ethnic, social, cultural, and linguistic backgrounds relate as brothers and sisters in love. The church is the new humanity; it is one body, a community of the reconciled through whom God demonstrates his wisdom to the earthly authorities and the principalities and powers of darkness in the heavenly realms. All these facets of the church are essential to the mission of the church in society.

Two of the Greek notices have been discovered: "No foreigner may enter within the barrier and enclosure round the temple. Anyone who is caught doing so will have himself to blame for his ensuing death."

12   Under the law, the Jews considered the Gentiles unclean. Christ had abolished the requirements of the law like circumcision and eating clean and unclean food which distinguished between Jews and Gentiles.

13   Andrew Lincoln, *Ephesians* (Dallas, TX: Word Books, 1990), 161–162. "If the Church in Ephesians 2 stands for the overcoming of the fundamental division of humanity into either Jew or Gentile, it stands for the overcoming of all divisions caused by tradition, class, color, nation, or group of nations. Anything less would be a denial of that nature of the Church which this writer takes as axiomatic."

14   The word translated "chief cornerstone" is ambiguous: some have taken this to refer to a stone set high in the building rather than cornerstone. Thielman takes the view that Paul could have intended both meanings: "He is paradoxically, the 'topmost foundation stone'" (Thielman 2010, 181–183).

15   Tom Wright, *Justification: God's Plan and Paul's Vision* (London: SPCK, 2009), 149.

1 Peter

Peter uses a number of Old Testament metaphors, but he applies them to the churches in Asia Minor, which are predominantly Gentile.[16] They were facing hostility from non-Christians because they had stopped indulging in debauchery, drunken orgies, and idolatry with them (4:3–4). These activities would have taken place during the imperial festivals and trade association meetings.[17] When they withdrew from their relationships with non-Christians, they suffered abuse from them (2:12, 15; 3:16; 4:14). Peter uses metaphors to teach them about their identity and place in God's plan.

1 Peter 2:4–12

In 2:4–8, Peter likens Jesus to a living stone, chosen by God but rejected by the Jews.[18] Christians too are like living stones, rejected by men but chosen by God (1:1; 2:9). In their suffering, they find their identity and solidarity with Christ.

As living stones, they are being built into a spiritual house to be a priesthood. In itself, the house can be understood as a household. They have received "new birth" (1:3; 2:2). As "obedient children," they call God their Father (1:14, 17); they are "the household of God" (4:17). Within this household, they must love one another deeply like brothers (1:22; 2:17; 3:8; 4:8).

The church is also a holy priesthood, offering sacrifices to God (2:5). This must be seen in the light of other Old Testament metaphors in 2:9–10. The Israelites were a kingdom of priests, serving as mediators between God and the nations (Ex 19:6). They were also a holy nation, distinct from other nations (Ex 19:6). In Isaiah 43:20–21, God refers to Israel as "my people, my chosen, the people I formed for myself that they may proclaim my praise." In using this cluster of Old Testament metaphors, Peter stresses the mission of the church: to proclaim publicly God's redemptive acts to those who do not know him.

---

16   By Asia Minor, I refer to the five provinces of Pontus, Galatia, Cappadocia, Asia, and Bithynia (1 Pet 1:1). Together with other Old Testament references (1:16; 2:4–10, 22, 24; 3:6, 10–12, 14; 4:18; 5:5), the terms by which Peter addresses the Christians in 1:1 have given rise to the view that Peter's readers are Jews, as Jews would be most familiar with these Old Testament quotations and allusions. But this does not militate against a predominantly Gentile audience, as Gentiles would have been instructed in the Old Testament after their conversion. Michaels notes "the Jewishness of 1 Peter" but argues that Peter was writing primarily to Gentile Christians in Asia Minor. J. Ramsay Michaels, *I Peter* (Waco, TX: Word Books, 1988), xlv–li.

17   Plutarch writes of the fondness of men for gathering on "festal days and banquets at the temples, initiations and mystic rites, and prayer and adoration of the gods": Mor 169D. These refer to the festivals in honor of local gods and the celebration of the imperial cult, where people assembled to offer sacrifices to the gods and the emperor and participated in the feasting and games that followed. Association meetings were also the place for feasting and merrymaking. These meetings were often rowdy, so much so that complaints had been brought against them. The rules of an association of gypsum merchants provided that "regularly on the twenty-fifth of each month, they shall drink six pints of beer each": P Mich V245 (AD 47). It is not surprising that the rules and regulations of some associations enjoined members to "take your ease without ill-temper," to maintain "tranquillity and propriety," and to appear on feast days "in your most decent clothes." Ramsay MacMullen, *Roman Social Relations* (New Haven, CT: Yale University Press, 1974), 78.

18   In the Old Testament, God is often described as the Rock (Deut 32:4; 2 Sam 23:3; Isa 26:4; 30:29; Ps 19:14; 62:7). Jesus is the living stone in that he is alive and is able to give life.

If they are to fulfil this missional role, Christians must not return to the former lifestyle they shared with the pagans (2:11; cf. 4:3–4). Instead, they must "live such good lives among the pagans that, though they accuse you of doing wrong, they may see your good deeds and glorify God on the day he visits us" (2:12). Peter uses two further metaphors to depict how Christians are to live among non-Christians: aliens (*paroikoi*) and strangers (*parepidemoi*) in the world (2:11; 1:1, 17).[19] Upon conversion, they had withdrawn from their relationships with non-Christians, who treated them like aliens and strangers in their own community and households (4:3–4).[20]

Peter exhorts them to live as aliens and strangers among the pagans and do good to them. Doing good and good works are predominant themes in 1 Peter.[21] This is Peter's strategy for how they are to relate with non-Christians, who are portrayed as hostile. By doing good, they can fulfil their missional purpose in the community and households where they live and work (2:13–3:6). He anticipates that their good works will disarm their critics and persecutors, and may win some of them over to Christ (2:12; 3:1–2).

Peter then instructs them how to live as aliens and strangers in three relationships: as citizens with non-Christian governing authorities and fellow citizens (2:13–17), as Christian slaves with non-Christian masters (2:18–25), and as Christian wives with non-Christian husbands (3:1-6). In the next section, I shall discuss the first of these relationship to show how Peter's strategy of silencing hostility by doing good would work out.

1 Peter 2:13–17

Peter exhorts Christians in Asia Minor to submit for the Lord's sake to the governing authorities. The emperor was the head of political power and the guarantor of peace in the empire.[22] Thus his well-being was vital for the welfare of his subjects, who expressed their loyalty through participation in the imperial cult.[23] In many instances, the initiative for establishing the cult came from the people themselves.[24] Everyone, from the governor to the

---

19   For a literal meaning of aliens and strangers, see John Elliott, *A Home for the Homeless: A Social-Scientific Criticism of 1 Peter, Its Situation and Strategy* (Minneapolis, MN: Fortress Press, 1990).

20   "It was precisely the precarious legal status of foreigners that provided the closest analogy to the kind of treatment Christians could expect from the hostile culture in which they lived." Paul Achtemeier, *1 Peter* (Minneapolis, MN: Fortress Press, 1996), 174.

21   The verb "to do good" appears in 2:14, 15, 20; 3:6, 17; 4:19; "good works" in 3:11, 13, 16; "good" appears twice in 2:12.

22   Klaus Wengst, *Pax Romana and the Peace of Jesus Christ,* trans., John Bowden (London: SCM Press, 1987), 46–47.

23   There were more than eighty imperial temples in the cities in Asia Minor (Simon Price, *Rituals and Power: The Roman Imperial Cult in Asia Minor* (Cambridge: CUP, 1984), 135). Dio Cassius (AD 150–235) wrote: "This practice [of imperial cult], beginning under him [Augustus], has continued under other emperors, not only in the case of Hellenic nations but also in that of all the others, in so far as they are subject to the Romans": Dio Cassius, 51.20.7.

24   Dio Cassius, 51.20.6–7. It was at the request of the people of Asia and Bithynia around 29 BC that Augustus allowed them to build sanctuaries in Ephesus and Nicaea respectively, which were dedicated to the cult of Roma and Julius Caesar. Deputations from eleven cities of Asia were sent in AD 26 to plead with Emperor Tiberius for the honor of erecting a temple in honor to himself, Livia, and the Senate.

slave, participated in imperial festivals, which were held regularly.[25] Prayers and sacrifices were offered to the emperor in the imperial temples.[26] They would then process through the streets; householders along the streets placed sacrifices on altars outside their houses, the doors of which were adorned with laurels and lamps. People in festive clothes would enjoy the banquets and gladiatorial shows paid for by the rich and elite.

Upon conversion, Christians in Asia Minor could no longer participate in the imperial festivals. They become subjects of "the ignorant talk of foolish men" (2:15). Their neighbors and fellow citizens would have treated them like aliens and strangers, accusing them of disloyalty to the emperor and not caring for the well-being of the community.[27]

Under these circumstances, Peter exhorts Christians to submit to the governing authorities "for the Lord's sake." Christians could submit by being good citizens and obeying the laws, thus showing their commitment to the community.[28] While they could not participate in imperial festivals, they could do good through public benefactions, demonstrating their care for the well-being of their fellow citizens.[29] In this, Peter might have envisaged the church as a whole performing acts of public benefaction, rather than a few individual rich members.

---

25   Imperial worship was so widespread by the early second century AD that when the Roman authorities sought a means by which men and women could categorically denounce Christianity and profess their attachment to the emperor and the gods, they required them to make oaths and sacrifices to or on behalf of the emperors: Pliny, Ep. 10.96.

26   Divine honors were paid to emperors as early as 49 BC. An inscription from Ephesus honoring Julius Caesar reads: "The cities of Asia and the [communities] and the country districts (honor) Gaius Julius, son of Gaius, Caesar, Pontifex Maximus, Imperator and consul for the second time, descendant of Ares and Aphrodite, the god who has appeared visibly and universal savior of the life of human beings." The city of Myra in Lycia honored the emperor Tiberius as "the exalted god, son of exalted gods, lord of land and sea, the benefactor and savior of the entire world." Hans-Josef Klauck, *The Religious Context of Early Christianity*, trans., Brian McNeil (Edinburgh: T&T Clark, 2000), 290. For divine honors on other emperors, see Klauck 2000, 290–312.

27   Cities honored the emperor with expectations of privileges and benefits from him. For Christians not to participate in the imperial festivals would put these expectations in jeopardy. When the people of Aezani in Phrygia sent envoys to offer their good wishes to Tiberius upon his accession to the throne, Tiberius replied in a letter saying, "Having known] long since of your [devotion and] affection for me it was also with the greatest pleasure that on the present occasion I received [from] your envoys [the decree which] demonstrates the good will of the city towards me. I shall [accordingly] endeavor [to the best of] my ability to play my part in promoting [your interests on all] occasions on which you request [my help]": Barbara Levick, *The Government of the Roman Empire: A Sourcebook* (London: Croom Helm, 1985), 118.

28   The phrase "praise those who do good" in 1 Peter 2:14 means "to praise those who were properly obedient," those who do not commit any wrong.

29   Bruce Winter, *Seek the Welfare of the City: Christians as Benefactors and Citizens* (Grand Rapids: Eerdmans, 1994), 26–40. Winter shows from his study of ancient benefaction inscriptions that doing good refers to public benefactions. He finds that in the ancient world there were established conventions for publicly recognizing and commending benefactors. Someone would move a motion in the Council that a benefactor be granted certain honors. When approved, this particular benefactor would be honored in a public ceremony, and the erection of an inscription in a public place would bear witness to the event. These benefactions include supplying grain in times of necessity, forcing down the price by selling it in the market below the asking rate, erecting public buildings or adorning old buildings, refurbishing the theater, widening roads, helping in the construction of public utilities, going on embassies to gain privileges for the city, and helping the city in times of civil upheaval.

In this respect, Harland uses an analogy from the participation of some Jewish associations in the Diaspora in civic life.[30] He distinguishes between "participation within civic networks of benefaction, including honors for emperors or elites with imperial connections, and cultic activities in honor of the emperors or imperial family as gods."[31] An example of the former was the dedication of inscriptions to emperors. But cultic rituals and sacrifices would be inappropriate for them. Harland sees the first kind of activities honoring the emperor as compatible with Christian beliefs, provided no cultic element was involved. Peter's exhortation to "do good" and "honor the king" (2:12–17) must involve "actual concrete behaviors" that can be observed by people in authority and others as good and worthy of commendation.[32] Like Jewish groups, the church as a whole could set up an inscription to dedicate a structure or building, and pray regularly for the emperor whenever they meet together in worship.

Seneca gives some examples of good deeds: helping someone with money; paying someone's debt; giving land in order that by its fertility the price of grain may be lowered; giving a loaf of bread in a time of famine; pointing out a spring of water to a thirsty man; giving useful advice; helping someone with influence; protecting someone's reputation; attending to one who is sick.[33] Christians could do these good deeds to show their care for their non-Christian neighbors and fellow citizens.

In Graeco-Roman society, doing good was especially pertinent to one's response towards one's enemies. In answer to the question, "How shall I defend myself against my enemy?" Plutarch replied:

> By proving yourself good and honorable. What, think you, would be their state of mind if you were to show yourself to be an honest, sensible man and a useful citizen, of high repute in speech, clean in actions, orderly in living, outdo your enemies in diligence, goodness, magnanimity, kindly deeds, and good works. These are the things which, as Demosthenes puts it "retard the tongue, stop the mouth, constrict the throat, and leave one with nothing to say."[34]

Peter knew the social conventions of his day and anticipated a similar outcome: "For it is God's will that by doing good you should silence the ignorant talk of foolish men" (2:15).

As a chosen people, a royal priesthood and a holy nation, the church in Asia Minor bear witness to God's redemptive acts to those who do not know him. By likening Christians to aliens (*paroikoi*) and strangers (*parepidemoi*) in the world, Peter shows how Christians could do good to disarm their critics and win some of them over to Christ.

---

30   Philip Harland, "Honouring the Emperor or Assailing the Beast: Participation in Civic Life among Associations (Jewish, Christian, and Other) in Asia Minor and the Apocalypse of John," *Journal for the Study of the New Testament,* July 2000, vol. 22, 77: 99–121.

31   Harland, "Honouring the Emperor," 111.

32   Harland "Honouring the Emperor," 115.

33   Seneca, Ben. 1.2.4-5; 2.35.3; 3.8.2-3; 3.9.2-3. The treatise was probably written sometime between AD 56 and 62.

34   Plutarch, Mor. 88B.

Conclusion

The church, as God's field, God's building, and God's temple, belongs to God. The church is God's temple, where the Holy Spirit dwells. The head-body metaphor stresses the intimate relationship between Christ and the church. This intimacy is also expressed in the image of the church as the bride of Christ, through his self-sacrificing love for the church.

The church is one new humanity, one body, comprising Jews and Gentiles, slave and free. Within this unity, there is "functional diversity."[35] Different gifts are given to the church so that the church may grow into maturity. The church is a family where members relate to each other as brothers and sisters, whose lives must be marked by love. The church is a community of the reconciled, a model of what true community is meant to be. The church is a royal priesthood, a holy nation, and God's chosen people, the continuation of God's people in the Old Testament, and bears a similar role in relation to the world. The church as a royal priesthood has a missional purpose: the church must make God known to the world, and call people to repent and believe in Jesus Christ. Christians must not withdraw from society, even though they may be like aliens and strangers, alienated from the rest of society because of their faith. In their hardship, they can experience Christ's identification with their suffering. Nevertheless, they must continue in their relationships with non-Christians and do good to them. The church is the "one body" through which God manifests his wisdom to both earthly authorities and the principalities and powers of darkness in the heavenly realms. As Christ is "head over all things," so the church too is above "all things," and expresses the fullness of Christ.

Questions for Reflection:

1. What biblical metaphors for the church are relevant for your specific context? Are there other ways of describing and comparing the church that may be more culturally understandable for people in our days?
2. Poh says that "a metaphor in Scripture is more than description or emotion; it highlights theological truth." How is that shown in her explanation of the different metaphors? How far can we go in making theology of these "images" of the church?
3. What is your preferred metaphor for the church? Why?

References

Achtemeier, Paul. 1996. *1 Peter.* Minneapolis, MN: Fortress Press.

Clowney, Edmund P. 1984. Interpreting the Biblical Models of the Church: A Hermeneutical Deepening of Ecclesiology. In Donald A. Carson, ed. *Biblical Interpretation and the Church: Text & Context.* Exeter: Paternoster.

---

35 Wright, "The Church," 226.

Dunn, James. 1992. The Body of Christ in Paul. In *Worship, Theology and Ministry in the Early Church: Essays in Honour of Ralph P. Martin*, eds. M. J. Wilkins and T. Paige. Sheffield, UK: JSOT Press.

Elliott, John. 1990. *A Home for the Homeless: A Social-Scientific Criticism of 1 Peter, Its Situation and Strategy.* Minneapolis, MN: Fortress Press.

Harland, Philip. 2000. Honouring the Emperor or Assailing the Beast: Participation in Civic Life among Associations (Jewish, Christian and Other) in Asia Minor and the Apocalypse of John. *Journal for the Study of the New Testament* 22(77): 99–121.

Klauck, Hans-Josef. 2000. *The Religious Context of Early Christianity*, trans., Brian McNeil. Edinburgh: T&T Clark.

Lee, M.V. 2006. *Paul: The Stoics and the Body of Christ.* Cambridge: CUP.

Levick, Barbara. 1985. *The Government of the Roman Empire: A Sourcebook.* London: Croom Helm.

Lincoln, Andrew. 1990. *Ephesians.* Dallas, TX: Word Books.

MacMullen, Ramsay. 1974. *Roman Social Relations.* New Haven, CT: Yale University Press.

Michaels, J. Ramsay. 1988. *I Peter.* Waco, TX: Word Books.

Minear, P.S. *Images of the Church in the New Testament* (Nashville, TN: Westminster John Knox Press, 1960).

Price, Simon. 1984. *Rituals and Power: The Roman Imperial Cult in Asia Minor.* Cambridge: CUP.

Stott, John. 1979. *The Message of Ephesians.* Nottingham, UK: IVP.

Thielman, Frank. 2010. *Ephesians.* Grand Rapids, MI: Baker Academic.

Travers, Michael E. 2007. The Use of Figures of Speech in the Bible. *Bibliotheca Sacra* 164(3): 277–290.

Wengst, Klaus. 1987. *Pax Romana and the Peace of Jesus Christ*, trans., John Bowden. London: SCM Press.

Winter, Bruce. 1994. *Seek the Welfare of the City: Christians as Benefactors and Citizens.* Grand Rapids: Eerdmans.

Wright, Tom. 2009. *Justification: God's Plan and Paul's Vision.* London: SPCK.

———. 2002. *Paul for Everyone: The Prison Letters: Ephesians, Philippians, Colossians and Philemon.* London: SPCK.

Wright, Christopher J.H. 2006. The Church. In *The New Lion Handbook: Christian Belief*, ed. A. E. McGrath. Oxford: Lion Hudson.

Eileen Poh lectures in Biblical Studies at Discipleship Training Centre in Singapore. Her doctoral thesis (from King's College London) examines the social relationships between Christians and non-Christians in Asia Minor in the second half of the first century AD.

CHAPTER 5

THE ESSENCE OF THE CHURCH

The One, Holy, Catholic, and Apostolic Church in God's Purposes

Paul Coulter

Refining the Essence

Disillusionment with church is reaching epidemic levels among Christians in the global North and, in an increasingly globalized world, the ripples of this uncertainty must surely be felt elsewhere. A new post-Christian context has sparked conversations about the relationship between church, kingdom, and mission and has ignited a fresh interest in church renewal and church planting. Such a time presents exciting opportunities to follow where the Spirit blows (John 3:8), but there is also a danger of being blown around by false winds (Eph 4:14). We must understand the essential nature of the church to appreciate its place in God's purpose. This chapter aims to assist missional practitioners and theorists in both global North and South to refine the essence of the church—its vital ingredients—in order to serve God more faithfully in diverse contexts.

The Pure Essence: Devotion to Christ

The church is both human and divine. *Ekklēsia* can be translated both as a gathered human *assembly* and a called-out divine *congregation*.[1] Jesus described his church in both terms: as a gathering of people in his name but also constituted by his presence in the midst (Matt 18:20). Acts describes the church's origins through both the human agency of the apostles Christ commissioned and the divine agency of the Spirit he promised.

The church is, thus, essentially defined by its relationship to Jesus, and one powerful New Testament image of this reality is that of bride. It is rooted in Old Testament descriptions of Israel as the wife of Yahweh (Jer 2:2; Ezek 18; Hosea 1:2), developed in Jesus' parables about an eschatological wedding feast (Matt 22:1–14; 25:1–13), stated in the epistles (Eph 5:25–27), and brought to glorious fulfilment in Revelation, where the Lamb's bride comprises God's people from both old and new covenants (19:6–9; 21:2; 22:17). Paul likens his ministry of church-initiation to matchmaking in 2 Corinthians 11. He had promised the

---

1   G. C. Berkouwer, *The Church*, trans. J. E. Davison, (Grand Rapids, MI: Eerdmans, 1976), 19–24.

believers to Christ as a virgin bride (verse 2) and so urges them to maintain their "sincere and pure devotion to Christ" (verse 3). To follow a different Jesus, a different Spirit or a different gospel would be spiritual adultery (verse 4). The Trinitarian pattern of Paul's words should not be missed: sincere devotion must be towards the true historical Jesus, dependent upon the true Spirit, and trusting in "God's gospel" (verse 7).

Here, then, is the pure essence of the church: a community gathered in devotion to Christ in expectation of eschatological union with him. The church is, thus, the foretaste of the ultimate gathering of God's people. It is uniquely the Trinitarian community in which Christ's lordship is celebrated, the Spirit's presence manifested, and God's truth proclaimed. As such, the church, although it is not the sole location of God's action in the world, is central in his purposes.

Describing the Essence: Four Dynamic Words

As a growing church contextualized the apostles' witness to the historic Jesus into the Greek-speaking Roman world, it responded to inadequate understandings of his person by formulating creeds. Amidst Christological debates, four undisputed words described the church's self-understanding: "one, holy, catholic, and apostolic."[2] The qualities expressed by these words find a firm basis in the New Testament. At the end of the one Gospel that records Jesus' comments about the church (Matt 16:18; 18:10), Jesus commissions his apostles (Matt 28:18–20) to make disciples (*holy* people) from all nations because of Christ's universal (*catholic*) authority by baptizing them into the triune name (*one* people) and teaching them to obey what he had taught them (passing on the *apostolic* message). The resulting community of baptized disciples in continuity with the apostles would be the sign, instrument, and foretaste of Christ's presence and reign "to the very end of the age."[3]

As the church began at Pentecost through the Spirit-empowered activity of these same apostles, they engaged in four core practices that embody the four words (Acts 2:42). In *breaking bread* they remembered Jesus, declared his death and anticipated his coming (1 Cor 11), thus expressing *oneness* in his body (1 Cor 10:17). Their *prayer*, following the kingdom-seeking pattern Jesus had taught them (Matt 6:9–13) was that they might be God's *holy* servants as Jesus had been (Acts 4:29–30). Their *fellowship*, flowing from devotion to Christ (1 John 3:11–18), expressed a *catholicity* (or wholeness) that was progressively widened as they overcame differences of wealth (Acts 2:44–45), culture (Acts 6:1–6), and ethnicity (Acts 15:1–35). Each of these instances of qualitative growth preceded quantitative growth (Acts 2:47; 6:7; 16:5)—increasing internal health (another English word from the same root as wholeness and catholicity) of the church contributed to external growth through inclusion of others. Lastly, the *apostles' teaching* ensured *apostolicity*—continuity with the real Jesus through the message of the apostles he appointed.

---

2   The words first appear together in the Chalcedonian-Nicean Creed (c. AD 381).

3   Lesslie Newbigin, *The Open Secret: Sketches for a Missionary Theology* (London: SPCK, 1978), 124; and Lesslie Newbigin, *The Gospel in a Pluralist Society* (London: SPCK, 1989), 233.

Ephesians, which describes the church as God's demonstration of his "manifold wisdom" to spiritual powers in the present age (3:10–11), also describes the qualities expressed in the creedal words. The church is *one* in seven unities (4:4–6) that share the Trinitarian pattern observed above in 2 Corinthians 11. This Trinitarian motif also flows through the images of the church elsewhere in Ephesians, each of which can make sense only on the singular—one household of God (2:19), one home of the Spirit (2:21–22), and one body (3:6) and bride (5:25) of Christ. The church is *holy* because it is chosen by God (1:4), cleansed by Christ (5:26) and sealed with the Spirit of holiness (1:13). The church is *catholic* because Christ, enthroned above every power, exercises his universal lordship on behalf of the church, which is his fullness—expressing him wholly (1:20–23). Consequently, in him Jew and Gentile form one new humanity (2:15). The church is *apostolic*, since it is founded on the apostles and prophets (2:20, echoing Matthew 16:18) and the gospel divinely revealed to them (3:5).

Although Ephesians demonstrates that each of the four qualities is the present possession of the church as a gift of the Spirit, growth in each is expected and requires the cooperation of believers: the *unity* of the Spirit must be maintained (4:3); *holiness* must be practiced (4:17ff.); *catholicity* ("fullness") must be grown towards (4:13); and *apostolicity* ("unity in the faith") must be attained (4:8–16). The invisible, divine dimension of the church becomes visible through human activity. The four words are, thus, dynamic concepts, expressing both the reality of what the church is and what the church must increasingly *become*. They are indicators of devotion to Christ and markers of health in the growth of the church, essential to its worship and its mission. They are implications of devotion to Jesus: submission to one Lord makes us *one*; Christ's fullness generates *catholicity*; he makes his bride *holy*. Meanwhile, *apostolicity* has a vital role in guaranteeing the other three qualities by ensuring our devotion is to the true Christ, the historic Jesus.[4]

The Essence Diluted and Recaptured

The abuse of the four creedal words by the European church in the centuries after Constantine has been widely acknowledged.[5] As the church followed the imperial pattern by adopting an increasingly centralized, institutional, hierarchical form, the four words were redefined: *apostolicity* as the authority of bishops claiming unbroken succession from the apostles; *catholicity* as the presence in every place of one institution; *holiness* as the gift of the church mediated through sacraments; and *unity* as rigid uniformity. The words, now misused to enforce submission to a self-serving church, actually became barriers to pure devotion to Christ.

---

4   Karl Barth, *Dogmatics in Outline,* trans. G. T. Thomson (London: SCM, 1949), 145; Karl Barth *Church Dogmatics, Volume IV: The Doctrine of Reconciliation, Part One.,* trans. by G. W. Bromley (Edinburgh: T&T Clark.. 1956), 714; Charles Conniry, "Identifying Apostolic Christianity: A Synthesis of Viewpoints," *Journal of the Evangelical Theological Society,* 37(2) (1994), 259–261.

5   Berkouwer, *The Church,* 12ff; Avery Dulles, *Models of the Church, 2nd ed.* (Dublin: Gill and Macmillan, 1988), 124–125; Hans Küng, *The Church,* trans. Ray and Rosaleen Ockenden (London: Burns and Oates, 1968), 263ff; Hans Küng, *Credo: The Apostles' Creed Explained for Today,* trans. John Bowden (London: SCM, 1993), 133ff; Charles Van Engen, *God's Missionary People: Rethinking the Purpose of the Local Church* (Grand Rapids, MI: Baker 1991), 61.

The leading Reformers, despite their break with Rome, believed that the essence of the church had been diluted in the preceding centuries, but not lost. They explained disunity in the visible church by distinguishing it from the invisible church "enrolled in Heaven" (Heb 12:23) and proposed "marks" by which the true church could be recognized: the right preaching of the word, the right practice of the sacraments (two rather than seven), and, in some cases, church discipline. Roman Catholic responses to the Reformation insisted that the four words were manifest only in the Roman Catholic Church. Although some more recent Catholic theologians have acknowledged that the church must be critiqued against the qualities embodied in the four words, differing understandings of apostolicity and catholicity remain the greatest barriers in ecumenical dialogue.[6]

The Protestant idea that the true church can be identified by "marks" has been blamed for shifting the focus from what the church is to what it does, contributing to unrestrained pragmatism.[7] This distortion is, however, the opposite of what the Reformers intended. They understood, as the earlier discussion of Acts 2:42 revealed, that the church is kept true to its essence through practices as well as doctrine and expected the "marks" to lead to faithfulness to Christ.[8] Attention to the "marks" can help eliminate false dichotomies between being and doing.[9] The "marks" can lead congregations to a fuller understanding of three of four creedal words: sacraments (baptism and communion) express *oneness*; biblical preaching maintains *apostolicity*; and the prayerful exercise of discipline enhances *holiness*.[10]

The three predominant "marks" were, however, flawed in their inattention to *catholicity*. Protestant churches too often elevated secondary theological formulations and activities (which are contextually determined) alongside core doctrine and practices (which should be universal across contexts). Systematized theologies and detailed confessions were added to the creeds and, as denominations developed, details of church organization and non-essentials were used as labels to distinguish one "church" from another. Catholicity receded into the background and ever-increasing fragmentation resulted. In the context of territorial wars of religion and the continued linking of church and State, the outward impulse of mission was neglected. Even when later Protestants recaptured a missionary vision, they often exported their divisions.

Evangelicalism emerged within eighteenth century Protestantism as a renewal movement with four defining emphases: *crucicentrism* (the centrality of Christ and his cross), *biblicism* (the functional authority of Scripture), *conversionism* (expectation of personal faith

---

6   Dulles, *Models*, 127–137; Richard R. Gaillardetz, *Ecclesiology for a Global Church: A People Called and Sent* (Maryknoll, NY: Orbis, 2008): xx–xxi.

7   Craig Van Gelder, *The Essence of Church: A Community Created by the Spirit* (Grand Rapids: Baker, 2000), 57.

8   Berkouwer, *The Church*, 15; Reinhard Hütter, "The Church," in *Knowing the Triune God: The Work of the Spirit in the Practices of the Church,* eds. James Buckley and David Yeago (Grand Rapids: Eerdmans, 2001), 35; Van Engen, *God's Missionary People*, 63.

9   Donald Bloesch, *The Church: Sacraments, Worship, Ministry, Mission* (Downers Grove, IL: IVP, 2002), 39.

10   Jürgen Moltmann, *The Church in the Power of the Spirit: A Contribution to Messianic Ecclesiology,* trans. by Margaret Kohl (New York: Harper and Row, 1975), 341; Lesslie Newbigin, *The Household of God: Lectures on the Nature of the Church* (London: SCM, 1953), 50ff.

and transformation) and *activism* (commitment to service and mission).[11] Evangelicalism, reflecting post-Enlightenment individualism, ignited an individual devotion to Christ that fuelled vigorous personal piety and mission. While *biblicism* preserves *apostolicity* and *conversionism* promotes personal *holiness*, evangelicalism's *transdenominational* nature and individualistic bent, caused *oneness* and *catholicity* to be interpreted primarily in a spiritual sense to the neglect of their visible expressions.[12] Activism was channelled into "parachurch" agencies, supported through voluntary donations, and the predominant evangelical conception of "church" became the "local church" as a voluntary congregation. Evangelicalism, although it has restored some sense of belonging to the whole church, has an underdeveloped ecclesiology.[13]

Renewing the Essence in the Present

Various proposals have been made concerning the relationship of the four creedal words to mission. Some criticize them as incomplete and propose complementary words to add a missionary orientation.[14] Others see the fault not as a deficiency in the words but in the excessively inward orientation they were given by the institutional church of Christendom.[15] Based on their biblical roots, I have argued that the four words, as dynamic qualities, describe both the health and the mission of the church. Stated simply, mission is of the essence of the church. Each of the four words can enrich evangelicalism, helping to correct its ecclesiological deficit, and shape the contours of contemporary mission.

Oneness must be a visible reality, rather than only a theoretical commitment, if the church is to be a present sign to the world of Christ's love for his bride (John 13:35, 17:23). Positively, evangelicalism's elevation of the person and cross of Christ above all other theological commitments creates a powerful doctrinal core that has forged *unity* in diversity across ecclesiological and theological divides. Negatively, unreflective activism has too often permitted self-loving empire builders to hide behind a guise of serving God. The oneness of the church challenges evangelicals to adopt a default position of cooperation in mission with all who are in Christ and challenges us to consider mergers of congregations and organizations. It provokes us to reimagine settled congregations and so-called "parachurch" agen-

---

11   David Bebbington, *Evangelicalism in Modern Britain: History from the 1730s to 1980s* (London: Routledge 1989), 2–3.

12   Edmund Clowney, *The Church: Contours of Christian Theology* (Downers Grove: IVP, 1995), 110; Doug Gay, *Remixing The Church: The Five Moves of Emerging Ecclesiology* (London: SCM, 2011), 111.

13   George Vandervelde, "Ecclesiology in the Breach: Evangelical Soundings," *Evangelical Review of Theology, 23(1)* (1999), 30; Kevin Vanhoozer, "Evangelicalism and the Church: The Company of the Gospel," in *The Futures of Evangelicalism: Issues and Prospects*, eds. Craig Bartholomew, Robin Parry and Andrew West (Leicester: IVP, 2003), 41.

14   Martyn Atkins, "What is the Essence of the Church?" in *Mission-Shaped Questions: Defining Issues for Today's Church*, ed. Steven Croft (London: Church House Publishing, 2008); Howard Snyder, "The Marks of Evangelical Ecclesiology" in *Evangelical Ecclesiology: Reality or Illusion*, ed. by John G. Stackhouse Jr (Grand Rapids: Baker Academic, 2003), 22–23; Van Gelder, *The Essence of the Church*, 113ff.

15   Archbishop's Council, *Mission-Shaped Church: Church Planting and Fresh Expressions of Church in a Changing Context*, 2nd edn. (London: Church House Publishing, 2009), 98–99; Dulles, *Models*, 127–129; Moltmann, *The Church*, 337ff.; Van Engen, *God's Missionary People*, 65ff.

cies as two interdependent aspects of the one church. Oneness also suggests a reconceiving of "local church" as the whole church in a locality.

If oneness is valued, the core practices that supremely celebrate the church's oneness and renew its devotion to Christ—baptism and communion—will have central importance. The taking of bread and the cup (whatever type of bread and whatever is in the cup) must not be sidelined by less central practices, whether preaching or praise. Only a truly united church can point postmodern people, who are skeptical that there is any grand narrative with any settled destination, towards the eschatological horizon of the unity of all things under Christ. Our oneness in Christ compels us to make Christ known through declaring the true story of the world, the good news that Jesus Christ, crucified and risen, is Lord and Savior. Oneness places evangelism at the heart of mission.

Holiness is also essential for the church's mission. Evangelicalism recognizes correctly that holiness starts with the radical conversion of individuals that only the Holy Spirit effects. We are in danger, however, of thinking that holiness to God—being set apart for God—means withdrawal from the world when, in fact, it means serving the world for God's sake as Christ did. God's holy people will be profoundly countercultural, but will also sacrificially lay down their lives for the world. Our devotion to Christ spurs us on to follow his example in doing good to all as we have opportunity (Gal 6:10). Holiness requires acts of compassion as an essential element of mission.

Catholicity in its quantitative dimension has been extended through evangelical missions. The activist impulse contributed to the growth of the church globally, so that it is now a truly international phenomenon. Qualitative catholicity has, however, been more problematic. Some early evangelical missions failed to adequately distinguish the transcultural message of the gospel from the cultural baggage of missionaries. Although we now realize that the gospel must be contextualized into every culture, the risk today is that we fail to appreciate the degree to which the gospel creates its own culture. Evangelicals have sometimes extracted the propositional truths of the gospel from the narrative of a man who lived in a culture that is foreign to both the missionary and the unreached people. That true story displaces all lesser accounts of ultimate reality and when, through faith, it becomes our story, it recreates the values he embodied in our relationships with one another. The gospel restores wholeness and health to incomplete and diseased cultures.

Understood in this light, the idea of an ethnically or culturally homogeneous congregation is exposed as an oxymoron. Catholicity is of the essence of the church and it must be expressed not only through fellowship between congregations, but also within them. Homogeneous congregations may exist as a temporary compromise when people from unreached groups come to faith, but they should yearn for ways in which to embrace others and to move towards wholeness. Growth in discipleship will entail movement towards the eschatological vision of God's people, gathered from all ethnic groups and cultures, but given the markers of a new culture: a new song, a new identity and a new purpose (Rev 5:9–10). To resist or deny this possibility is to deny the reconciling power of the gospel. Only as the church demonstrates it catholicity, embodied in heterogeneous Christian communities, can it engage in the third dimension of mission, acts of justice on behalf of the oppressed and marginalized.

Apostolicity is essential as the church seeks to be one, holy, and catholic in mission. It includes submission to the authority of God's Word in Scripture, which will enable us to prioritize practices and doctrines that are of "first importance" (1 Cor 15:3) and to find resolutions to debates about everything else without compromising oneness, holiness, or catholicity. The apostolic testimony to Jesus, recorded in Scripture, is the norming standard as we encounter cultural differences and seek faithfulness. Evangelicals must to add to our biblicism the concern for continuity with the historic church that is also part of apostolicity. The gospel did not descend afresh from heaven to Wesley, Whitefield, Edwards, Spurgeon, Moody, Graham, or Stott—it was transmitted across the generations in an unbroken line stretching back to the apostles. Whatever the errors and inadequacies of the church in past generations, contemporary Christians stand in continuity with it, and the church of the present must learn from the church of the past and not ignore its legacy for good and ill. In the context of mission this means church planting must not proceed in reaction against or competition with existing congregations. Competitiveness and sectarianism is as much an enemy of apostolicity as unorthodox teaching.

Conclusion

The essence of the church is devotion to Christ. This devotion is created as people from all nations become his disciples through baptism and teaching (Matt 28:18–20). It is maintained through core practices of the church—communion, prayer, fellowship, and teaching (Acts 2:42). It is expressed in four creedal words which should be more than theoretical affirmations, stored on the theological shelf and dusted off occasionally to be used in prefaces to joint statements. They are invisible gifts created by the Spirit, but become visible signs pointing to Christ through the church's practices in and for the world. The one church declares the gospel of one Savior. The holy church serves its redeemer through acts of compassion. The catholic church represents the universal Lord in a ministry of justice and peacemaking. The apostolic church continues the mission of the apostles whose words, in Scripture, are its foundation. The one, holy, catholic, and apostolic church, devoted to Christ as a pure virgin, will be and do these things until the bridegroom comes.

Questions for Reflection:

1. How does the image of the church as the bride of Christ inform your understanding of life, ministry, and mission? What would change if you thought of life as marriage preparation, church as a wedding rehearsal, and mission as matchmaking?

2. In what ways has the denomination, congregation, or agency within which you primarily serve neglected the essence of the church? Which of the four words have been most valued and which have been neglected?

3. How can the church in post-Christian Europe and North America renew the essence of the church in its mission? What lessons can it learn from or teach to the church in the global South as it does so?

4. In your local context how can you begin to develop a missional understanding of church that appreciates the significance of all four words for the health and mission of the church? How can you integrate the three dimensions of mission identified in this chapter—evangelism, compassion, and justice?

References

Abraham, William J. 2001. I Believe in One Holy, Catholic, and Apostolic Church. In *Nicene Christianity: The Future for a New Ecumenism*. Ed. Christopher R. Seitz. Grand Rapids: Brazos.

Archbishop's Council. 2009. *Mission-Shaped Church: Church Planting and Fresh Expressions of Church in a Changing Context*, 2nd edn. London: Church House Publishing.

Atkins, Martyn. 2008. What Is the Essence of the Church? In *Mission-Shaped Questions: Defining Issues for Today's Church*. Ed. Steven Croft. London: Church House Publishing.

Barth, Karl. 1949. *Dogmatics in Outline*. Trans. G.T. Thomson. London: SCM.

———. 1956. *Church Dogmatics, Volume IV: The Doctrine of Reconciliation, Part One*. Trans. G.W. Bromley. Edinburgh: T&T Clark.

Bebbington, David W. 1989. *Evangelicalism in Modern Britain: History from the 1730s to 1980s*. London: Routledge.

Berkouwer, G.C. 1976. *The Church*. Trans. J.E. Davison. Grand Rapids: Eerdmans.

Bloesch, Donald G. 2002. *The Church: Sacraments, Worship, Ministry, Mission*. Christian Foundations. Downers Grove: IVP.

Clowney, Edmund P. 1995. *The Church: Contours of Christian Theology*. Downers Grove: IVP.

Conniry, Charles J. 1994. Identifying Apostolic Christianity: A Synthesis of Viewpoints. *Journal of the Evangelical Theological Society*, 37(2): 247–261.

Dulles, Avery. 1988. *Models of the Church*, 2nd edn. Dublin: Gill and Macmillan.

Gaillardetz, Richard R. 2008. *Ecclesiology for a Global Church: A People Called and Sent*. Theology in Global Perspective. Maryknoll: Orbis.

Gay, Doug. 2011. *Remixing the Church: The Five Moves of Emerging Ecclesiology*. London: SCM.

Humphrey, Edith. 2003. One, Holy, Catholic, and Apostolic: Awaiting the Redemption of Our Body. In *Evangelical Ecclesiology: Reality or Illusion?* Ed. John G. Stackhouse. Grand Rapids: Baker.

Hütter, Reinhard. 2001. The Church. In *Knowing the Triune God: The Work of the Spirit in the Practices of the Church*. Eds. James J. Buckley and David S. Yeago. Grand Rapids: Eerdmans.

———. 2004. *Bound to Be Free: Evangelical Catholic Engagements in Ecclesiology, Ethics and Ecumenism*. Grand Rapids: Eerdmans.

Küng, Hans. 1968. *The Church*. Trans. by Ray and Rosaleen Ockenden. London: Burns and Oates.

———. 1993. *Credo: The Apostles' Creed Explained for Today*. Trans. by John Bowden. London: SCM.

Moltmann, Jürgen. 1975. *The Church in the Power of the Spirit: A Contribution to Messianic Ecclesiology*. Trans. Margaret Kohl. New York: Harper and Row.

Newbigin, Lesslie. 1953. *The Household of God: Lectures on the Nature of the Church*. London: SCM.

———. 1978. *The Open Secret: Sketches for a Missionary Theology*. London: SPCK.

———. 1989. *The Gospel in a Pluralist Society*. London: SPCK.

Snyder, Howard. 2003. The Marks of Evangelical Ecclesiology. In *Evangelical Ecclesiology: Reality or Illusion*. Ed. John G. Stackhouse Jr. Grand Rapids: Baker Academic.

Van Engen, Charles. 1991. *God's Missionary People: Rethinking the Purpose of the Local Church*. Grand Rapids: Baker.

Van Gelder, Craig. 2000. *The Essence of the Church: A Community Created by the Spirit*. Grand Rapids: Baker.

Vandervelde, George. 1999. Ecclesiology in the Breach: Evangelical Soundings. *Evangelical Review of Theology*, 23(1): 29–51.

Vanhoozer, Kevin J. 2003. Evangelicalism and the Church: The Company of the Gospel. In *The Futures of Evangelicalism: Issues and Prospects*. Eds. Craig Bartholomew, Robin Parry, and Andrew West. Leicester: IVP.

Volf, Miroslav. 1998. *After Our Likeness: The Church as the Image of the Trinity*. Grand Rapids: Eerdmans.

Paul Coulter is a lecturer in practical theology and missiology in Belfast Bible College. He is engaged in doctoral studies on church planting by evangelicals in Northern Ireland, podcasts such as the "Restless Wonderer," visits churches as a Bible teacher and trainer, and serves on the Northern Ireland Executive Committee of the Evangelical Alliance. His professional background is in medicine and he has previously worked in church-based ministry in both cross-cultural and same-culture settings. He is the husband of a Chinese Malaysian wife and father to two young children.

CHAPTER 6

THE CHURCH AS GOD'S AGENT

A Study in Reflecting the Trinity

Peter Rowan

Troublesome Theological Baggage?

The doctrine of the Trinity was hammered out in the context of cross-cultural mission.

"It is indeed a significant fact that the great doctrinal struggles about the nature of the Trinity, especially about the mutual relations of the Son and the Father, developed right in the midst of the struggle between the church and the pagan world. These Trinitarian struggles were indeed an essential part of the battle to master the pagan worldview at the height of its power and self-confidence." Many Christians tend to steer clear of the doctrine not because they wish to deny it, but because "it has usually been regarded as a venerable formulation handed down from the past, or perhaps … a troublesome piece of theological baggage which is best kept out of sight when trying to commend the faith to unbelievers."[1]

For this reason, while most Christians will be Trinitarian in creed they may not necessarily be so in experience. They struggle to articulate its practical relevance for personal faith, never mind its connection with mission. But far from being "a piece of theological baggage," this doctrine is of central importance.

In his book *The Orthodox Church*, Timothy Ware reminds us that "Orthodoxy believes most passionately that the doctrine of the Holy Trinity is not a piece of 'high theology' reserved for the professional scholar, but something that has a living, practical importance for every Christian."[2] This is the spirit in which we should approach our topic.

Trinity and Mission: Latin Terms to Lausanne Commitments

It is worth remembering that until the sixteenth century the term "mission" was used to describe the activity of the Trinity—the Father's sending (missio) of the Son and the Father and the Son's sending (missio) of the Holy Spirit. We have the Jesuits to thank for extend-

---

1   Lesslie Newbigin, *Trinitarian Doctrine for Today's Mission* (Carlisle: Paternoster; [1963] 1998), 34–5.
2   Timothy Ware, *The Orthodox Church* (London: Penguin, [1963] 1991), 216.

ing the term "mission" beyond the activity of the Trinity to include the church spreading the Christian faith. It is always helpful to keep this order in mind: that the church's mission is always an extension of God's prior mission.

The twentieth century saw something of a revival of Trinitarian theology, and this has influenced missiological thinking—that mission is first of all God's mission and flows from the initiative and community of the Trinity. This larger perspective is good medicine for missionaries and churches who too often succumb to an introverted self-centeredness and have the propensity to limit the scope of the biblical mission. How true that, "We invite God's blessing on our human-centered mission strategies, but the only concept of mission into which God fits is the one of which he is the beginning and the end."[3]

In recent years evangelicals have been thinking hard about the Trinitarian basis of mission. The World Evangelical Fellowship's Mission Commission Consultation in Iguassu, Brazil in 1999, saw Ajith Fernando give a series of Bible readings on the theme "Grounding Our Reflections in Scripture: Biblical Trinitarianism and Mission." The Iguassu Affirmation contained a commitment to ongoing reflection on "Trinitarian foundation for mission."[4]

A more accessible and probably more influential expression of the *missio Trinitatis* is found in *The Cape Town Commitment of the Third Lausanne Congress on World Evangelization* which took place in Cape Town, 2010. The document's confession of faith and call to action are expressed within a Trinitarian framework using the covenant language of love. The Cape Town Commitment is a wonderfully clear and succinct vision of integral mission set within a Trinitarian framework.

The Church: Icon and Representative of the Trinity

There is an inherent danger of constructing our understanding of mission using isolated biblical texts. An understanding of what it means for the church to reflect the Triune God of mission requires a larger, altogether more comprehensive vision of God shaped by an engagement with the whole counsel of God. But we have to begin somewhere, and perhaps there's no better place than John's Gospel. Anastasios of Androussa writes that

> The starting point of any apostolic activity on our behalf is the promise and order of the Risen Lord in its Trinitarian perspective: "As the Father has sent me, even so I send you ... Receive the Holy Spirit" (John 20:21–22). The love of the Father has been expressed through the sending of the Son. "For God so loved the world that he gave his only Son ... For God sent the Son into the world" (John 3:16–17).[5]

---

3   Christopher J.H. Wright, "An Upside-Down World: Distinguishing Between Home and Mission Field No Longer Makes Sense," *Christian Vision Project* (www.christianvisionproject.com/2007/01/an_upsidedown_world {accessed 20/11/2007).

4   William Taylor, ed, *Global Missiology for the Twenty-first Century: The Iguassu Dialogue* (Grand Rapids: Baker; 2000), 19.

5   Anastasios of Androussa, "Orthodox Mission: Past, Present, Future," in *Your Will Be Done: Orthodoxy in Mission*, ed. George Lemopoulos (Geneva: WCC Publications, 1998), 79–81; cited in N.E. Thomas, *Classic Texts in Mission and World Christianity* (Maryknoll, NY: Orbis, 1995), 119.

John 3:16 has been described as "The inexhaustible, key gospel verse" laying out simply, yet profoundly "God's immanent nature and economic expression in the world."[6]

In the fourth Gospel, God is the sending God. John the Baptist is sent by God to bear testimony to Jesus; Jesus is sent to do the Father's will and to make him known. The Father and the Son send the Holy Spirit who continues the witness and work of Jesus in the world. And finally, the disciples are sent to accomplish the mission of Jesus, empowered by the Holy Spirit.

On first glance, it seems that the only one in John's Gospel who is not sent is the Father, but in reality the incarnation reveals the Father as both sender and sent. The key person at the center of all the sendings is Jesus. He is "the flaming center of the Christian message."[7] Remove him and the church has nothing to say and no mission to the world. "Every other mission," observes Köstenberger, "is derivative of the mission of Jesus: the mission of the Baptist, the Spirit, and the disciples."[8] And the disciples receive this commissioning not as isolated individuals but as a community. Of all the so-called classic missionary texts of the New Testament, Jesus' words of commissioning—"as the Father has sent me so I am sending you" (John 20:21)—are surely the clearest in terms of the church being sent as the representative of the Trinity. The immediate context is Trinitarian and the wider context of the fourth Gospel has already taken up the theme of representation in 13:20, where being a representative of Jesus is also, indirectly, to be a representative of the Father. "The sending of the church is intimately linked to the sending activity of the Trinity. It is not by human authority, but through the authority of the Triune God, who as Father sends, as Son redeems, and as Spirit empowers."[9]

Our understanding of what it means for the church to represent and reflect the Triune God who is missionary is also part of what it means for us to be made in the image of God. We most often apply this individually, but there is a corporate dimension which is not always present in our discussions on church and mission. Orthodox theology recognizes "the church as a whole is an icon of God the Trinity, reproducing on earth the mystery of unity in diversity."[10] So what does it mean for the whole church to image the whole-ness of the triune God, in bringing the whole gospel to the whole world?

Reflecting the Trinity in Building Community

Pursuing Partnership and Unity
The relationality and interdependence of the Trinity is to be reflected in how we pursue partnership with other Christians, churches, and organizations.

---

6   J. Corrie, ed., *Dictionary of Mission Theology: Evangelical Foundations* (Nottingham : IVP, 2007), 399.

7   C.E. Braaten, *The Flaming Centre: A Theology of the Christian Mission* (Philadelphia, PA: Fortress Press, 1977), 2.

8   A.J. Köstenberger and P.T. O'Brien, *Salvation to the Ends of the Earth: A Biblical Theology of Mission* (Downers Grove, IL: IVP, 2001), 209.

9   C. Ott, S.J. Strauss, and T.C. Tennent, *Encountering Theology of Mission: Biblical Foundations, Historical Developments, and Contemporary Issues* (Grand Rapids, MI: Baker Academic, 2010), 73.

10   Ware, *The Orthodox Church*, 244.

As the letter to the Ephesians explains, the church is a multiethnic community, and in this new humanity "is the promise that this society mirrors as in a microcosm the hope of the world and the universe, at present divided and at odds with its creator."[11] In the New Testament, "God's reconciling work in his people during the present age is presented as a pilot scheme for the realization of his saving purpose."[12] This means that a foretaste of God's ultimate reconciling work is already present in creation—in the church. The working out of this eschatological vision into the concrete ministry and mission of the church must surely include demonstrating visible, experienced unity. This, writes Hastings, is "the most powerful dynamic in mission." Reform movements within the church therefore need to be tempered, so that "emerging churches and church plants ... do all they can to remain within the catholicity of the church. Jesus calls the church to missional effectiveness by working for unity."[13]

Seeking to maintain gospel integrity and seeking to achieve the unity of the church are not mutually exclusive goals. Indeed, the former probably requires the latter. As Kevin Vanhoozer puts it, "The Truth of the gospel ranks higher in the evangelical order of priorities than does visible church unity. It may be time, however, to rethink our priorities."[14]

Sometimes it is those situations closest to home that we struggle with most. Vinoth Ramachandra writes of a visit to Seoul to take part in a conference on reconciliation.

> I was impressed by the passionate intensity of my South Korean friends' prayers for unification with their North Korean kinsmen. Every day, groups of South Korean Christians gather in the de-militarized zone to pray for the unification of the peninsula. But I saw no comparable passion for the unity of the church in South Korea. Indeed they must have found my questions regarding Christian unity and partnership in mission as baffling as I did their lack of interest in the latter.[15]

There is a sense in which churches belong to each other. Every church is part of the body of Christ. Every church is to reflect the relationality and interconnectedness of the Trinity in its pursuit of partnership and unity. We have all been called "into the fellowship of his Son, Jesus Christ our Lord" (1 Cor 1:9). Churches may differ in terms of organizational structure and worship patterns, and yet there is "one body and one Spirit... one hope... one Lord, one faith, one baptism, one God and Father of all" (Eph 4:4–5).

Partnership is not simply a useful idea in carrying out the task of mission. It expresses something of the essence of what the church is, and reflects the Trinity in our relationships. "Within world Christianity, 'partnership' expresses a relationship between churches based

---

11   R. Martin, *Reconciliation: A Study in Paul's Theology* (London: Marshall, Morgan & Scott, 1981), 232.

12   F.F. Bruce, "Some Thoughts on Paul and Paulinism," in *Vox Evangelica* 7:14 (1971), 14.

13   R. Hastings, *Missional God, Missional Church: Hope for Re-Evangelizing the West* (Downers Grove: IVP, 2012), 115.

14   K. Vanhoozer, "Evangelicalism and the Church: The Company of the Gospel," in *The Futures of Evangelicalism: Issues and Prospects,* eds. C. Bartholomew, R. Parry and A. West (Downers Grove, IL: IVP, 2003), 40–99.

15   V. Ramachandra, "Foreword," in *Proclaiming the Peacemaker: The Malaysian Church As an Agent of Reconciliation in a Multi-Cultural Society,* P. Rowan (Oxford: Regnum, 2012), xi–xii.

on trust, mutual recognition, and reciprocal interchange … It is a term designed to show how different parts of the church belong to one another and find their fulfilment through sharing a common life."[16]

When Paul writes to the Corinthians and connects them with "churches everywhere that call on the name of our Lord Jesus Christ—their Lord and ours" (1 Cor 1:2), he is reminding the Corinthians that they are part of a larger body. They are not the only pebble on the beach. Our local contextual expressions of church need to be balanced with their catholicity—the practical outworking of their theological connection to "churches everywhere."

Building Reconciled Communities

What distinctive form should church communities take, particularly in contexts of ethnic and cultural diversity? How can a congregation become the dynamic expression of the triune God in terms of unity in diversity? One answer, particularly in ethnically diverse contexts, is for a local church to express the way Christian identity transcends ethnic and cultural boundaries.

Let me illustrate this from the Malaysian context. Since Malaysia's independence, many have pinned their hopes on the education system to provide the necessary foundations for racial integration, and on the local school as a place where such integration can be fostered and seen in action, preparing each generation for the reality of *bangsa Malaysia*.[17] However, research has shown that in this aspect at least, the education system has largely failed.[18] Therefore, where in Malaysia can a racially reconciled community be seen in action? As Christians we ought to be able to point to the local church. In reality however, most congregations are as racially segregated as the society around them. Denison Jayasooria has called for the breaking down of racial barriers within the Christian community:

> While it is true to affirm the importance of an individual's or community's cultural, linguistic, or racial background, those who have found new life in Jesus are a radical community … Within our Malaysian context where there is racial and linguistic polarization, the Christian community should set a model of inter-ethnic relations. However the tragic reality is, many large denominations operate like the Barisan Nasional. As a radical step forward, should not our churches drop labels like "Chinese Church," "Tamil Church," etc. … There must be the breaking down of racial barriers and myths.[19]

16   J.A. Kirk, *What Is Mission?* (London: DLT, 1999), 184.

17   The goal of National Unity gave birth to the phrase "bangsa Malaysia," first used by the former Malaysian Prime Minister, Mahathir Mohammad in 1991. "Bangsa" is a Malay word meaning "race, nationality; belonging to a race, or nationality." Bangsa Malaysia means "Malaysian nationality," "Malaysian people," or "united Malaysian people."

18   See Lee Hock Guan, "Globalisation and Ethnic Integration in Malaysian Education," in *Malaysia: Recent Trends and Challenges,* eds. Saw Swee-Hock and K. Kesavapany (Singapore: Institute of South East Asian Studies, 2006), 230–259.

19   D. Jayasooria, *Social Transformation: Theology and Action* (Kuala Lumpur: Malaysia Care, 1990).

The gospel transcends the barriers of race, ethnicity, and culture, making the church the most inclusive community on earth. In its local expression it therefore has the potential to become a community of hope in a fragmented world. In Malaysia, the church has the task of not only proclaiming the message of reconciliation to all Malaysians, but of embodying the concrete implications of that message in its community life, so that Malaysians of all races can look at a local church and see the gospel fleshed out in a racially reconciled group of people who can work, worship, and witness together. This is one dimension of what it means for the church to reflect the Trinity: a unity in diversity. Such a model of reconciliation will find various pathways opening up for reconciliation and peacebuilding initiatives to be carried out within the wider community. Richard Dorall recognizes that the unique, multiethnic make-up of the church in Malaysia creates possibilities:

> The most striking feature of Malaysia's non-Christian religions is their ethnic exclusivity. Only Christianity is multiethnic, reflecting closely in its membership the overall ethnic composition of Malaysia … Christianity, then, is uniquely placed to make major contributions to genuine multiracial living in Malaysia.[20]

In diverse and fragmented communities, church planting strategies should contain the goal of seeing churches birthed that reflect the community of the triune God—churches which demonstrate how the gospel has the power to bring diverse peoples together, forming them into reconciled communities. Church planting strategies where this intentionality is absent risk distorting the gospel itself: "The moment we make 'planting churches within people groups' the aim of Christian mission, even in heterogeneous geographical areas, we inevitably distort the gospel so that it no longer confronts the idolatries of politics and culture. It no longer challenges converts to identify with the 'outsider' and even the 'enemy.'"[21]

It may be the case that working with one particular ethnic group is a useful starting point in evangelism and in the early stages of church planting, but there are significant theological reasons why it is necessary for new Christians and young congregations to understand early on in their spiritual pilgrimage that they are part of the whole people of God, the multiethnic, multicultural people of God, and that the gospel requires us to demonstrate the social implications of the doctrine of reconciliation and the doctrine of the Trinity.

Conclusion

In the early fifteenth century, the Russian iconographer, Andrei Rublev, painted a famous icon of the Trinity. It is based on the Genesis 18 narrative which describes Abraham being visited by three angels. In the icon these angels are depicted as God the Father, Jesus, and the Holy Spirit seated around a table, and the Trinity is pictured inviting us into their mysterious community where there is a space at the table. The icon's purpose is to remind the believer of the call to go deeper into the divine life. And this is the key to our becoming God's agents in mission and reflecting the triune God.

---

20   R.F. Dorrall, *Religion and Ethnicity in Malaysia: A Preliminary Analysis of Data in the 1980 Population and Housing Census of Malaysia,* unpublished, no date given.

21   H. Peskett and V. Ramachandra, *The Message of Mission* (Leicester: IVP, 2003), 204.

The Genesis 18 narrative contains the promise to Abraham that "all nations will be blessed through him," a promise that finds fulfilment as the Patriarch keeps "the way of the Lord" (Gen 18:19)—a common theme in Old Testament ethics and one which is carried over into the New Testament with the pattern of discipleship seen in the Gospels and in Paul (e.g., Eph 5:1ff). As with Abraham, so with us: in the context of a sinful world, God calls his people to be characterized by the way of the Lord, the way of mirroring the Triune God in the totality of life. And as we live that kind of life, God's mission to the nations is fulfilled.

Questions for Reflection:

1. Interpretations of the Trinity have tended to produce certain emphases in how Christians have understood mission. In theological literature, there are three main interpretations of the Trinity: the "immanent," the "economic," and the "social." What missional paradigm might emerge from each of these, and how might a breadth of Trinitarian perspective encourage a more integrated understanding of mission?

2. "Cultural diversity should in no way militate against the unity of the Church ... Such diversity in fact should serve the unity." (David Bosch). Do you agree? In the area of church planting, give examples of how we might balance contextuality with catholicity.

3. How important to you is visible church unity in relation to the missionary task that you are particularly concerned with?

References

Anastasios of Androussa. 1998. Orthodox Mission: Past, Present, Future. In *Your Will Be Done: Orthodoxy in Mission.* Ed. George Lemopoulos. Geneva: WCC Publications.

Braaten, C.E. 1977. *The Flaming Centre: A Theology of the Christian Mission.* Philadelphia, PA: Fortress Press.

Bruce, F.F. 1971. Some Thoughts on Paul and Paulinism. In *Vox Evangelica* 7(14).

Corrie, J. ed., 2007. *Dictionary of Mission Theology: Evangelical Foundations.* Nottingham: IVP.

Dorrall, R.F. n.d. *Religion and Ethnicity in Malaysia: A Preliminary Analysis of Data in the 1980 Population and Housing Census of Malaysia.* Unpublished, no date given.

Guan, Lee Hock. 2006. Globalisation and Ethnic Integration in Malaysian Education. In *Malaysia: Recent Trends and Challenges.* Eds. Saw Swee-Hock and K. Kesavapany. Singapore: Institute of South East Asian Studies.

Hastings, R. 2012. *Missional God, Missional Church: Hope for Re-Evangelizing the West.* Downers Grove: IVP.

Jayasooria, D. 1990. *Social Transformation: Theology and Action.* Kuala Lumpur: Malaysia Care.

Kirk, J.A. 1999. *What Is Mission?* London: DLT.

Köstenberger, A.J. and P.T. O'Brien. 2001. *Salvation to the Ends of the Earth: A Biblical Theology of Mission*. Downers Grove, IL: IVP.

Martin, R. 1981. *Reconciliation: A Study in Paul's Theology*. London: Marshall, Morgan & Scott.

Newbigin, Lesslie. 1998. *Trinitarian Doctrine for Today's Mission*. Carlisle: Paternoster.

Ott, C., S.J. Strauss and T.C. Tennent. 2010. *Encountering Theology of Mission: Biblical Foundations, Historical Developments, and Contemporary Issues*. Grand Rapids, MI: Baker Academic.

Peskett, H. and V. Ramachandra. 2003. *The Message of Mission*. Leicester: IVP.

Ramachandra, V. 2012. Foreword. In *Proclaiming the Peacemaker: The Malaysian Church as an Agent of Reconciliation in a Multi-Cultural Society*. P. Rowan. Oxford: Regnum.

Taylor, William, ed. 2000. *Global Missiology for the Twenty-first Century: The Iguassu Dialogue*. Grand Rapids: Baker.

Thomas, N.E. 1995. *Classic Texts in Mission and World Christianity*. Maryknoll, NY: Orbis.

Vanhoozer, Kevin. 2003. Evangelicalism and the Church: The Company of the Gospel. In *The Futures of Evangelicalism: Issues and Prospects*. Eds. C. Bartholomew, R. Parry and A. West. Downers Grove, IL: IVP.

Ware, Timothy. 1991. *The Orthodox Church*. London: Penguin.

Wright, Christopher J.H. 2007. An Upside-Down World: Distinguishing Between Home and Mission Field No Longer Makes Sense. *Christian Vision Project*. www.christianvisionproject.com/2007/01/an_upsidedown_world.

Peter Rowan is from Northern Ireland and has worked with OMF International since 1998. After teaching missiology in Malaysia for ten years he returned to the UK in 2009 to serve as National Director for OMF International (UK), a role he shares with his wife, Christine. A graduate of All Nations College, he holds a PhD in missiology.

CHAPTER 7

THE CHURCH AND MISSION IN THE NEW TESTAMENT

Paul Joshua Bhakiaraj

The New Testament as a whole is a record and expression of the life of the church in mission. Right from the day of Pentecost, where it began, to the vision of the end times, the background to the writings and the very writings themselves implicitly represent and even explicitly speak of a church in mission or, as the case may be, of a church not realizing her genuine identity of a community set apart and sent into the world on behalf of the mission of God. The New Testament is, in essence, a missionary document and New Testament theology is essentially a missionary theology. This is the basic assumption that forms the background to these reflections that follow. I will seek to argue that the Scriptures exhort us not to be thinking of church *and* mission, as if they were two separate aspects of the Christian life that one can choose to participate in if it so suits us, but rather as biblically saturated Christians we ought to be thinking of a church *in* mission of which we are an integral part. Mature Christian discipleship will see missiology and ecclesiology walking hand-in-hand and not existing independently of each other.

The Importance of the Whole Bible's Story

We will do well to recognize that the New Testament cannot be understood without reference to the Old Testament, and more particularly so if the focus is on the church in mission. One can only understand the church, her identity and role, if she is seen in the context of the whole Bible's narrative and not exclusively from the New Testament writings alone. For it is right at the beginning of the biblical narrative that we find God's overall purposes expressed and at its end we find a vision of the consummation of that agenda. If the people of God, the church, are part of that plan, as we see for example in Ephesians 3:10–12, then the entire flow of Scripture in which we see that purpose being worked out will be vital for our understanding and practice. Even though there are numerous genres, historical periods, and authors that give shape to and situate the writings of Scripture, the Bible forms an organic whole: that organic whole being given to it by the *missio Dei,* or the mission of God.

The Bible not only describes for us the working out of that *missio Dei,* through the warp and woof of the Israelites and subsequently of the church in the Greco-Roman world, but is in fact occasioned by it. We have the Bible because God in his love decided to first create the world, and second create a people through whom he desired to reveal to the world himself and his overall purposes. In a sense, the Bible is a by-product of that activity of God in the world through his people. That activity of God, the *missio Dei*, forms the backdrop to the Scriptures. The entire biblical record is situated in the outworking of the *missio Dei*; it is what gives the entire biblical narrative its primary framework. Accordingly, as Christopher Wright has suggested, it would be more appropriate to talk of the missional basis for the Bible rather than a biblical basis for mission.[1] That is to say mission is not just a subject that is found in the Bible, but the Bible itself is a result of the mission of God and *missio Dei* is what the Bible as a whole is all about. He helpfully expresses his intention in making such an assertion thus:

> I want them to see not just that the Bible contains a number of texts which happen to provide a rationale for missionary endeavour, but that the whole Bible is itself a "missional" phenomenon … The writings, which now comprise our Bible, are themselves the product of, and witness to, the ultimate mission of God … So a missional reading of such texts is very definitely not a matter of, first, finding the "real" meaning by objective exegesis, and only then, secondly, cranking up some "missiological implications" as a homiletic supplement to the "text itself." Rather, it is to see how a text often has its origin in some issue, need, controversy, or threat which the people of God needed to address in the context of their mission. The text in itself is a product of mission in action.[2]

When it comes to the New Testament we may therefore say that it is a record and expression of mission in action, just as the Old Testament was, though in a qualitatively different way. In this reckoning, mission, in the first instance, does not derive from the command of Jesus, though that is important, but is motivated by and patterned on the very God whom Christians worship and serve. This God is by nature a missionary; the Father sends his son and the Father and Son send the Spirit and altogether they send the church. Mission therefore derives supremely from the character and nature of the Triune God. This nature and character which is in turn stamped on the church creates and calls this body of Christ to be a church *in* mission.

Church in Mission: The New Testament Church's Experience

Valuable and instructive patterns of mission in action are visible as we look more closely into the early church's experience, particularly the narrative found in the Acts of the Apostles. In Acts 1:6–7, as we learn about the curiosity of the disciples regarding eschatological times and dates, we are also told of Jesus' overall reliance on God's appointed time: "He said to them: 'It is not for you to know the times or dates the Father has set by his own authority.'" In placing this at the start of his second volume, Luke signals that the grand plan the mis-

---

1   Christopher J.H. Wright, *The Mission of God: Unlocking the Bible's Grand Narrative* (Downers Grove, Il,: IVP, 2006), 29.

2   Christopher J.H Wright, *Truth with a Mission: Reading All Scripture Missiologically*, Grove Booklet Series (Cambridge: Grove Books, 2005).

sion of God is following, of which his second volume is a record, is set by God the Father and not dictated by human events or actors. Luke affirms that God is in control and he will accomplish his work in his time. Not long after that in Acts 2:17 we find that idea reiterated. Peter explains the significance of Pentecost using the Joel prophecy (Joel 2:28), "In the last days, God says, I will pour my Spirit on all people." Notice it is emphasized that this is God's will being accomplished in the pouring of the Holy Spirit and that this was occurring in God's own time. Both the purpose and the timing find their origins in God. This idea finds another echo in Acts 1:8. Here God sends the Holy Spirit to empower his disciples to be his witnesses "to the ends of the earth." The desire of God is that his agenda, which graciously includes all the earth, will be accomplished in his own time. Just as we observe in the Old Testament, God chooses his people for his purposes. As these Scriptures attest, mission follows God's prerogative because it is his mission.

Having observed this central point, it may be worth pondering over the stark contrast between the differing conceptions expressed in Acts 1:6 and Acts 1:8. While the former, preferred and even expected by the disciples, was founded on the centripetal action of Israel at the center and the nations coming toward them in order to find God, the latter, following God's plan, was fuelled by a centrifugal conception of the people of God, endowed with his Spirit, going into all the nations to make disciples, thereby fulfilling his agenda. Now that Christ had been resurrected and ascended and that the Spirit had descended, the older conception of mission was reversed, giving way to a new conception. In this new era God was doing a new thing to bless all the nations. The Old Testament remains crucial to the understanding of the *missio Dei*. While there is a significant transformation to those ideas and practices (e.g., 1 Pet 2:4–9, where clear reference to Old Testament ideas are evident), yet it remains extremely significant. It certainly was that overall agenda, as expressed in Genesis 12, for example, that was being accomplished, yet it was now being done through the specific agency of his church.

The disciples, who constituted the church, had to learn that the prime actor in this mission that they were invited to participate in was the God they worshiped and served. In these two significant events—the sending of the Spirit and the launching of the church—God was accomplishing his agenda in the world. Both the giving of the Spirit and the simultaneous inauguration of the church was to be seen as part of the missionary plan of God. The New Testament church that was born on the day of Pentecost, therefore, learned right from the beginning that the formation of this reality, called the church, was integrally tied to mission. The church implied mission. In their early experience of this new era in which God was acting specially to further his mission, the disciples came to understand that the church and mission were not two separate tasks but rather one vocation. The Holy Spirit was given as the empowerment, the *dunamis,* for mission to the church who was invited to bear witness to the ends of the earth. Both the *charis* and the calling had mission written all over it. If the church was therefore formed by the indwelling of the Holy Spirit, and the Holy Spirit was, among other things, the Spirit of mission, could the church be characterized by anything else other than mission?

Though there are clear signs that this was understood in part by the early church, it took some direct orchestration by God himself for that mission to move beyond certain human boundaries. While there may have been passionate missionary activity among the Jews, in the reluctance of the early church to move beyond the safe environs of Jerusalem and Judaism we find evidence of a less than comprehensive grasp of what that *missio Dei* was all about. We observe in the narrative that though the promise and invitation of Acts 1:8 was heard loud and clear, less clear was moving that promise and invitation from Jerusalem to Judea and Samaria and even beyond to the ends of the earth. We seem to find little intention of going beyond the boundaries circumscribed by Jewish geographical, social, religious, and other such conventions and propriety. This is clearly exemplified, for example, in the narrative of the interaction between Peter and Cornelius found in Acts 10.

It is evident that the Spirit of God was active in the life of Cornelius, the Roman centurion. His devout and holy life expressed in his prayers and his care for the poor expressed in his alms-giving came up as an offering to the Lord (Acts 10:1–4). Yet, as the narrative explains, the apostles had a difficult time in accepting the work of God outside their fold. Notwithstanding the supernatural communication methods that God had to employ to get through to Peter, he was reluctant to transgress conventional Jewish boundaries. It was not without some struggle that he then goes to minister to Cornelius and his family and there observes first-hand the abundant grace and supernatural power of God at work, "even among the Gentiles" (Acts 10:45). God was leading the predominantly Jewish church outward to the world at large inhabited predominantly by Gentiles. This transgression of Jewish religious, cultural, and geographical boundaries was not an easy process, but just as God worked in and through Peter he accomplished his work among the leaders of the early church as well, who acceded to this transformation as described in Acts 11:18. Under the superintendence of God himself, the church was being transformed from a primarily Jewish entity into a church *in* mission, a church for others.

This Acts 1:8 principle of a church in mission, a church for others, finds expression once again in the narrative, particularly within the life of the church in Antioch (Acts 11:19ff). Whereas it took a supernatural vision in the case of Peter, it takes a bout of persecution (Acts 8:1, 11:19) for the realization of this calling at Antioch. As they are persecuted and thus scattered across Asia minor, some followers of Christ willingly participate in the work of God among the nations as they share the good news to Greeks also (Acts 11:20). The selfsame struggle that plagued the Apostles in Jerusalem is also active here. It took men from Cypress and Cyrene to step outside their comfort zone and realize their calling to be a church in mission, a church for others. As we will observe in the narrative that explains what transpired, such missional identity and actions transform the church in the New Testament. And such transformation meets the approval of Barnabas, the son of encouragement, and later Saul-turned-Paul who came and served with this church in Antioch (Acts 11:22–16). They not only served for a year in the church there but, in due course, they were commissioned on their first missionary journey. The missionary journeys which became so significant for the expansion of the gospel and the establishing of the church around Asia minor was launched by the church in Antioch and not Jerusalem. In these and other ways the church in Antioch, we may say, set in place a pattern of a church *in* mission for posterity and thus represents for the worldwide church a model to live in and live out.

Missionary Ecclesiology

This brief theological reading of the experience of the early church has been instructive in alerting us to the integral relationship that exists between church and mission. Now let us briefly survey the development of theological thought that has caught up with and been reckoned with a biblical understanding. At the start of the twentieth century, the church, theologically speaking, was seen by many as existing in the West, and mission was seen as that which was done in the rest of the world. There seemed to be a distinction that was drawn between the two. Over time, however, this conception of the church underwent a radical change. Among Protestants this idea was first challenged at the International Missionary Council Conference held in Jerusalem in 1928 and was later given up at Tambaram in 1938. In Willingen 1952, the concept of *missio Dei* came into prominence. As a consequence the entire church was seen as being called to participate in God's mission. Whereas in the Roman Catholic Church it was not until Vatican II (1962) that we saw a move away from the centrality of the institutional church. The document *Lumen Gentium* expressed this integral vision of mission and the church.

This idea that the church on earth is by its very nature missionary, since, according to the plan of the Father, it has its origin in the mission of the Son and the Holy Spirit, gained greater prominence. According to the concept of *missio Dei*, mission is in the first instance the work of God sending Jesus and the Spirit for the redemption of the world. This then leads to the recognition that the church is taken up into God's mission as an instrument of that work of God. The Willingen conference made this memorable statement: "There is no participation in Christ without participation in his mission to the world. That by which the church receives its existence is that by which it is also given its world-mission. 'As the Father has sent me, even so send I you'" (John 20:21).[3] Mission was thus not seen as something that members of the church do in far-away lands, rather the church was understood as a function of God's mission, serving the purpose of God in the world. To place the church as a subset under God's mission is therefore to say that God's mission is the framework that provides the church its orientation. This understanding has gained wide acceptance such that it is called "the new conciliar understanding of mission" and is perhaps the most widely recognized idea in the conversation about missionary ecclesiology.[4]

To be sure this Trinitarian understanding of mission, as noted, poses a challenge to traditional ecclesiology. Theology has long thought of mission as an activity that takes place only after the church is constituted, as "one among several functions of the church," and in unreached and far-away lands.[5] A one time Bishop of the church of South India, Lesslie Newbigin explains that "the very general belief of Christians in most churches … that the church can exist without being a mission involves a radical contradiction of the truth of

---

3   Norman Goodall, *Missions Under the Cross* (Edinburgh: Edinburgh House, 1953), 190.

4   Veli-Matti Kärkkäinen, *An Introduction to Ecclesiology* (Downers Grove, IVP Academic, 2002), 151.

5   Wilbert R. Shenk, *Changing Frontiers of Mission* (New York: Orbis Books, 1999), 7.

the church's being."[6] Bosch makes a similar claim: "It is impossible to talk about the church without at the same time talking about mission. One can no longer talk about church and mission, only about the mission of the church."[7] Consequently we now recognize that a contemporary theology of mission rooted as it is in the mission of the Trinitarian God, will affirm that the church does not so much have a mission as much as mission has a church. The church is either missionary in its very being or it is not the church.

The missionary church that is being spoken of here, one must be clear, does not only mean the church in the West. On the contrary it refers to the church around the world. This theological idea does not discriminate between so-called older churches and younger churches; between established and emerging churches. All churches, wherever they happen to be located and whatever stage of their life they happen to be in, are in essence part of the missionary church. Consequently, as the World Council of Churches' Commission on World Mission and Evangelism expressed in its 1963 meeting in Mexico City, mission is now on "six continents."[8] We should not speak about "sending churches" and "receiving churches." Mission happens wherever the church is; it is how the church exists. Indeed mission is from everywhere to everywhere.[9]

Although it represents a challenge to conventional theology, it is gratifying that this theological emphasis on the *missio Dei*, which affirms that God is the agent of mission, and the church's calling to participate in that *missio Dei* finds echoes in recent ecumenical documents issued at their significant events. The Edinburgh 2010 *Common Call* describes the church as a sign and symbol of the reign of God, called "to witness to Christ today by sharing in God's mission of love through the transforming power of the Holy Spirit."[10] And in a similar vein the *Cape Town Commitment* issued at the Lausanne III Congress says that the mission of God flows from the love of God: "World evangelization is the outflow of God's love to us and through us."[11] So it appears that the idea that God has called the church in every situation to be a missionary church has brought about significant changes to the way the church is being viewed. This bodes well for the twenty-first century church around the world as it experiences numerous changes and faces numerous challenges on many fronts.

Conclusion

With our re-reading of the Scriptures and reflection on the development of theological thought, I have been seeking to demonstrate that church and mission are integrally tied to each other. David Bosch quite appropriately wrote: "The *missio Dei* institutes the *missiones ecclesiae*."[12] The church has come into being as a result of mission and hence mission ought

---

6   Lesslie Newbigin, *The Household of God: Lectures on the Nature of the Church* (London: SCM Press, 1953), 170.

7   David Bosch, *Transforming Mission: Paradigm Shifts in Theology of Mission* (Maryknoll, NY: Orbis Books, 1991), 372.

8   See R.K. Orchard, ed., *Witness in Six Continents: Records of the CWME; Mexico City 1963* (London: Edinburgh House Press, 1964).

9   Michael Nazir-Ali, *From Everywhere to Everywhere: A Worldview of Mission* (London: Collins, 1990).

10   http://www.edinburgh2010.org/fileadmin/Edinburgh_2010_Common_Call_with_explanation.pdf.

11   http://www.lausanne.org/content/ctc/ctcommitment.

12   Bosch, *Transforming Mission*, 391.

to characterize the whole of Christian existence. The identity of the church as a missionary community is given to it by its Lord, and thus participates in God's mission because it cannot do otherwise. We may accordingly say that unless we see the body of Christ as a missionary church, we are not seeing the real church. In the light of all this can we continue to labor under the notion of the church *and* mission? Should we not rather seek to be active members of the church *in* mission?

Questions for Reflection:

1. The author emphasizes the need to keep church and mission "integrally tied." What is the biblical basis for that affirmation, according to him? Are there other biblical references that come to your mind, supporting the same thought?
2. How would you explain the term "church in mission," based on Paul Joshua's text?
3. In what way has later missiological reflection about the role of the church in mission influenced your context and congregation?

References

Bosch, David. 1991. *Transforming Mission: Paradigm Shifts in Theology of Mission.* Maryknoll, NY: Orbis Books.

Goodall, Norman. 1953. *Missions Under the Cross.* Edinburgh: Edinburgh House.

Kärkkäinen, Veli-Matti. 2002. *An Introduction to Ecclesiology.* Downers, Grove: IVP Academic.

Nazir-Ali, Michael. 1990. *From Everywhere to Everywhere: A Worldview of Mission.* London: Collins.

Newbigin, Lesslie. 1953. *The Household of God: Lectures on the Nature of the Church.* London: SCM Press.

Orchard, R.K., ed., 1964. *Witness in Six Continents: Records of the CWME; Mexico City 1963* London: Edinburgh House Press.

Shenk, Wilbert R. 1999. *Changing Frontiers of Mission.* New York: Orbis Books.

Wright, Christopher J.H. 2005. *Truth with a Mission: Reading All Scripture Missiologically.* Grove Booklet Series. Cambridge: Grove Books.

———. 2006. *The Mission of God: Unlocking the Bible's Grand Narrative.* Downers Grove, IL: IVP.

Paul Joshua Bhakiaraj, PhD, is a Commended Worker and an Elder at the Tamil Brethren Church. He serves as Professor of Theology at South Asia Institute of Advanced Christian Studies (SAIACS), Bangalore, India. Among other affiliations he is an Associate of the Mission Commission of the World Evangelical Alliance, a member of the Lausanne

Theology Working Group and a part of the International Steering Group of the International Fellowship of Mission as Transformation (INFEMIT). He has published widely in journals and in books such as *Atlas of Global Christianity* (Edinburgh, 2010) and *Oxford Handbook of Christianity in Asia* (Oxford, 2014); he is also involved in an itinerant preaching and teaching ministry.

CHAPTER 8

THE PILGRIM CHURCH

David D. Ruiz M.

The church is described as the community of those who are called by God to be his people, according to Acts 2:39. As we see in the calling of the apostles, Jesus Christ himself selected a particular twelve from the larger group of his disciples and clarified their purpose: "*so that they might be with him* to become his people and with the purpose that *he might send them out to preach*" (Mark 3:14 ESV, emphasis mine). This is the starting point of a church on the move, a community of people who believe in Christ and understand that the church is also called to be sent. As Engelsviken writes, "It is not possible to be a disciple of Jesus and belong to his church without also being called to mission."[1] In the last meeting at the mountain of Galilee, the risen Lord Jesus Christ confirmed for them that this calling to be sent is for the whole church and the prime means to disciple the nations.

As we know, the apostolic church from the start was a church on the move. We see the church advancing with the purpose of filling the known earth with the gospel of Jesus Christ, to make disciples, and to see them advancing in the commitment to share it with everyone everywhere. The book of Acts confirms that the church is a pilgrim by its very nature. At the very core of this book is the sense of advance, not only in the development of the church but also in its geographical expansion. It shows how the church advanced from Jerusalem to Rome, the heart of the empire, a model of its progression into all the nations. The epitome of the pilgrimage is when we understand that Christians are "a pilgrim people on the way through this world toward the final goal of the church, which is perfect communion with God 'face to face,' and to serve and worship him forever in his new creation (Rev 7:9–17; 21:1–5; Rom 8:22–23)."[2]

With Peter's first sermon in Acts 2, we observe how the church starts on the move. Among those three thousand who received his word were Parthians, Medes, Elamites; people from Cappadocia, Pontus, Asia, Phrygia, Pamphylia, Egypt; and people from the parts of Libya, Rome and beyond who would carry with them the church as they returned to their home places. However, the first massive mobilization of the church is registered in Acts 8. This magnificent chapter helps us understand what the church did when they were moving, how they engaged in the process of discipling the nations, and how they measured the success

---

1   T. Engelsviken, "Church/Ecclesiology," in *Dictionary of Mission Theology*, ed. John Corrie (Downers Grove, IL: IVP, 2007), 51–55.

2   Engelsviken, "Church/Ecclesiology," 51–55.

of this task. This chapter alone reminds us to reflect and rediscover the degree to which the concept of pilgrimage is at the very nature of the church.

The Pilgrim Nature of the Church

Before we engage with the events of Acts 8, Acts 1:8 has already introduced us to the pilgrim nature of the church. This core passage is like a roadmap for a journey starting in Jerusalem, and that journey must continue to the end of the earth, wherever it is located—then or today.

The apostolic journey started in Jerusalem because it "was the center for the followers of Jesus the Messiah for just under forty years: from the death and resurrection of Jesus of Nazareth in April AD 30 and the Feast of Pentecost … until the beginning of the Jewish revolt against the Romans in AD 66/67 when the Christians from Jerusalem left the capital and fled to Pella in Transjordan."[3] The next geographical center for the apostolic church was Antioch, as we read in Acts 8:4. Step by step the church in Antioch becomes influential in the development of the church, especially defining the nature of discipleship. Paul became part of this process and they succeeded in such a way that "the disciples were first called Christian at Antioch" (Acts 11:26).

They also understood well what "therefore go" meant. So, after the laying on of hands by the church in Antioch and then led by the Holy Spirit, the first intentional missionaries were sent out into Asia Minor—today's eastern Turkey. This is an important shift in church history: "from accidental church planting to intentional church planting" and "the planting of new churches become intentional, the product of focused activity by people set aside for this particular mission."[4] The most critical contribution of this new geographical center was also to help define the church of Jesus Christ as a universal body formed by Jews and Gentiles. As a result of their initiative, the first document of Christian distinctives was written, shared and accepted by the whole church. This we read with clarity in Acts 15 at the Jerusalem Council.

The geographical center continues to shift and grow, for soon Corinth and later Ephesus appear to be the next centers of the early church. The Apostle Paul established a base in Ephesus for his missionary activity and an important part of his writings was produced there. It was during this time that the ministry to Gentiles was recognized as part of the plan of God. "This mystery is that the Gentiles are fellow heirs, members of the same body, and partakers of the promise in Christ Jesus through the gospel" (Eph 3:6 ESV).

In the *Atlas of Global Christianity*, Johnson and Chung present the time-geography movement of the church's center of gravity; "After AD 100 Christianity grew to the West, then back to the East and finally in the north-western direction that would define the bulk of

---

3   Eckhard Schnabel, *Early Christian Mission, vol. 2* (Leicester: Apollo, 2004), 1489.
4   Bob Logan, "The Birth of Intentional Church Planting," in *The Mission of God Study Bible*, ed. Ed Stetzer and Philip Nation (Nashville: Holman, 2012), 1154.

Christian history."[5] They imagine, as Latourette, Winter, and Walls did in their moment, the "drama of Christian expansion": the church of Jesus Christ as pilgrim in its very *nature*—it is on the move all the time and all directions en route to the New Jerusalem.[6]

The pilgrimage of the church is connected with human mobility. Starting at Babel, human societies began moving everywhere. Human mobility aligns with the purpose of the Lord to fill the earth with his glory. People move, sometimes intentionally and other times forced by circumstances; migration is an historic human reality and not simply a problem for modern societies. Today Christians are paying attention to migrations and diasporas and thinking about the missional consequences. However, by not recognizing pilgrimage and diaspora as part of the nature of the gospel people, we run the risk of missing one of the ways in which the Lord sends out his gospel messengers.

The Pilgrim Church Influences Every Area of Human Need with the Gospel

A fresh reading of Acts 8 reinterprets the famous phrase "the whole gospel." At the beginning of its pilgrimage, the gospel was so incarnated in every one of the believers that wherever they went, they naturally were exposed as disciples. They had to be ready to share the gospel. This means that everything that happened to them was understood in the "discipleship category" as they met at the temple, as they worshiped the Lord, as they moved in the market place. In all places and spaces they exhibited integrity and commitment and as they were persecuted and martyred they commended their lives to the Lord, for as we see in Acts 8, they were persecuted as they went about preaching the word!

We discover four gospel outcomes in the church's first experience of being scattered:

They preached the word (8:4). The main activity of the disciples as they fled was to testify about Christ, who he is and what he has done. Life was uncertain and threatened; they don't know about tomorrow but they do know about the faithfulness of the Lord from the first day, so they naturally speak about him. When they thought they were settled or planted they became scattered again, and in each place they arrived they began to bear fruit as they bore witness to Christ.

They proclaimed Christ (8:5,35). As they stay longer in Samaria, the need for a more systematic teaching became clear and Phillip emerges as a preacher and teacher among them. His role was to bring clarity regarding the person of Jesus Christ and his work. Christ is proclaimed as a process of revelation rather than as an event. Just like Jesus did in Luke 24:27–44 they explained who Christ is, as messiah and king, as sacrificial Lamb of God, and what it all meant to use the whole Scripture in parallel to their personal experience with the Lord. Philip did the same later in verse 44 with the Ethiopian pilgrim official. Starting from Isaiah he explained the whole gospel and confirmed what was later written in Romans 1:16:

5   Todd Johnson and Kenneth Ross, eds., *Atlas of Global Christianity* (Edinburgh: Edinburgh University Press, 2009), 50.

6   Johnson and Ross, *Atlas of Global Christianity*, 50.

the gospel "is the power of God for salvation to everyone who believes, to the Jew first and also to the Greek."

They proclaimed the good news of hope (8:7). The gospel is much more than information about Christ and the plan of salvation. It is also a source of hope for the poor, freedom for the slaves, and healing for the infirm. As the pilgrim church arrived every place on earth, transformation started. We read in Acts 8, "The crowds paid attention with one mind to what Philip said," but they also saw the power of Christ in action among the disciples and the loving hand of Christ represented as they provided for the needs of the people of Antioch: "For unclean spirits, crying out with a loud voice, came out of many who had them, and many who were paralyzed or lame were healed" (Acts 8:7).

The gospel brought joy to people (8:8,39). The birth of Jesus was announced by the angel as good news of great joy for all the people. The church's pilgrimage makes effective the promise of the angels, and in the middle of their own sufferings people in Judea and Samaria receive hope through the proclamation of a new world order under the authority of Jesus Christ and his will as law. People turned and enveloped their lives in renewed hope and become full of joy. As N. T. Wright said, "The new world which was born when Jesus died and rose again comes to fresh life in the hearts, minds, and lifestyle of the listeners, or at least some of them."[7]

Its Pilgrim Nature Pushes the Church to the Ends of the Earth

In Acts 8:4 we read that "the ones who were scattered preached the word wherever they went." In this verse we see two important ideas emerging that will define the pilgrim nature of the church. First, the carefully chosen word that describes the persecution, "scattered." It is the same world that in Hebrew we know as *jezreel*. It means "scattered," but it also means "planted."[8] It's a wonderful picture, like Jesus taking the seed of the church and throwing it out to Judea and Samaria. By scattering the disciples, the Lord plants them in Judea and Samaria to become fruitful; from there they "preached the word."

The second important idea is that the church was "scattered" with a purpose: to spread the seed of the gospel and show the power of the Holy Spirit to transform. This is how the journey of the church was experienced by the disciples. They understood persecution from a different perspective and not as an unnecessary accident. Rather, it came by design from the Lord to share the gospel with others. This clarity ignites in them love for the people there and courageously they give the most valuable gift they have, the gospel of Jesus Christ. So, they preach the word as they move. They confirmed what Paul would later write in Romans 8:28, "all things works for the good."

In every town and city they preached the gospel, even in Samaria, a region traditionally rejected and excluded by the Jews. Judea and Samaria were separated by deep tribal, historical

---

7   N. T. Wright, *Paul for Everyone: Romans Part I* (Louisville, KY: Westminster John Knox Press, 2004), 12.
8   James Montgomery Boice, *Acts, An Expositional Commentary* (Grand Rapids, MI: Baker Books, 1997), 133.

and religious differences that made Jews look down on the Samaritans and not want to deal with them at all (John 4:9).[9] Judgment was the natural response of the disciples toward Samaritans when they were rejected at the entrance to a village of Samaritans as they headed to Jerusalem with Jesus (Luke 9:52–55). But in Acts 8, when disciples visit and preach to them, the gospel is given a warm reception by Samaritans. The preaching didn't stop there. The persecuted disciples continued to preach in every town and village they passed as they fled (11:19). In every village, the process was the same; they arrived in flight, preached the gospel and moved on. Interestingly, the two apostles that had been sent by the church in Jerusalem preached the gospel in many villages of the Samaritans on their way back to Jerusalem (8:25). It is as if they were ignited with passion to share the gospel after they observed what the church did, especially in Samaria.

At every level of society. The disciples understood that salvation was for everyone. As they experienced in Jerusalem, the early followers of Jesus demonstrated that everyone is in need of salvation. The gospel is for everyone no matter what his or her social, cultural, educational, or ethnic reality; and they intentionally shared the gospel in such a way that in the process men and women (Acts 8:12), rich and poor, persons of influence in society or not (8:13), important government officials, and even diplomats (8:27) would believe in Christ and become part of the church in Samaria. They also became part of that dynamic process of making disciples. These verses helps us to understand the meaning of Revelation 22:17, "The Spirit and the bride say, 'Come.' And let the one who hears say, 'Come.' And let the one who is thirsty come; let the one who desires take the water of life without price." The church in its pilgrimage is like an invitation traveling everywhere and saying, "come." *And* everyone who accepts the invitation becomes part of the church and immediately joins the church in its pilgrimage and add his voice to the invitation's cry of the church, "come"! For all people who hear and accept, the invitation is, "take the water of life without price."

To every linguistic group and ethne. Their commitment to share the gospel with everyone, everywhere helped the church in Samaria, and especially Phillip, to both understand the ministry and their role in it. In just one verse we can see how this perspective changed Philip's ministry, location, and role: "Now an angel of the Lord said to Philip, 'Rise and go toward the south to the road that goes down from Jerusalem to Gaza.' This is a desert place. And he rose and went. And there was an Ethiopian, a eunuch, and a court official of Candace, queen of the Ethiopians, who was in charge of all her treasure. He had come to Jerusalem to worship" (Acts 8:26, 27). In the middle of a "successful" and "effective" ministry, Philip left behind Samaria, his popularity, his church, and his comfort zone. He left behind his own future plans for ministry and his new flock to travel alone to the desert (26), to watch and eventually to share the gospel with a pilgrim Ethiopian, a rejected eunuch, who was looking for God and in need of a word from God. Geographic, ethnic, or positional distance was not an obstacle at all for Phillip to obey. And then, contrary to what we expected, he didn't return to Samaria but continued sharing the gospel in other areas in need. In his journey, the church's success is measured by obedience to the Great Commission mandate, not by numbers.

---

9   Boice, *Montgomery,* 133.

Only the pilgrim church has the courage to act like the church in Samaria. Only when all members are actively involved in sharing the gospel to everyone and everywhere, when the church believes that the Lord knows and lets their members go, confident that he will be provide the replacement.

This is the core: the pilgrim church is the community of believers in Jesus Christ who, moved by the Holy Spirit, participates with all its members and all its resources to make the supernatural gospel of Jesus Christ available to all people and ethnicities, both in its local geographies and to the ends of the earth.

The Pilgrim Nature of the Church Invites Her to Raise Her Eyes and Keep Her Focus on Her Eternal Destination

The pilgrimage of the church of Jesus Christ has a clear destination: the new Jerusalem. The holy city in Revelations 21:1–4 is perfect and complete. It is the unifying city that gathers "my scattered people" (Zeph 3:9–13). The New Jerusalem is both the place and the moment that completes the journey started in Genesis 12 to its final destination. Only then will we arrive to the New Jerusalem, the city where "all will call on the name of the Lord, all will serve in unity and worship him." It is a place where, finally, it will be OK to settle, to stop, and to rest because as the Apostle John wrote: "I heard a loud voice from the throne saying, 'Behold, the dwelling place of God is with man. He will dwell with them, and they will be his people, and God himself will be with them as their God'" (Rev 21:3).

Abraham understood that the pilgrim nature of his calling led to a destination. Hebrews 11:9–10 explains clearly: "By faith he went to live in the land of promise, as in a foreign land, living in tents with Isaac and Jacob, heirs with him of the same promise. For he was looking forward to the city that has foundations, whose designer and builder is God" (Heb 11:9, 10). Raising his eyes, Abraham was able to see that his journey would lead him to discover God acting in unexpected ways and in unexpected places. Hebrews 11 makes the contrast clear: Abraham didn't build cities, he built altars. His altars were milestones that marked the path of the pilgrimage and registered the places where he met with God and saw God act. The church of Jesus Christ is also called to raise her eyes and to consider herself a pilgrim. Moving all the time and everywhere, living with constant surprise, we discover—all the time and all along the way—that he was already there before us, and he is already moving in the places where we will ultimately arrive.

What is important is that, most of the time, when we think about missions, we tend to think that it is we who share the knowledge of the Lord to the nations. We find it easy to forget that the Lord was already moving everywhere before us through his Spirit. Even when we personally carry and share the gospel, most of the time as soon as we arrive we discover that God had already been moving there in a variety of ways. This perspective allows us to know God at each stop (each altar) on the journey where we see the Lord working.

We must not think of ourselves as bringing the light to every place. Rather, we come there to stop for a while, pay attention, and to see what the Lord is already doing. Then, we help the people respond to the question, "What does it mean?" as the Apostles did in Acts 2 when the church started in Jerusalem.

Conclusion

The church/churches (i.e., universal and local) in all of its forms continues on the move today. This pilgrimage takes the church all the way from Jerusalem to the New Jerusalem, but before they arrive, they must journey through every nation of the earth. The journey of the church must lead the church to all the nations.

As the church continues on the move, its members will get the full picture of them as both a community on the move as well as the main actors of the advance of the gospel. As Justo Gonzales wrote: "The largest part of the expansion of Christianity in the centuries that preceded Constantine took place not as a result of the work of people exclusively dedicated to that task but thanks to the constant testimony of hundreds and thousand of merchants, slaves, and Christians condemned to exile who went on witnessing to Jesus Christ wherever life took them, and in that way created new communities in places where the 'professional' missionaries had not arrived as yet."[10]

For the church to become effective in her obedience to the Great Commission, we must recover her pilgrimage mentality. We need to remember, as Jesus prayed in John 17:16, "They are not of the world, just as I am not of the world." We are here with a purpose, as Jesus continued praying in John 17:18, "As you sent me into the world, so I have sent them into the world" to "make it know your name" and show in our life the power of the gospel to transform.

When we finally arrive at the New Jerusalem and we end our pilgrimage, then we will be transformed from a pilgrim church to the very body of Jesus Christ. As we read in Revelation 21:3, "Behold, the dwelling place of God is with man. He will dwell with them, and they will be his people, and God himself will be with them as their God." Then we will be united to him that is our head and there will be no more need for us to move because the perfect plan of the Lord will be fulfilled since the people that he built for his name are finally with him. Hallelujah!

Questions for Reflection

1. David Ruiz says that the very nature of the church is to be pilgrim. What are the implications today of that understanding of the church? Is there a risk that we lose the sense of pilgrimage as Christians, particularly in places where life on earth is very good and comfortable?

2. The author reminds us of the importance of mission done by those who were scattered and migrated to other places due to a variety of motives. How do we evaluate the expansion of the gospel in our days? How much are diaspora groups part of our

---

10   Justo González, *Historia de las Misiones* (Buenos Aires: La Aurora, 1970), 59.

missionary strategy? Do we receive Christian migrants from other countries with this mission potential in mind?

3.   What does it mean in your context that the church is pilgrim? How are you moving into local society and to the ends of the earth? In what way can the vision of the New Jerusalem as final destination be of inspiration to your local community and to your personal life?

References

Boice, James M. 1997. *Acts*. Expositional Commentary. Grand Rapids, MI: Baker Books.

Engelsviken, T. 2007. Church/Eclesiology. In *Dictionary of Mission Theology*. Ed. John Corrie. Downers Grove, IL: IVP.

Escobar, Samuel. 2007. *Cómo Comprender la Misión: De Todos los Pueblos a Todos los Pueblos*. Buenos Aires: Ediciones Certeza Unida.

France, R.T. 1989. *Matthew: Evangelist and Teacher*. Guernsey: Paternoster Press.

González, Justo L. 1970. *Historia de las Misiones*. Buenos Aires: La Aurora.

Hastings, Ross. 2012. *Missional God, Missional Church: Hope for Re-evangelizing the West*. Downers Grove, IL: IVP.

Johnson, Todd and Kenneth Ross. 2009. *Atlas of Global Christianity*. Edinburg: Edinburg University Press.

Küng, Hans. 2012. *Existencia Cristiana*. Madrid: Trotta.

Ruiz, David D. 2005. *La Transformación de la Iglesia*. Miami: Patmos.

Schnabel, Eckhard J. 2004. *Early Christian Mission*, vol. 2. Leicester: Apollo.

Wright, N.T. 2004. *Paul for Everyone: Romans Part I*. Louisville: Westminster John Knox Press.

David D. Ruiz M. is from Guatemala and holds an MA in Mission Studies from All Nations, UK. Married to Dora Amalia and father of three children, David has worked as a pastor and executive director of COMIBAM (The Ibero American Mission Cooperation). Currently he is an Associate Director of the WEA Mission Commission and Vice President for Global Ministries of Camino Global.

CHAPTER 9

GOD'S MISSION AND THE CHURCH'S MISSION

Hannes Wiher

Recently, the evangelical movement has demonstrated a new interest in the Trinitarian foundation of pastoral ministry and mission.[1] In this regard, the publication of two major missiological books has revived the old debate on *missio Dei*: Christopher Wright's *The Mission of God* (2006), and Timothy Tennent's *Invitation to World Missions: A Trinitarian Missiology for the Twenty-first Century* (2010).[2] There are, however, major theological difficulties at the heart of this debate. One of these difficulties is connected to the Latin origin of the term, which means "the mission of God" or literally "the sending of God."[3] Furthermore, the notion of the *missio Dei* is founded on the church fathers' reflection on the doctrine of the Trinity, which in itself is complex.

Later on, the debate reappears in the consideration of the Trinitarian foundation of the church's mission. After the Second World War and during the period of decolonization and the independence of the "mission churches" in the South, the term was reintroduced into theological discussion. This time, however, it was linked to a new concept of mission, tied to issues around colonialism and ecclesiocentrism. At this turning point the expression *missio Dei* seemed to have resolved the "fundamental crisis of mission" by giving it a new and more theological foundation to serve as an element of convergence between the different theological persuasions.[4] What happened after that seemed more like a "Copernican

---

1   For an overview see Jason Sexton, "The State of the Evangelical Trinitarian Resurgence," *Journal of the Evangelical Theological Society* 54, 4 (2011), 787–805; for pastoral theology and mission, 802f.

2   Christopher J.H. Wright, *The Mission of God: Unlocking the Bible's Grand Narrative* (Leicester, UK: IVP, 2006). Timothy Tennent, *Invitation to World Missions: A Trinitarian Missiology for the Twenty-first Century* (Grand Rapids, MI: Kregel, 2010).

3   For an introduction to the concept of *missio Dei*, cf. David J. Bosch, "Mission as Missio Dei," in *Transforming Mission: Paradigm Shifts in Theology of Mission* (Maryknoll, NY: Orbis, 1991), 389–393.

4   The term "fundamental crisis of missions" has been coined by Georg F. Vicedom, *Missio Dei – Actio Dei*, ed. Klaus W. Müller (Nurnberg: VTR, 2002), 178–180. First ed. of *Missio Dei* (Munich: Kaiser, 1958) and of *Actio Dei* (Munich: Kaiser, 1975). English translation: *The Mission of God: An Introduction to a Theology of Mission*, ed. Gilbert A. Thiele and Dennis Hilgendorf (St. Louis: Concordia Press, 1965). So the hope or the evaluation of Johannes Verkuyl, *Contemporary Missiology* (Grand Rapids, MI: Eerdmans, 1978), 203; R C. Bassham, "Mission Theology: 1948–1975," *Occasional Bulletin of Missionary Research 4, 2* (1980), 56; T. Engelsviken, "Convergence or Divergence? The Relationship between Recent Ecumenical and Evangelical Mission Documents," in *Swedish Missiological Themes,* no. 2 (2001), 202–207.

revolution" in mission theology as each theological school of thought defined the term *missio Dei* as it desired.[5] Contrary to what was hoped, it became the cause of division and the basis for multiple deviations in the theology of mission.

In order to better understand the issues involved, we propose to review the history of the concept of *missio Dei*. However, the objective of this article is not to resolve all the problems inherent in this concept, but rather to outline its historical development in relation to the Trinity and to highlight the issues linked to a Trinitarian foundation of mission theology and practice from an evangelical perspective. First, we will reflect on some linguistic difficulties in regard to the concept. Secondly, we will review the concept in its Catholic context, and then, thirdly, in its critical assimilation by Protestant theology and the ecumenical movement. Fourthly, we will present its reception by the evangelical movement before concluding with an evaluation and a practical application.

Linguistic Considerations

A first element of debate is found in the linguistic construction of the genitive. Intuitively, the objective genitive comes to the foreground, leading us to think in terms of the "mission given to God." But the question naturally arises: How could God be the object of the sending? At first sight, the term with the connotation of an objective genitive is a non-sense. However, the expression can also mean that God is the subject of mission: it is God who sends, who is the initiator of mission. In this way, the construction would then be interpreted in the sense of a subjective genitive. A study of the occurrence of the term in the Latin translation of the Bible and the use by the church fathers can help orient our interpretation.

In the Latin Vulgate, the verbal form *mitto* "to send" can indicate the sending of the persons of the Trinity as well as the sending of the disciples. Examples of this usage can be seen in some New Testament passages that use the Latin form of the verb "to send": "But when the time had fully come, God sent (*misit*) his Son, born of a woman, born under law, to redeem those under law, that we might receive the full rights of sons. Because you are sons, God sent (*misit*) the Spirit of his Son into our hearts, the Spirit who calls out, 'Abba, Father'" (Gal 4:4–6). "As you sent (*misisti*) me into the world, I have sent (*misi*) them into the world" (John 17:18). "Again Jesus said, 'Peace be with you! As the Father has sent (*misit*) me, I am sending (*mitto*) you'" (John 20:21). These texts indicate the different sendings of the persons of the Trinity in the Bible: The Father has sent the Son (John 3:16), and, together with the Son, the Spirit (John 14:16, 26; 15:26; 16:7). The Son and the Spirit send, in their turn, the disciples and the apostles (Matt 28:16–20; Mark 16:15–18; Luke 24:46–49; John 20:21–22; Acts 1:8; 13:1–4).

Even if these biblical occurrences are, without doubt, the basis of later reflection, from the point of view of theological terminology it is more important to look at the use of the terms *missio* and *missio Dei* in the literature of the church fathers, which serves more as the

---

5   The expression is linked to *missio Dei* by John G. Flett, *The Witness of God: The Trinity, Missio Dei, Karl Barth, and the Nature of Christian Community* (Grand Rapids: Eerdmans, 2010), 157.

foundation for later developments.[6] The genesis of the term *missio Dei* is essentially situated in the reflection on the doctrine of the Trinity. The *Thesaurus Linguae Latinae* cites examples from Ambrose and Augustine. Augustine can say: "The sending of Christ is thus the incarnation" (*Christi ergo missio est incarnatio*), and "this activity [of the Father] is called the sending of the Holy Spirit" (*haec… operatio… missio spiritus sancti dicta est*).[7] In these two occurrences *missio* is used in the sense of being sent (objective genitive). Augustine insists: "Only the Father cannot be said to be sent" (*Solus Pater non legitur missus*). Thus, in Augustine's view, *missio Patris* (the sending of the Father) could not indicate the sending of the Father (objective genitive), but only the sending by the Father (subjective genitive or author's genitive). The *Thesaurus* gives only one example of *missio Patris*: "As the Son has been known of the world through the sending by the living Father [*viventis Patris missionem*], thus the name of the Father has equally been known of the world and men through the living Son."[8]

These examples show that the church fathers use more frequently the objective genitive for the sending of the Son and of the Spirit (*missio Filii, missio Spiritus sancti*). The Father sends first the Son, and together with the Son (*filioque*), the Spirit. Thus, at the eleventh Council of Toledo (675) it is declared: "We believe that the Holy Spirit is sent by the two as the Son has been sent by the Father…"[9] But the Father is never sent. He is the initiator of mission. Thus, the church fathers' reflection on the Trinity does not favor the development of a concept like *missio Dei*: the triune God cannot be sent but is only the one who sends. The meaning of the expression *missio Dei* must therefore primarily be in reference to an author's genitive. Having said this, is it not the sending of the Son and of the Spirit, so crucial for salvation history, which has prepared the way for the development of this concept? This observation has lead Georg Vicedom in his reflection on the Trinity and the *missio Dei* to a further conclusion: "In order to render justice to the biblical conception, *missio Dei* must also be understood as an *attributive genitive*. God is not only the one who sends but also the one who is sent."[10]

In the English speaking world, the concept *missio Dei* has been introduced in its English form "*mission of God*" or "*God's mission.*" In this linguistic space, the reception of the concept has been less complicated than in continental Europe, where the critical Protestant voices manifest themselves especially in Germany and Holland. This linguistic analysis leads us to consider what the great theologians have thought about the relationship between Trinity and mission.

---

6   In this section, I follow partly Helmut Rosin, *Missio Dei: An Examination of the Origin, Contents and Function of the Term in the Protestant Missiological Discussion* (Leyden: IIMO, 1972), 12–16.

7   *Thesaurus Linguae Latinae* (Munich: Saur, 2002–2007).

8   "*Sicut enim per viventis Patris missionem mundo innotuit Filius, ita per viventem Filium, Patris nomen mundo et hominibus innotuit…*" (Ps. Vigil. Thaps. c. Marivad. 1, 68, 396c).

9   "*Hic igitur Spiritus Sanctus missus ab utrisque sicut Filius a Patre creditur…*" *Enchiridion Symbolorum*, ed. Heinrich Denziger (Freiburg-im-Breisgau: Herder, 1947), 277. The *filioque* is mentioned for the first time at the third Council of Toledo (589).

10   Vicedom, *Missio Dei – Actio Dei*, 33.

The Catholic Concept

In this section, we do not pretend to discuss all the problems linked to the doctrine of the Trinity. Rather, we want to explore the relationship between this doctrine and the concept of mission, and how this reflection has influenced mission theology. The introduction of the term Trinity is attributed to Tertullian (ca. 155–220) who has articulated the doctrine in an "economic" perspective.[11] He described God as three "distinct" but "inseparable" persons and one substance (*una substantia*), leaving many aspects undefined. The debate between Arius (256–336) and Athanasius (293–373) and the important contribution of the Cappadocian theologians (Basil of Caesarea, Gregory of Nazianzus, and Gregory of Nyssa) prepared the way for the conclusions drawn at the Council of Chalcedon (381). But it is Augustine of Hippo (354–430) and later Thomas Aquinas (1224/1225–1274) who had the most influence on relating the doctrine of the Trinity to the church's mission. Their work laid the foundation for important concepts in this regard. As is often the case in the development of ideas, the pioneers establish the principal contours for future discussion.

Trinity and Mission: Augustine and Thomas Aquinas

Augustine reflects about the Trinity in all of his writings. His "magnum opus" on the question is *De Trinitate*. The mark of the Council of Nicaea is felt from the first pages of this seminal work: "How can one say that there are not three gods, but only one God?"[12] In order to answer this question, Augustine develops the notion of "psychological analogy" (*analogia entis*). Starting from Genesis 1:26 ("Let us make man *in our image*"), Augustine sees in the unity of man's inner life (his psychology) the most important vestige of the Trinity left in creation. Among these remnants, Augustine discerns several triads, including for example, the memory, the intelligence, and the will of a person.[13] He stresses the fact that the three "functions" of the soul are connected to one another and yet remain distinct. It is to be noted that the concept of analogy between the divine and the human will take a certain importance in the later debate.

Augustine's main contribution in the controversy with modalism is to have generalized in the West the notion of *relationship* as a means of distinction between the divine persons.[14] In this view, it is not through what they are or possess that the divine persons distinguish themselves, but through their relationship with the two other persons of the Trinity.[15] The Augustinian relational analogy (*analogia relationis*) between the divine and the human will play an important role.

---

11   Systematic theology distinguishes "immanent Trinity" from "economic Trinity," immanent Trinity being concerned with the nature of God (who God is), and the economic Trinity with his action in the plan of salvation (*oikonomia* "plan," literally "household") and in the role played by each of the three divine persons.
12   *Trin*. I, V, 8. All citations are taken from Augustine, *De Trinitate*, trans. Edmund Hill, 5 vols. (Brooklyn: New City, 1991).
13   Trin. X-XV. Other triads are: being, knowing, willing (Conf. XIII, 11, 12); reason, knowledge, love (*Trin*. IX, 2–5).
14   According to modalism, the Trinity has three modes of appearance; God manifests himself in the form of Father, Son, and Spirit.
15   *Trin*. V.

Furthermore, the Augustinian restriction concerning the Trinity is very well known due to its adoption by the Reformers in order to prevent speculation. Augustine affirms: "The external works of the Trinity are indivisible" (*opera trinitatis ad extra sunt indivisa*). He further explains: "[A]s the Father possesses the essence in himself [*a se*], he acts equally by himself [*a se*], and the Son acts through the Father and the Spirit acts and operates through both of them."[16] In so doing, Augustine introduces a distinction between the immanent and the economic Trinity and takes a position, which has had many implications for later theological thought. Essentially, this distinction creates two ontological levels within the Trinity. In this regard, Augustine writes:

> [A]nd just as being born means for the Son his being from the Father, so his being sent means his being known to be from him. And just as for the Holy Spirit his being the gift of God means his proceeding from the Father, so his being sent means being known to proceed from him [the Father].[17]

This implies that the economic Trinity is related specifically to knowing God. The sending of the divine persons (i.e., their mission) is relegated to an inferior ontological level with only an epistemological value.[18] Once this distinction is made, the concept of procession, which belongs to the immanent Trinity, receives a greater importance than that of the mission of the divine persons, which belongs to the economic Trinity.[19]

Thomas Aquinas takes up Augustine's theological reflection on the Trinity and develops it. He assigns questions 2 to 26 in book I of the *Summa Theologica* to the one God: He is infinite (q. 7–8), perfect (q. 4–6), immutable and eternal (q. 9–10). Questions 27 to 43 concern the triune God and operate a distinction between the divine persons. In question 27, Aquinas defines the procession of the divine persons: the first procession is the *generation* of the Son, an immanent act in relation to the Father, situating the verb at the Father's interior. The second procession is a *spiration*, identified with the Holy Spirit.[20]

In question 43, Aquinas defines the mission of the divine persons. By "sending" of a divine person he understands the eternal procession of the sent person with a temporal effect produced in creation. This suggests that Aquinas, just as Augustine, makes a distinction between procession and mission. Why this distinction? Aquinas starts with this affirmation: "A divine person cannot be properly sent. For one who is sent is less than the sender.[21]" Then, Aquinas more precisely affirms: "Mission implies inferiority in the one sent when it

---

16 *Trin.* IV, XX, 29.

17 Ibid.

18 Epistemology (from Greek *épistème* "knowledge" and *lógos* "discourse") describes either the field of the philosophy of science that studies the particular sciences, or the theory of knowing in general. In the latter case, it asks the question: How can we know?

19 The biblical basis for this concept is found for example in John 15:26: "When the Counselor comes, whom I will send to you from the Father, the Spirit of truth who goes out (*procedit*) from the Father, he will testify about me."

20 *ST* Ia, q. 27, a. 1–4. The citations are taken from Thomas Aquinas, *Summa Theologica*, 5 vol. (Westminster, MD: Christian Classics, 1981).

21 *ST* Ia, q. 43, a. 1, obj. 1.

means procession from the sender as principle ... But in God mission means only procession of origin."[22] He concludes by saying: "As the Father does not proceed from anybody else, he cannot be sent; this pertains only to the Son and to the Holy Spirit.[23]

It is easy to see the consequences of this philosophic-theological system: the movement of God towards his "economy" is a secondary development apart from what he is from all eternity. It does not belong to the essence of God to reveal himself. Maintaining the concept of procession at the higher ontological level of the immanent Trinity while relegating mission to the lower ontological level of the economic Trinity will have tragic consequences for the theology of mission. It will be marginalized. The logical consequence of this breach is seen in the important place given to the concept of analogy.

Adaptation by Ignatius of Loyola

This dichotomy between the immanent and the economic Trinity, between being and action, and finally between the divine and the human, has also resulted in the unfortunate separation of human missionary action from God's action. Thus, at the beginning of the Catholic missionary movement, Ignatius of Loyola (1491–1556), founder of the Order of the Jesuits, considers the sending of missionaries by the Pope in terms of the "mission of the church" (*missio ecclesiae*), which for Loyola is a separate movement from the *missio Dei*. Through this new term (*missio ecclesiae*), he introduces an independent concept from the *missio Dei* which was interpreted, as we have seen, in the perspective of the divine processions. The objective in the *missio ecclesiae* is to plant the church where it does not yet exist. Thus, the concept of "church planting" (*plantatio ecclesiae*) appears in the debate. This ecclesiocentric concept of mission was adopted by the Protestant missionary movement in the middle of the nineteenth century and dominated about a hundred years until a theological definition through the new concept of *missio Dei* replaced it in the middle of the twentieth century.

Critical Resumption by Hans Urs von Balthasar

From 1965 on, Hans Urs von Balthasar (1905–1988) published his *Trilogy*, a monumental work of fifteen volumes. He based his theo-missiological approach on a Trinitarian theology of mission placed in the central table of a "triptych."[24] Part I of his *Trilogy* presents a "theological aesthetic" of European literature, philosophy, and culture.[25] The aesthetic aspect consists in the fact that God lets us see his beauty in the different aspects of culture through "the eyes of faith." In part II, von Balthasar portrays a divine "theo-drama" in which he presents the elements of God's action in history by exposing the themes of a classical treaty of theology, including the doctrine of the Trinity.[26] In the third table, von Balthasar develops a "theological logic" which results from a comparative study of culture and of fundamental

---

22   *ST* Ia, q. 43, a. 1, obj. 1.
23   *ST* Ia, q. 43, a. 1, obj. 1.
24   Hans Urs von Balthasar, *My Work: In Retrospect* (San Francisco: Ignatius Press, 1993).
25   Hans Urs von Balthasar, *The Glory of the Lord: A Theological Aesthetics*, 7 vol. (San Francisco: Ignatius Press, 1982–1991).
26   Hans Urs von Balthasar, *Theo-Drama: Theological Dramatic Theory*, 5 vol., (San Francisco: Ignatius Press, 1988–1998). Cf. the similar conception of Kevin J. Vanhoozer, *The Drama of Doctrine: A Canonical-Linguistic Approach to Christian Theology* (Louisville: John Knox, 2005).

theology, presented in the first and second part of his *Trilogy*.[27] His Trinitarian theology is situated in the central piece of the triptych, and is based on God's love as the focal point of mission.[28] Peter Henrici, the international coordinator of *Communio* publications, comments on von Balthasar's approach and sums up the centrality of God's love in the mission in the following way:

> God's acts have their origin in his love of which they are the manifestation: Trinitarian love, between the Father and the Son and the Holy Spirit. The Father is the loving origin of all that is: the Son receives, already according to an intra-Trinitarian mode, the mission of love in loving obedience and brings it to the world in the Holy Spirit who leads and accompanies him. The Son transmits this mission to the Apostles and to all those who listen to them. Consequently, Christian life must essentially be seen as a life in mission. From the unique mission of Jesus Christ multiple individual missions will be deployed in their "Catholic" diversity.[29]

Faithful to this mission rooted in the theological reflection on the Trinity, von Balthasar links God's love to the history of European thought. Following the pattern of the church fathers (especially Augustine, Origin, Irenaeus, Gregory of Nyssa, and Maximus the Confessor), who transformed Greek philosophy into a Christian theology, von Balthasar undertakes the colossal task to analyze two thousand five hundred years of European thought. He considers that after European Christianity had decided to adopt Plotinus' comprehensive philosophy, the turning point in this history came in Nietzsche's dialogue with Kierkegaard and Dostoyevski, a dialogue between two worldviews, Christian and non-Christian.[30] Henrici sees in von Balthasar's work a theology of European culture.[31] His originality consists in the formulation of a Trinitarian theology as the result of a dialogue between fundamental theology and the context. For Balthasar, the human being and the metaphysical Being are dialogical. Henrici evaluates the dialogical aspect of von Balthasar's Trilogy in the following way:

> The dialectic is solitary as any other pure thought; it is only through dialogue that the human being opens himself to the other, also to God. All drama is in its essence dialogical, and because the theological esthetic opens up to the dialogical being of God and to the intra-Trinitarian dialogue between the Father and the Son, it prepares for the theo-drama in which it finds its accomplishment. This is the meaning of theology: to justify this reflection in a Trinitarian way … When all the historical and dramatic events are seen as manifestations of an acting God's love, the history

---

27   Hans Urs von Balthasar, *Theo-Logic: Theological Logical Theory* (San Francisco: Ignatius Press, 2000).

28   God's love in mission is also the focus of the Cape Town Commitment (2010). See http://www.lausanne.org.

29   Peter Henrici, "Hans Urs von Balthasar's Trilogy: A Theology of European Culture," *Communio: International Catholic Review 32, 2* (2005). As I could not get hold of the English version, the two citations are my translation from the German (original) version of this article, *"Communio,"* in *Internationale Katholische Zeitschrift* 34, 2 (2005), 117–127, see p. 121 (the page references are from the German version).

30   von Balthasar, *The Glory of the Lord*, summed up by Henrici, "Trilogy," 122.

31   So the subtitle of Henrici's article "Trilogy."

of European ideas receives a new interpretation which only makes visible its deeper meaning.[32]

In summary, it is important to notice that the dichotomy between the intra-Trinitarian and the extra-Trinitarian dialogue, between the "mission of God" and the "mission of the church," which was so prominent in Aquinas' thought, has disappeared in von Balthasar's presentation.

Reception by the Protestant Movement

As far as Protestantism is concerned, the Reformers reacted to scholastic theology with its speculations on the inner life of the Trinity. They recalled Augustine's warning that the external works of the Trinity are inseparable from God's being. In this line of thought, Jacques Matthey remarks: "Who are we to know the inner life of God?"[33] Consequently, the Reformers have said very little about the immanent Trinity. Nevertheless, according to Martin Luther (1483–1546), mission is essentially the work of the triune God and its goal is the construction of the reign of God. In the perspective of the general priesthood of all believers, Luther sees the church, and every baptized believer, as essential divine instruments for the accomplishment of mission through the Word of God.[34] For the same reason, the theology of John Calvin (1509–1564) said so little concerning the Trinity that Pierre Caroli, a Protestant pastor from Lausanne, accused Calvin, Viret, and Farel of Arianism in 1536.[35] The Protestant debate about *missio Dei* did not begin, however, before Karl Barth's important contribution. We will now study the relationship between the Trinity and mission in Karl Barth's dialectic theology and present a brief history of the introduction of *missio Dei* in the ecumenical movement.

Critical Resumption by Karl Barth

In his *Church Dogmatics*, written from 1931 on, Karl Barth (1886–1968) takes up critically the Catholic theology on the Trinity.[36] He refers to it more than any other Protestant theologian, but handles it at the same time very freely. Eberhard Busch, who has written the preface to the last volume of the French edition, writes on Barth: "His doctrine of the Trinity sets a final point to the traditional doctrines insofar as these

---

32　Henrici, "Trilogy," 126.

33　Jacques Matthey, "God's Mission Today: Summary and Conclusions," *International Review of Mission* 92, 4 (2003), 582.

34　Cf. James A. Scherer, ed., *Gospel, Church, and Kingdom: Comparative Studies in World Mission Theology* (Minneapolis: Augsburg Publishing House, 1987), 55; idem, "The Lutheran Missionary Idea in Historical Perspective," in *That the Gospel May Be Sincerely Preached throughout the World: A Lutheran Perspective on Mission and Evangelism in the 20th Century*, ed. James A. Scherer (Stuttgart: Kreuz, 1982), 1–29.

35　Arianism is the heresy of Arius, condemned at the Council of Nicaea (325), according to which the Son is not eternal and does not possess the same nature as God the Father. The Son has thus an intermediary status between God and men. Calvin defended his position on the Trinity in *Confessio de Trinitate propter calumnias P. Caroli.*

36　Karl Barth, *Church Dogmatics,* 4 vol. (Edinburgh: T. & T. Clark, 1956–1969, 1975) [abridged hereafter as *CD*].

dealt with God beyond Revelation." [37] Barth founds his whole theology on the Revelation of God. For him, the revealed God cannot be different from the hidden God. Busch notes:

> Barth has distanced himself courageously from a long tradition through the radicalism of his conception: *in all his works,* God is no other than the God who reveals himself in Jesus Christ, even in his work of Creation and consummation, according to the old rule, dear to Barth, *opera trinitatis ad extra sunt indivisa* ... Even if one needs to maintain the distinction between God "a se" [in himself] and God "pro nobis" [for us], between the "hidden God" and the "revealed God," ... even if Barth can speak of the "aseity"[38] of God, one needs to conclude strictly that the hidden God "a se" is *the same* as the revealed God "pro nobis. "[39]

By concluding that God, from all eternity, has to be in himself Father, Son, and Spirit, Barth avoids modalism. By this approach, Barth distances himself not only from the distinction between immanent and economic Trinity, but also from the concept of "psychological analogy" (*analogia entis*), logical consequence of the first. The sending of the divine persons becomes thus the vehicle of God's revelation, maintaining a prime importance for God's revelation and the plan of salvation. For Barth, the divine revelation proceeds exclusively from the being and action of God himself. It is impossible, declares Barth, to "ascribe the event of revelation to God, and yet attribute to humanity the instrument and point of contact for it. "[40]

However, when God reveals himself to us, the human being has to be able to receive this revelation by faith. Despite the fact that Barth refuses to enter into the logic of natural theology[41] and is in this point strictly opposed to Emil Brunner, he has to postulate a certain correspondence between God and the human being, a "point of contact. "[42] In order to do this, and strictly in the perspective of the *sola fide* of the Reformers, Barth introduces the concept of the "analogy of faith" (*analogia fidei*).[43] Through the relationship between the

---

37   Eberhard Busch, "Un Magnificat Perpétuel," in Barth, *Dogmatique,* index général et textes choisis, 1980, 18. This preface has not been included in the English edition for reasons explained in *CD*: Index Volume, v.

38   From Latin *Deus a se,* "God in himself."

39   Busch, "Un Magnificat Perpétuel," 22 (emphasis in the original).

40   *CD* I/2, 280.

41   Barth's definition of natural theology permits us to understand his position: "Natural theology is the doctrine of humanity with God existing outside God's revelation in Jesus Christ. It works out the knowledge of God that is possible and real on the basis of this independent union with God and its consequences for the whole relationship of God, world, and humanity ... A natural theology which does not strive to be the only master is not a natural theology." *CD* II/1, 168, 173.

42   See Barth's discussion in *CD* I/2, 557 (quoting W. Gass, *Geschichte der protestantischen Dogmatik: In ihrem Zusammenhang mit Theologie überhaupt,* vol. 2 [Berlin: Reimer, 1854], 88). For Brunner's position concerning the concept of "point of contact," see Emil Brunner, "Die Frage nach dem 'Anknüpfungspunkt' als Problem der Theologie," *Zwischen den Zeiten* 10 (1932): 505–509.

43   Von Balthasar remarks that Augustine's psychological analogy (*analogia entis*) and Barth's analogy of faith (*analogia fidei*) do not exclude each other, but are complementary, the second one being a concept that encompasses the first. Hans Urs von Balthasar, *"Analogia fidei,"* in *The Theology of Karl Barth: Exposition and Interpretation* (San Francisco: Communio Books, Ignatius Press, 1992 [1st German edition 1951]). Five years later, Barth seems to have come closer to von Balthasar's position. Karl Barth, *The Humanity of God,* Conference held at the Swiss Pastoral Society at Aarau, September 25, 1956 (Richmond: John Knox Press, 1960).

triune God and the human being created in his image, there is a rapprochement of
the two despite the radical dichotomy between the Creator and his creature. In this
sense, Barth can speak of Christian theology as "theanthropology."[44] The believer
receives a noble task at the side of God:

> Everything that can be said about our participation in the being and work of
> Jesus Christ, here in the depth as such, properly consists only in this: It lies in
> the nature of what happens there in God, in the eternal continuation of the
> reconciliation and revelation accomplished in time, that it, in full reality, also
> happens here to and in us. ... Our participation in the being and work of Jesus
> Christ must not follow as a second thing, but is, as the one thing which must
> be accomplished, wholly and utterly accomplished in Him.[45]

In this participation in the work of God which is essentially that of Christ, the task of
regenerated man is one of service in fellowship with God. So Barth can say:

> If God requires and makes possible that He should be served by the creature,
> this service itself means that the creature is taken up into the sphere of divine
> lordship. We have always to remember that God's glory really consists in His
> self-giving, and that this has its center and meaning in God's Son, Jesus Christ,
> and that the name of Jesus Christ stands for the event in which humanity, and
> in humanity the whole of creation, is awakened and called and enabled to par-
> ticipate in the being of God ... [T]he self-declaration of God is true and real,
> which means that God Himself is God in such a way that He wills to have the
> creature as a creature with Him, that He does not will to be God without it,
> without claiming it, but also without being personally present to it.[46]

This participation extends necessarily to the Christian community which Barth sees
as a missionary community: "The community is as such a missionary community, or
she is not the Christian community."[47] And again: mission, which is "the sending or
sending out to the nations to attest the gospel," is the "very root of the existence and
therefore of the whole service of the community."[48] Announcing the kingdom of
God is the community's authentic work, her "*opus proprium.*"[49] Not living up to this
calling has severe consequences for the community:

> [T]he community which has not existed in the interim period as a *missionary*
> community as such, whose witness has not been *invitational* and *persuasive*
> according to the measure of her power, with the return and final revelation

---

44   Barth, *The Humanity of God.*
45   *CD* II/1, 157–158 (adapted translation).
46   *CD* II/1, 670.
47   *CD* III/4, 504f. (adapted translation).
48   *CD* IV/3, 2, 872.
49   *CD* III/4, 506.

of her Lord will be banished into the darkness, where there can be only wailing and gnashing of teeth instead of the promised banquet.[50]

By distancing himself from the dichotomy between immanent and economic Trinity, Barth sets a high value on the sending (mission) of the people of God. This refers back to God himself who becomes a "missionary" God;[51] through fellowship with him, the Christian community becomes a missionary community; finally, for Barth, theology becomes a Trinitarian and missionary theology.[52] Despite the fact that Brunner had accused Barth of thinking as a church theologian, while Brunner considered himself to think as a missionary theologian,[53] Barth seems to have succeeded in articulating God's being and action together, church and mission together, and God and man together in the task of reconciliation. Finally, Barth's dialectic theology, with its categorical refusal of natural theology, seems to design successfully a Trinitarian foundation of mission, even though it may be perceived as being removed from missionary realities.[54]

Barth's influence on the Catholic theologian Karl Rahner (1904–1984) became apparent after Vatican II. Rahner took up Barth's conceptions of revelation and Trinity and formulated the following thesis: The economic Trinity is the immanent Trinity and vice versa.[55] Barth himself never goes so far. In his analysis, God as the Creator remains the completely other. In this sense, Barth speaks about the "aseity" of God. Even though Rahner and Barth conceive of revelation in a similar way, their point of departure and their methodologies are different. While Barth puts his accent on God's Revelation, Rahner starts from the conviction that all theological declarations are basically anthropological.

Evidently, Barth adopted a different approach than von Balthasar to the relationship between theology and culture. Barth takes the Alsatian Benedictine monk during the First World War as example who continues to celebrate the Magnificat while a French bomb breaks through the roof of his monastery.[56] For Barth, theology has to be attached to its object "as if nothing had happened."[57] In contrast to Barth, and following the example of the church fathers, von Balthasar starts his Trilogy with an analysis of European thought.

---

50   *CD* III/2, 507 (emphasis in the original).

51   Barth himself never uses this term in contrast to other theologians, e.g. John Stott, "Our God Is a Missionary God," in *The Contemporary Christian: Applying God's Word to Today's World*, vol. 2 (Leicester, UK: IVP, 1992); Samuel Escobar, "We Believe in a Missionary God," in *A Time for Mission* (Leicester, UK: IVP, 2003).

52   *CD* IV/4, 100.

53   Emil Brunner, "Toward a Missionary Theology," *Christian Century 66, 27* (1949): 817. See also his autobiographical remark: "In distinction to Barth ... my theological thinking was, from the very start, dominated by the endeavor to preach the gospel to the 'pagans.'... This was the reason why I was so much interested in the 'Anknüpfungspunkt,' the point of contact, between man's mind as such (what theologians call the 'natural man') and the Word of God." Emil Brunner, "A Spiritual Autobiography," *Japan Christian Quarterly* (July 1955): 242.

54   For a more detailed discussion of Karl Barth's theology in the perspective of *missio Dei*, see the PhD thesis of John G. Flett, *The Witness of God: The Trinity, Missio Dei, Karl Barth, and the Nature of Christian Community* (Grand Rapids, MI: Eerdmans, 2010).

55   Karl Rahner, *The Trinity* (Freiburg-im-Breisgau: Herder & Herder, 1970), 22.

56   Barth, *Das Wort Gottes und die Theologie: Gesammelte Vorträge 1* (Munich: Kaiser, 1924), 109.

57   Barth, *Theologische Existenz Heute, Heft 1* (1933): 3, quoted by Busch, "Un Magnificat perpétuel," 9.

Development in the Ecumenical Movement

Karl Barth's lecture at the Brandenburg Mission Conference held at Berlin on April 11, 1932, is generally considered the starting point for the adoption of the concept of *missio Dei* and the Trinitarian grounding of mission by the ecumenical movement. The title of his lecture was: "Theology and mission in our present situation."[58] In his address, Barth develops simply his conception of the missionary community as a reflection of the action of the triune God as presented above:

> [M]ust not the most faithful, the most convinced missionary think seriously about the fact that the concept *"missio"* in the ancient church was a term from the doctrine of the Trinity, the designation of the divine self-sending, the sending of the Son and of the Holy Spirit into the world?[59]

However, it has to be noted that Barth never mentions the term *missio Dei* or an idea which could come close to it. Moreover, the detailed development of his conception in his *Church Dogmatics* dates from after the Conference of the International Missionary Council (IMC) at Willingen (1952).

It is usually assumed that Barth influenced Karl Hartenstein (1894–1952), who was the director of the Basel Mission from 1926 to 1939. However, even if Hartenstein was influenced by Barth's thought, it seems that Hartenstein followed Oscar Cullmann and Dietrich Bonhoeffer more. Several reasons lead us to this conclusion. First of all, Hartenstein writes in a lecture presented in 1927 on the question, "What has Karl Barth's theology to tell missions?" that Barth was "not a close friend of missions."[60] In a similar way, Walter Freytag (1899–1959), professor of missiology at Kiel and Hamburg, referring to Hartenstein, comments that "a Barth student who strongly advocated mission appeared to be nothing more than a contradiction."[61] Further, Hartenstein did not follow the dominant position of German missiology which puts a special emphasis on the grounding of the churches in the indigenous culture (in German *Volkstum*). Following Cullmann and Freytag, Hartenstein developed a salvation-historic approach to the theology of mission by integrating certain ideas of Barth, especially the overarching idea that God himself is the sovereign agent of mission.

It is generally recognized that the Missionary Conference at Willingen (1952) was the great turning point in the theology of mission. Its theme was "The Missionary Obligation of the Church," and much emphasis was given to the concept of *missio Dei*. After the two world wars of the twentieth century and the ejection of

---

58   Karl Barth, "Die Theologie und die Mission in der Gegenwart," *Zwischen den Zeiten 10, 3* (1932), 189–215.

59   Ibid., 204.

60   Karl Hartenstein, "Was Hat die Theologie Karl Barths der Mission Zu Sagen?" *Zwischen den Zeiten 6* (1928), 59.

61   Walter Freytag, "Mitglied im Deutschen Evangelischen Missionsrat und Missionstag und bei den Tagungen der Ökumene," in Karl Hartenstein: *Ein Leben für Kirche und Mission,* ed. Wolfgang Metzger (Stuttgart: Evangelischer Missionsverlag, 1953), 296.

missionaries from China in 1950–51, it became clear that the Christian colonial powers had lost their credibility. At the same time, it was the period of decolonization in the southern hemisphere, when the "young" churches became conscious of their maturity and dynamism. It was a moment of radical questioning, a "fundamental crisis of mission." As churches were now found on all the continents, the geographical definition of mission according to the slogan "from the West to the rest" became obsolete.

The moral failure of Western churches resulted also in the questioning of the ecclesiocentric conception of mission. It was necessary to find a new theological foundation and framework for mission thinking and practice. A Trinitarian grounding seemed the most appropriate to the two most influential groups at the conference of Willingen. On the one side, it was the American preparatory group under the leadership of Paul Lehmann, professor at Princeton Theological Seminary, who published the report "Why Missions?"[62] This group was under the strong influence of H. Richard Niebuhr (1894–1962), professor at Yale Divinity School. Niebuhr presented a realized eschatology and a theological standpoint which he characterized as "Trinitarian, that is to say it is neither Christocentric, nor spiritualistic nor creativistic but all of these at once." He declared his approach to be "theocentric."[63] His juxtaposition of Christocentrism and Trinitarianism seems to be a reaction to Barth. Helmut Rosin and David Bosch think that this American report, together with the WCC study "The Missionary Structure of the Congregation" under the direction of Johannes Hoekendijk, have been decisive for the genesis of the *missio Dei* formula.[64] On the other side was the German group under the direction of Hartenstein and Freytag with its salvation-historic approach and a rather sympathetic attitude towards Barth. This group was afraid of the strong influence of the liberal American group. This tension between the liberal American current and the Pietistic German position was not new. It dates to the first IMC conferences. Hartenstein illustrates this reticence well in his report on the IMC conference at Tambaram in 1938 when he says that the American emphasis on the reign of God offers "a comprehensive password with which to wage the war to realize God's kingdom in all areas of social and political life."[65] The Trinitarian foundation proposed by the American group permitted inclusion of other subjects on their agenda like an orientation towards the reign of God, God in action in creation, and the concept of the missionary congregation.

---

62   "Why Missions? Report of Commission I on the Biblical and Theological Basis of Missions," *Paul L. Lehmann Collection* (Princeton: Princeton Theological Seminary, 1952). The complete text of the report has never been published. An abridged version without the contentious elements has been published in Paul L. Lehmann, "The Missionary Obligation of the Church," *Theology Today 9, 1* (1952), 20–38.

63   Later published in H. Richard Niebuhr, "An Attempt at a Theological Analysis of Missionary Motivation," *Occasional Bulletin of Missionary Research 14, 1* (1963), 1.

64   Rosin, *Missio Dei*, 23; David J. Bosch, *Witness to the World: The Christian Mission in Theological Perspective* (London: Marshall, Morgan & Scott, 1980), 179f. See World Council of Churches Department on Studies in Evangelism, *The Church for Others, and the Church for the World: A Quest for Structures for Missionary Congregations* (Geneva: World Council of Churches, 1967).

65   Karl Hartenstein, "Tambaram, Wie Es Arbeitete," in *Das Wunder der Kirche unter den Völkern der Erde: Bericht über die Weltmissionskonferenz in Tambaram*, ed. Martin Schlunk (Stuttgart: Evangelischer Missionsverlag, 1939), 41f, quoted by Wilhelm Richebächer, "Missio Dei: The Basis of Mission Theology or a Wrong Path?" *International Review of Mission 92, 4* (2003), 603, n. 24.

The tensions rose so high that during the conference and in the redaction group of the final report, which included Russell Chandran, Hartenstein, Lehmann, and Hoekendijk, a consensus could not be found.[66] Expressed in ecumenical language, their report was "received but not adopted." In this impasse, Lesslie Newbigin's text was finally adopted. It affirms the grounding of the missionary calling of the church in the triune God by avoiding the contentious issues. The principal affirmation of the conference was this: "There is no participation in Christ without participation in his mission in the world. That by which the church receives its existence is that by which it is also given its world-mission. 'As the Father has sent me, even so I send you.'"[67]According to this declaration, which is based on the very large missionary mandate of the gospel of John (John 20:21), mission was conceived as the triune God's action in the world. This position is largely based on Hoekendijk's view, hiding the conflict with the salvation-historic perspective of the German group.[68]

It is remarkable that in all the discussions (as much as they can be traced) and in the final document, the formula *missio Dei* is absent. How then did the *missio Dei* enter into the Willingen conference? The first mention of *missio Dei* appears in a report that Hartenstein wrote after the conference. In this report, he confirms his position, which he held before the conference, with a deep concern to maintain the salvation-historic perspective on mission.[69] His main affirmation links the action of the triune God with that of the church: "From the '*missio Dei*' alone comes the '*missio ecclesiae*.' That locates mission in the broadest conceivable framework of salvation history and of God's plan of salvation."[70] His premature death some weeks after Willingen leaves many questions open as to the development of his thought. However, it was not Hartenstein's report which popularized the concept of *missio Dei*, but rather the book of Georg Vicedom (1903–1974) entitled *Missio Dei*.[71] Vicedom was professor of missiology at the Lutheran Missiological Seminary Augustana at Neuendettelsau (Germany) 1956–1972. In his book, Vicedom presents an evangelical Lutheran theology of mission in the perspective of salvation history and of the reign of God. In order to safeguard the classical missionary mandate, Vicedom introduces a distinction between the (general) *missio Dei* and the *missio Dei specialis*. The first describes God's action in creation

---

66   Norman Goodall, ed., *Missions Under the Cross* (London: Edinburgh House, 1953), 244.

67   Ibid., p. 190.

68   L. A. Hoedemaker, "The People of God and the Ends of the Earth," in *Missiology: An Ecumenical Introduction*, ed. F. J. Verstraelen et al. (Grand Rapids: Eerdmans, 1995), 165.

69   Karl Hartenstein, "Übergang und Neubeginn: Zur Tagung des Internationalen Missionsrats in Willingen," *Zeitwende 24, 4* (1952): p. 334-345; idem, "Theologische Besinnung," in *Mission Zwischen Gestern und Morgen*, ed. Walter Freytag (Stuttgart: Evangelischer Missionsverlag, 1952), 51–72. For an evaluation, see Bosch, *Transforming Mission*, 391f.

70   Hartenstein, "Theologische Besinnung," 62.

71   Georg F. Vicedom, *Missio Dei: Einführung in eine Theologie der Mission* (Munich: Kaiser, 1958). English translation: *The Mission of God: An Introduction to a Theology of Mission*, ed. Gilbert A. Thiele and Dennis Hilgendorf (St. Louis: Concordia Press, 1965). Vicedom traces the later development of ecumenical and evangelical theology of mission in a complementary work: *Actio Dei: Mission und Reich Gottes* (Munich: Kaiser, 1975). Georg F. Vicedom, *Missio Dei – Actio Dei*, ed. Klaus W. Müller, (Nurnberg: VTR, 2002). The citations are taken from this later edition.

and history, while the second indicates specifically the redemptive action of the Son and the Spirit.[72]

Thus, the first two missiologists who propagated the *missio Dei* formula were conservative German missiologists. They were concerned with protecting the traditional perspective on the church's mission, while at the same time placing it within a larger theological framework. Despite this fact, for Helmut Rosin, the new term is "a Trojan horse through which the (unassimilated) 'American' vision was fetched into the well-guarded walls of the ecumenical theology of mission."[73] For John Flett it represents retrospectively a "Copernican revolution" for the theology of mission.[74] According to Hoedemaker, it "symbolizes the fact that the pre-critical and in a sense pre-theological discourse on mission (in what is called the 'Warneck era') is past. And in fact, the boundary line was passed by Willingen ... All in all, the harvest has been poor. The formula *missio Dei* ... is too open in all directions to be fruitful for a treatment of the problems."[75]

The development after the Willingen conference confirms the fact that the formula is a sort of "comprehensive password." If *missio Dei* represents a consensus, it is limited to the terminology. As far as content is concerned, there is divergence of interpretation. On the one hand, we have already mentioned the salvation-historic approach of Hartenstein, Freytag, and Cullmann. In this line of thought, *missio Dei* becomes, in an attenuated and derived sense, a synonym for the salvation history of God's election to mission from Abraham down to the church. Close to this conception is the one, often defended by evangelical groups, which makes a fundamental distinction between salvation history and world history. Georg Sautter is a representative of this position.[76] On the other hand, the concept can also describe the dynamic relatedness of the reign of God and the world in which the church is no more than a function of the apostolate and a messenger of shalom. As main representative we can mention Hoekendijk.[77] A similar approach is the one that sees in the *missio Dei* the expression of God's action in history. In this line of thought, we have already mentioned the American preparatory report for Willingen with H. Richard Niebuhr as a main representative. One can also mention the Catholic conception of the church as sacrament of the unity of humankind and institution for the salvation of humanity. In summary, the formula *missio Dei* still serves as a "comprehensive password" and allows for all these divergent interpretations.

Despite this note of caution, the formula has had a salutary effect on systematic missiology by promoting a Trinitarian grounding to mission. This foundation replaces the geographical and ecclesiocentric definitions of mission by a theological definition. Bosch sums this

---

72   Vicedom, *Missio Dei – Actio Dei*, 59–62.

73   Rosin, *Missio Dei*, 26.

74   Flett, *Witness of God*, 157.

75   Hoedemaker, "The People of God," 164f. (emphasis in the original).

76   G. Sautter, *Heilsgeschichte und Mission* (Giessen: Brunnen, 1985).

77   E.g. Johannes C. Hoekendijk, "Zur Frage einer Missionarischen Existenz," annexe in *Kirche und Volk in der deutschen Missionswissenschaft* (Munich: Kaiser, 1967), 297–354.

up very concisely: "Mission has its origin in the heart of God."[78] *Missio Dei* puts the emphasis on the fact that church and mission have their foundation in the sending of the triune God. In its perspective, the challenge is not the extension or expansion of the church or of Christianity, but a participation in the relationship God has with the world. The downside of this new conception of mission is that it can lose its substance. In a "horizontal" perspective, it can be identified with a historical process or with historical movements, as the ecumenical movement propagated in the 1960s through the concepts of "humanization" and "revolution" or through "liberation" in the 1970s. In a Universalist perspective, it could also be seen as a general relatedness between God and humanity that would make all missionary work a pointless exercise. In a "vertical" perspective, missiology could lose its Christocentric accent and blend into pneumatology, eschatology, or ecclesiology, or in a diffuse Trinitarianism.[79] Despite all these inconveniencies, the different Christian confessions (Catholic, Orthodox, Ecumenical, Protestant, evangelical) have adopted the concept of *missio Dei* in the course of the last fifty years.[80] For some, this indicates that a consensus has been established between the theological persuasions.[81] Thus, Willingen has indeed become a turning point for the theology of mission.[82]

Reception by the Evangelical Movement

We will now study the reception of *missio Dei* by evangelicals. The development in the ecumenical movement after the Willingen conference frightened the majority of evangelicals. At the climax of the theological deviations presented in the preceding section, the evangelical movement separated from the ecumenical movement.[83] The point of departure was the Lausanne I Congress in 1974.

In the English speaking world, evangelicals have followed non-evangelical theologians in using the English form "mission of God," without necessarily questioning the complexity of the issues which are attached to the expression. After distancing themselves for several decades, evangelicals have started to accept tacitly the "new consensus." The Trinitarian grounding of mission made its entry into the text of

---

78   Bosch, *Transforming Mission*, 392.

79   Cf. Hoedemaker, "The People of God," 164f.

80   The documents of the different movements testify of this fact. Several documents of the Second Vatican Council (1962–1965), e.g. the *Decree on Mission: Ad Gentes* (1965), § 2 and 9; Adam Wolanin, "Trinitarian Foundation of Mission," in *Following Christ in Mission: A Foundational Course in Missiology*, ed. Sebastian Karotrempel et al. (Boston: Pauline, 1996); Anastasios of Androussa, "Orthodox Mission: Past, Present, Future," in *Your Will Be Done: Orthodoxy in Mission* (Geneva, WCC, 1989); WCC, *The Nature and Mission of the Church* (1982), § 9; David J. Bosch, *Witness to the World: The Christian Mission in Theological Perspective* (Atlanta: John Knox, 1980), 179f, 239–248; "The Iguassu Affirmation," in *Global Missiology for the 21st Century: The Iguassu Dialogue*, ed. William D. Taylor (Grand Rapids: Baker, 2000), 15–21.

81   Bosch, *Transforming Mission*, p. 390f; Engelsviken, "Convergence or Divergence?" 202–207.

82   For a more detailed discussion of the events around the Willingen conference, see Flett, *Witness of God*, 123–162.

83   Jacques Matthey speaks of "contextual interpretations" which led to the separation of the ecumenical and evangelical movement. Matthey, "God's Mission Today," 580.

the Iguassu Affirmation (1999), a meeting of the World Evangelical Alliance Mission Commission,[84] and also into the Cape Town Commitment (2010), the declaration of the Lausanne III Congress.[85] Both texts avoid the Latin expression *missio Dei*. This indicates that evangelicals have been the last to introduce the Trinitarian foundation of mission in their fundamental missiological texts. This delay is also apparent in the lack of evangelical reflection on the question. Regardless of the "evangelical Trinitarian resurgence,"[86] it is only recently that two evangelical missiologists have proposed substantial evangelical approaches to a Trinitarian grounding of mission.[87] The works come from Christopher Wright, Old Testament specialist and missiologist, as well as director of Langham Partnership (formerly John Stott Ministries) and former coordinator of the Theological Commission of the Lausanne Movement, and from Timothy Tennent, president of Asbury Theological Seminary and professor of world missions.

Christopher Wright's Hermeneutic Perspective

Christopher Wright's book *The Mission of God* (2006) is one of the first books focusing on the *missio Dei* without practically using the Latin term. A popular extension of Wright's thinking on the church's mission can be found in *The Mission of God's People: A Biblical Theology of the Church's Mission*.[88] In a more concise way, this theme has already been developed in the former book.

It is important to note that Christopher Wright's approach is that of an Old Testament exegete, not one of a systematic theologian. Wright does make reference to the debates on *missio Dei*, but develops independently his own concept of the "mission of God." The subtitle "Unlocking the Bible's Grand Narrative," indicates well that the general intention of the book is to demonstrate that the mission of God is the red thread going through the whole Bible. As a logical consequence, in part I Wright proposes to read the Bible with a "messianic and missional hermeneutic."[89]

---

84   "The Iguassu Affirmation," in *Global Missiology for the Twenty-first Century*, 17.

85   "Cape Town Commitment (2010)." Text online: www.lausanne.org.

86   Title of Sexton's article "The State of the Evangelical Trinitarian Resurgence."

87   See some other publications on Trinity and mission: Carl Braaten, "The Triune God: The Source and Model of Christian Unity and Mission," *Missiology* 18, 4 (1990),415–478; David E. Bjork, "Toward a Trinitarian Understanding of Mission in Post-Christendom Lands," *Missiology* 27, 2 (1999), 231–244; Stephen R. Holmes, "Trinitarian Missiology: Towards a Theology of God as Missionary," *IJST* 8 (2006), 72–90; John R. Franke, "God is Love: The Social Trinity and the Mission of God," in *Trinitarian Theology for the Church: Scripture, Community, Worship*, ed. Daniel J. Treier and David Lauber (Downers Grove: InterVarsity, 2009), 105–119; Robert K. Lang'at, "Trinity and Missions: Theological Priority in Missionary Nomenclature," in *Trinitarian Theology for the Church*, 161–81; Sexton, "The State of the Evangelical Trinitarian Resurgence," 803; John Jefferson Davis, "Practising Ministry in the Presence of God and in Partnership with God—The Ontology of Ministry and Pastoral Identity: A Trinitarian-Ecclesial Model," *Evangelical Review of Theology* 36, 2 (2012), 115–136.

88   Grand Rapids: Zondervan, 2010.

89   Christopher Wright defines the new term "missional" like this: "There are many biblical resources … that are profoundly enriching in our understanding of mission in its broadest sense (and especially the mission of God) that are not about sending missionaries. It is probably inappropriate therefore to refer to those texts and themes as 'missionary' … *Missional* is simply an adjective denoting something that is related to or characterized by mission, or has the qualities, attributes or dynamics of mission.

According to his definition, "a missional hermeneutic proceeds from the assumption that the whole Bible renders to us the story of God's mission through God's people in their engagement with God's world for the sake of the whole of God's creation."[90] With this missional hermeneutic he seeks to go beyond "biblical groundings" and "Trinitarian foundations" of mission towards a "missional Christocentrism."[91] Christ, the Son of God, is not only Lord and Savior, but also the one sent by God. According to Wright, a Christocentric theology has necessarily also to be missional. In this sense, Wright speaks in part II of "God with a mission" and of "Jesus with a mission," and in part III of "Israel with a mission" and of the "church with a mission." Part IV describes the "arena of mission": the earth, humanity, and the nations.[92] Wright reserves also a mission to humanity: the cultural mandate (Gen 1:28; 2:15).[93] His approach is holistic with no distinction between the classical cultural and missionary mandates. His conception of mission becomes very large with the risk that everything becomes mission and finally nothing remains mission.[94] A similar development with considerable implications has been observed in the ecumenical movement in the 1960s and 1970s.[95] One of the strengths of Wright's approach is to accentuate the aspects of continuity between Old Testament and New Testament. However, elements of discontinuity between the two testaments, for example the distinct concepts of "people of God" before and after the death and the resurrection of Jesus Christ, and the distinct missions of the different persons and groups sent in the two testaments are little discussed. Overall, Wright's contribution is very significant for the development of a more robust evangelical theology of mission as it seeks to set a history of salvation perspective within the framework of the mission of God.

Development by Timothy Tennent

Following the example of Christopher Wright, Timothy Tennent does make reference to the debates on *missio Dei*, but develops independently his own concept of the "mission of God." But contrary to Wright, Tennent adopts a systematic approach and mentions the Latin term. As the subtitle of his book *A Trinitarian Missiology for the Twenty-first Century* indicates, his intention is to ground his missiology on a Trinitarian foundation.[96] In part I, he establishes the link between *missio Dei* and the Trinity, a connection that the conference of Willingen did not succeed in accomplishing.[97]

Missional is to the word mission what covenantal is to *covenant* or fictional to *fiction*." Wright, *The Mission of God*, 24 (italics in the original).

90   Wright, *The Mission of God*, 51.

91   Ibid., 34 (title of the first section of chapter 1).

92   All are titles in chapter 2 and taken up later in the book

93   Ibid., 65.

94   We refer to the affirmation of the Anglican bishop Stephen Neill: "If everything is mission, nothing is mission." Stephen Neill, *Creative Tension* (London: Edinburgh House Press, 1959), 81.

95   Jacques Matthey speaks of a "'boundless' widening of the understanding of mission" in the 1960s. Matthey, "God's Mission Today," 580.

96   Timothy Tennent, *Invitation to World Missions: A Trinitarian Missiology for the Twenty-first Century* (Grand Rapids: Kregel, 2010).

97   Tennent, "A Trinitarian Missional Theology," and "A Trinitarian Framework for Missions," in *Invitation to World Missions*, 53–73, 74–101.

In this aspect, his approach is similar to that of Georg Vicedom.[98] Tennent builds on Wright's "missional hermeneutic"[99] which permits him to see the Bible as the story of the mission of God and of his people through the engagement of his people in God's action in creation and redemption. He proposes seeing mission as a joyful invitation to participate in the redemptive work of God. This conception of the Bible is close to Kevin Vanhoozer's concept of "theo-drama."[100] For Tennent it is important not to separate the mission of the church from God's mission, but rather to see the two as closely linked:

> Seeing the work of missions within the larger framework of *missio Dei* keeps the church from an unwarranted reductionistic view of soteriology that equates salvation with justification and fails to see the more comprehensive, holistic work of the triune God in regeneration, justification, sanctification, and final glorification, culminating in the New Creation.[101]

In part II of his book, Tennent presents the Father as the providential source and goal of the *missio Dei*. This approach permits him to develop a theology of creation, of revelation, and of culture. He insists on the fact that the God of creation is also the God of revelation. One of the originalities of the book is his Trinitarian theology of culture in the perspective of the New Creation.[102] In this regard, God the Father is the Source, the Redeemer, and the final goal of culture. God the Son is incarnated into sinful, human culture. Thus, God validates human culture despite the fall. In this way, our understanding of culture is protected from being either secularized or divinized. If God the Son is the model of the New Creation, the Holy Spirit is the agent of the New Creation, the transformer of culture. The perspective of the New Creation implies that the New Creation becomes the primary cultural identity of Christians, that the ultimate sense of every culture/religion (as reservoir of meaning) is grounded in the triune God, that in every culture the church is the witness of the New Creation, and that in its relativity and corruption the culture cannot be the source of absolute truth. Rather, culture is the context in which we can look for the "points of contact" for the communication of biblical truth so that the message becomes comprehensible and relevant for each milieu. In this perspective, in part III of his work, Tennent sees the history of mission and the cross-cultural communication of the gospel as reflections of the Incarnation. Finally, in part IV, he develops the theme of how the Holy Spirit renders the church capable of living its new identity permeated by the New Creation.

Reflecting on the role of the divine persons, Tennent goes farther than the Reformers who insisted on the non-division of the Trinity's works *ad extra*. However, Tennent warns against the deviations in this sense. For him, it is important that God executes his work in and through the church. Therefore, his slogan is: "*God-centered and church-focused missions*."[103] As an evangelical, he insists on the fact that "we no longer isolate soteriology from

---

98   Ibid., 55 and 56, n. 8.
99   Ibid., 60f.
100   Ibid., 61. Cf. Vanhoozer, *The Drama of Doctrine*.
101   Ibid., 73.
102   Ibid., "A Trinitarian 'New Creation' Theology of Culture," 159–190.
103   Ibid., 58f.

pneumatology and eschatology."[104] Tennent has thus offered a complementary approach to that of Wright.

Evaluation

The mainly passive use of the term *missio* by the church fathers and the predominance of the terms *missio Filii* and *missio Spiritus Sancti*, with their objective genitive construction, seems to indicate that the development of a concept with an active sense and a subjective genitive was not very likely. In addition, the definition of the concept by Augustine raises the problem of the dichotomy between God's being and action. The development in scholastic theology concentrates on the "divine processions" and adds a further dichotomy between the action of God and the church.

On the other hand, the recovery of the term in a particular politico-theological constellation around the missionary conference of Willingen without any link to the doctrine of the Trinity has permitted that the different theological persuasions could attribute all the meanings that they wanted to this ambiguous term. This fact has led Flett to call *missio Dei* a "Rorschach test."[105] He remarks:

> *Missio Dei's* ambiguous genealogy produces, in turn, a theological ambiguity. Willingen's Trinitarianism is an incidental development. This does not disqualify the significance of the basic theological move—the missionary act must be located in the triune being of God. It does, however, reveal that the lamented contemporary problems of *missio Dei* inhere within the original form of the concept and stem from its deficient Trinitarianism.[106]

Furthermore, concerning the origin of the contemporary concept, the popular link between Barth, Hartenstein, and Willingen cannot be supported.[107] Also, the consensus that the formula has permitted following Willingen concerns the term, rather than the content. For some, theological subjects like the "reign of God" and the "missionary church" that were in vogue in certain groups of the International Missionary Council around the middle of the twentieth century found a safe haven in this "comprehensive password." Others, such as the American preparatory group of Willingen, promoted a Trinitarian grounding, referring particularly to God's action in creation. For still others, notably Hartenstein, this "neologism" could safeguard a salvation-historic perspective of the theology of mission, as well as the priority of God's action in mission and the close relation between the action of God and the church. All this leads Rosin to speak of *missio Dei* as a "Trojan horse" through which all sorts of deviations have been welcomed into the theology of mission.[108]

---

104 Ibid., 101.
105 Flett, *Witness of God*, 76. The Rorschach test is a psychological test that consists of interpreting forms of colored patches.
106 Ibid., 161.
107 Ibid., 123–162, summary 161f.
108 Rosin, *Missio Dei*, 26.

A fundamental question in our debate touches the theme which was already discussed at the end of the Willingen conference: Was the missionary obligation of the church to be "understood primarily as derived from the redemptive purpose and acts of God or as derived from the nature of God Himself?"[109] This question delineates two options presented at the conference by Hartenstein and Lehmann: Is mission a reflex of faith (the American group) or a functional activity (the history of salvation group)? No doubt the background to this question is found in the dichotomy created by the church fathers between God's being and action, between the immanent and economic Trinity. This dichotomy between God's being and action also creates a corresponding dichotomy in the human response. At Willingen, all agreed to say that mission was essential to the nature of the church.[110] The tension centered, however, on the definition of this missionary nature. Flett sums up the issue as follows:

> Did the pattern of sending proceed from God's being, resulting in a missionary act that unfolded in historical process? Or did it proceed from God's act, resulting in a missionary act that unfolded in the institutional life of the church? While these positions appear very different, in actuality they trade on the fundamental Trinitarian breach of being and act, with the eschatological approach emphasizing the former and the ecclesiological approach emphasizing the latter. In that *missio Dei* attempts to ground mission in the doctrine of the Trinity, the doctrine attacks any such breach. It does not permit the kinds of activities grounded in natural theology and thus appears not to permit any human action. *Missio Dei*, in other words, eats away at itself. The foundational issue is Trinitarian, and any solution must begin there. It is a problem of God himself.[111]

How can one resolve the problem of dichotomy between being and action and ground mission successfully in the Trinity? It seems that Barth has traced a promising way forward: to eliminate the strict distinction between the immanent and economic Trinity. This approach permits us to see the revealed God in the God of all eternity, revealed at the same time in creation and in the sending of the Son and the Spirit, and thus to see together the Creator and Redeemer God, and equally see together church and mission. In our view, Wright and Tennent have attempted a good development of Barth's approach: to read the Bible as the story which reveals God's action in the world, with and through his people (a Christocentric and missional hermeneutic). In this way, one will be able to speak about the mission of God and of his people. But Marc Spindler warns us, however, not to see in a naïve way this common action of the divine and the human. He reminds us that this double dimension of mission will always remain a mystery. As man is a sinner, he can easily become an obstacle to the mission as God sees it. "It is probably for this reason that one cannot subscribe to the naïve identification of church and mission. The church is not only mission, but it can also be an obstacle to mission."[112]

---

109 Goodall, *Missions Under the Cross*, 244.
110 Ibid. See the affirmation, "the Church is missionary by its nature," in later Catholic and ecumenical documents: *Ad Gentes* (1965), § 2; WCC, *The Nature and Mission of the Church* (1982), § 9.
111 Flett, *Witness of God*, 162 (emphasis in the original).
112 Marc Spindler, *La Mission: Combat pour le Salut du Monde* (Paris: Delachaux et Niestlé, 1967), 94f.

On the other hand, by reacting against the social gospel of his time and against natural theology with its "points of contact," Barth has not found a good solution to help us to think correctly about the relationship between the divine and the human, between revelation and religion, between the supracultural and the cultural. The Catholic Church has given thought to this relationship between God and man in terms of analogy, and Barth in terms of correspondence, a concept close to analogy. However, it is necessary to go beyond these approaches. It is not sufficient to say that religion is a form of unbelief.[113] On this subject, it seems that Tennent has made a step forward in his consideration of a theology of culture in the perspective of the New Creation. However, it cannot be more than a preliminary approach to the problem. For Tennent, the supracultural God has entered fallen culture through his Son and transforms it through his Spirit. Even more, the triune God indwells the human being (John 14:17, 23; 1 Cor 6:19; Col 1:27).[114] And surprisingly, he expresses himself through very diverse cultural forms during the different historical periods and in the different geographical regions of the world. In this regard, a promising text is found in the World Evangelical Alliance Theological Commission's volume on contextualization, which studies this relation between divine revelation and human culture.[115] However, this will always remain a mystery. Finally, von Balthasar shows us in his Trilogy that a theo-socio-missiological approach may lead to fruitful results. This approach includes a theological and a cultural analysis (by using historical, philosophical, literary, sociological and anthropological tools) as well as a "theo-logical" synthesis.

In the final analysis, is *missio Dei* a term to be used or to be avoided? Should we follow Barth's and von Balthasar's efforts to avoid the term and to focus more on a Trinitarian grounding of the action of God and the church? Are Wright's and Tennent's evangelical attempts useful to link the concept of *missio Dei* with the Trinity, to develop the reflection on a Trinitarian foundation of mission, and beyond this foundation, a Christological and missional hermeneutic? Before attempting a concluding answer, we propose to apply the concept of *missio Dei* to a very familiar text, the Lord's Prayer.

The Lord's Prayer: An Application

The prayer that Jesus taught his disciples when they ask him how to pray, opens up in his first three requests a perspective that could be called "missionary": "Hallowed be your name, your kingdom come, your will be done on earth as it is in heaven" (Matt 6:9–10; Luke 11:2). The similar form of these three requests of which two use the imperative of the third person singular in the passive aorist tense, and one in the active voice, suggests that the three requests could refer to the same salvation-historic reality. Gerhardsson and Hagner mention a possible Hebrew parallelism (parallelismus membrorum) here between the three requests.[116]

---

113 *CD* I/2, § 17, 2.

114 The Catholic dogma speaks of the invisible mission of the Son and the Spirit in the soul of the believer where they come to dwell with the Father. *ST* Ia, q. 43, a. 5.

115 Matthew Cook et al., ed., *Local Theology for the Global Church: Principles for an Evangelical Approach to Contextualization* (Pasadena: William Carey Library, 2010).

116 B. Gerhardsson, "The Matthaean Version of the Lord's Prayer (Matt 6:9b–13): Some Observations," in *The New Testament Age*, FS B. Reicke, vol. 1, ed. W. C. Weinrich (Macon, GA: Mercer, 1984), 210, quoted by Donald A. Hagner, *Matthew 1–13*, WBC 33A (Dallas: Word, 1993), 148.

Typically, the "divine passive" indicates God's action. Here, in the Our Father, the believer who prays is called to participate in God's action. These observations could suggest that the believer who prays the Lord's Prayer is invited to participate in God's action. In this way, the first triplet of the Lord's Prayer seems to be an example of the imbrication between the action of the people of God and God's acts. Could the concept of "mission of God" (*missio Dei*) provide a useful model to think about the relationship between God and the believer as expressed in this prayer?

Conclusion

Certainly, the reflection on the Trinitarian foundation of mission is an important step forward for evangelical mission theology. Evidently, the Christological and missional hermeneutic of the Bible, based on the sending of the Son of God, will remain a subject of debate. There also needs to be much more serious thought given to the relationship or lack thereof between the divine activity and human action, between revelation and culture. In the final analysis, despite the potential of the resurgence of Trinitarian theology for evangelical mission thinking, we express our reservation concerning the use of the term *missio Dei*. If one wants to employ this expression, it would be important to explain it in the perspective of a Trinitarian grounding and framework for mission. However, if one does not have the possibility to explain the concept, it would be preferable to avoid this "comprehensive password" that can easily become a kind of "Trojan horse."

Questions for Reflection:

1. According to Hannes Wiher, evangelicals have had a tendency to avoid the use of the expression "*missio Dei*." Why has the term been more difficult to be accepted by evangelicals than to others? How much are you using the term to define mission and what is your understanding of it? Do you agree with the author's reservation in using the term?

2. How would you define a Trinitarian concept of mission? How has that concept developed in the history of the church and how is it related to the use of the expression *missio Dei*?

3. The use of the expression *missio Dei* has helped to change the focus in mission from the action the church doing things and sending to the action of God and that the church is sent into the world. How has that affected your understanding of mission? How would you describe the relationship between the divine activity and human action?

References

Anastasios of Androussa. 1989. Orthodox Mission: Past, Present, Future. In *Your Will Be Done: Orthodoxy in Mission*. Geneva: WCC.

Aquinas, Thomas. 1981. *Summa Theologica,* 5 vols. Trans. Fathers of the English Dominican Province. Westminster, MD: Christian Classics.

Augustine. 1991. *De Trinitate*. Trans. Edmund Hill. Brooklyn: New City.

Barth, Karl. 1924. *Das Wort Gottes und die Theologie: Gesammelte Vorträge 1*. Munich: Kaiser.

———. 1932. Die Theologie und die Mission in der Gegenwart. *Zwischen den Zeiten* 10(3).

———. 1933. *Theologische Existenz Heute*, Heft 1. Munich.

———. 1956–1969. *Church Dogmatics*, 4 vol. Edinburgh: T. & T. Clark.

———. 1960. *The Humanity of God, Conference held at the Swiss Pastoral Society at Aarau, September 25, 1956*. Richmond: John Knox Press.

Bassham, R.C. 1980. Mission Theology: 1948–1975. *Occasional Bulletin of Missionary Research* 4(2).

Bjork, David E. 1999. Toward a Trinitarian Understanding of Mission in Post-Christendom Lands. *Missiology* 27(2).

Bosch, David J. 1980. *Witness to the World: The Christian Mission in Theological Perspective*. London: Marshall, Morgan & Scott/Atlanta: John Knox.

———. 1991. Mission as Missio Dei. In *Transforming Mission: Paradigm Shifts in Theology of Mission*. Maryknoll, NY: Orbis.

Braaten, Carl. 1990. The Triune God: The Source and Model of Christian Unity and Mission. *Missiology* 18(4).

Brunner, Emil. 1932. Die Frage Nach dem 'Anknüpfungspunkt' als Problem der Theologie. *Zwischen den Zeiten* 10.

———. 1949. Toward a Missionary Theology. *Christian Century* 66(27).

———. 1955. A Spiritual Autobiography. *Japan Christian Quarterly*. July, 1955, 242.

Busch, Eberhard. 1980. Un Magnificat Perpétuel. In *Dogmatique*. Karl Barth, vol. I. Edinburgh: T&T Clark.

Cape Town Commitment. 2010. http://www.lausanne.org.

Cook, Matthew, et al., eds. 2010. *Local Theology for the Global Church: Principles for an Evangelical Approach to Contextualization*. Pasadena, CA: William Carey Library.

Denziger, Heinrich, ed. 1947. *Enchiridion Symbolorum*. Freiburg-im-Breisgau: Herder.

Engelsviken, T. 2001. Convergence or Divergence? The Relationship between Recent Ecumenical and Evangelical Mission Documents. *Swedish Missiological Themes no 2*.

Escobar, Samuel. 2003. We Believe in a Missionary God. In *A Time for Mission*. Leicester, UK: IVP.

Flett, John G. 2010. *The Witness of God: The Trinity, Missio Dei, Karl Barth, and the Nature of Christian Community*. Grand Rapids, MI: Eerdmans.

Franke, John R. 2009. God Is Love: The Social Trinity and the Mission of God. In *Trinitarian Theology for the Church: Scripture, Community, Worship*. Ed. Daniel J. Treier and David Lauber. Downers Grove: IVP.

Freytag, Walter. 1953. Mitglied im Deutschen Evangelischen Missionsrat und Missionstag und bei den Tagungen der Ökumene. In *Ein Leben für Kirche und Mission,* ed. Wolfgang Metzger. Stuttgart: Evangelischer Missionsverlag.

Gass, W. 1854. *Geschichte der Protestantischen Dogmatik: In Ihrem Zusammenhang mit Theologie überhaupt,* vol. 2. Berlin: Reimer.

Gerhardsson, B. 1984. The Matthaean Version of the Lord's Prayer. In *The New Testament Age.* FS B. Reicke, vol. 1, ed. W. C. Weinrich. Macon, GA: Mercer.

Goodall, Norman, ed. 1953. *Missions Under the Cross.* London: Edinburgh House.

Hagner, Donald A. 1993. *Matthew 1–13.* WBC 33A. Dallas: Word.

Hartenstein, Karl. 1928. Was hat die Theologie Karl Barths der Mission zu sagen? *Zwischen den Zeiten* 6.

———. 1939. Tambaram, Wie Es Arbeitete. In *Das Wunder der Kirche Unter den Völkern der Erde: Bericht über die Weltmissionskonferenz in Tambaram.* Ed. Martin Schlunk. Stuttgart: Evangelischer Missionsverlag.

———. 1952. Übergang und Neubeginn: Zur Tagung des Internationalen Missionsrats in Willingen. *Zeitwende* 24(4).

———. 1952. Theologische Besinnung. In *Mission Zwischen Gestern und Morgen.* Ed. Walter Freytag. Stuttgart: Evangelischer Missionsverlag.

Henrici, Peter. 2005. Hans Urs von Balthasar's Trilogy: A Theology of European Culture. *Communio: International Catholic Review* 32(2).

Hoedemaker, L.A. 1995. The People of God and the Ends of the Earth. In *Missiology: An Ecumenical Introduction.* Ed. F. J. Verstraelen, et al. Grand Rapids: Eerdmans.

Hoekendijk, Johannes C. 1967. Zur Frage einer Missionarischen Existenz. In *Kirche und Volk in der Deutschen Missionswissenschaft.* Munich: Kaiser.

Holmes, Stephen R. 2006. Trinitarian Missiology: Towards a Theology of God as Missionary. *IJST* 8.

Lehmann, Paul L. 1952. The Missionary Obligation of the Church. *Theology Today* 9(1).

Matthey, Jacques. 2003. God's Mission Today: Summary and Conclusions. *International Review of Mission* 92(4).

Neill, Stephen. 1959. *Creative Tension.* London: Edinburgh House Press.

Niebuhr, H. Richard. 1963. An Attempt at a Theological Analysis of Missionary Motivation. *Occasional Bulletin of Missionary Research* 14(1).

Rahner, Karl. 1970. *The Trinity.* Freiburg-im-Breisgau: Herder and Herder.

Richebächer, Wilhelm. 2003. *Missio Dei:* The Basis of Mission Theology or a Wrong Path? *International Review of Mission* 92(4).

Rosin, Helmut. 1972. *Missio Dei: An Examination of the Origin, Contents and Function of the Term in the Protestant Missiological Discussion.* Leyden: IIMO.

Sautter, G. 1985. *Heilsgeschichte und Mission.* Giessen: Brunnen.

Scherer, James A., ed. 1982. The Lutheran Missionary Idea in Historical Perspective. In *That the Gospel May Be Sincerely Preached throughout the World: A Lutheran Perspective on Mission and Evangelism in the 20th Century.* Stuttgart: Kreuz.

———. 1987. *Gospel, Church, and Kingdom: Comparative Studies in World Mission Theology.* Minneapolis, MN: Augsburg Publishing House.

Second Vatican Council. 1965. *Decree on Mission: Ad Gentes.*

Sexton, Jason. 2011. The State of the Evangelical Trinitarian Resurgence. *Journal of the Evangelical Theological Society* 54(4).

Spindler, Marc. 1967. *La Mission: Combat pour le Salut du Monde.* Paris: Delachaux et Niestlé.

Stott, John. 1992. Our God Is a Missionary God. In *The Contemporary Christian: Applying God's Word to Today's World,* vol. 2. Leicester, UK: IVP.

Taylor, William, ed. 2000. The Iguassu Affirmation. In *Global Missiology for the Twenty-first Century: The Iguassu Dialogue.* Grand Rapids: Baker.

Tennent, Timothy. 2010. *Invitation to World Missions: A Trinitarian Missiology for the Twenty-first Century.* Grand Rapids: Kregel.

Thesaurus Linguae Latinae. 2002–2007. Munich: Saur.

Thiele, Gilbert A. and Dennis Hilgendorf, eds. *The Mission of God: An Introduction to a Theology of Mission.* St. Louis, MO: Concordia Press.

Treier, Daniel and David Lauber, eds. 2009. *Trinitarian Theology for the Church: Scripture, Community, Worship.* Downers Grove, IL: IVP.

Vanhoozer, Kevin J. 2005. *The Drama of Doctrine: A Canonical-Linguistic Approach to Christian Theology.* Louisville: John Knox.

Verkuyl, Johannes. 1978. *Contemporary Missiology.* Grand Rapids, MI: Eerdmans.

Vicedom, Georg F. 1958. *Missio Dei: Einführung in eine Theologie der Mission.* Munich: Kaiser. English translation: 1965. *The Mission of God: An Introduction to a Theology of Mission,* ed. Gilbert A. Thiele and Dennis Hilgendorf. St. Louis: Concordia Press.

———. 2002. *Actio Dei: Mission und Reich Gottes.* Munich: Kaiser.

———. 2002. *Missio Dei – Actio Dei.* Ed. Klaus W. Müller. Nurnberg: VTR.

von Balthasar, Hans Urs. 1982–1991. *The Glory of the Lord: A Theological Aesthetics,* 7 vols. San Francisco: Ignatius Press.

———. 1988–1998. *Theo-Drama: Theological Dramatic Theory* 5 vols. San Francisco: Ignatius Press.

———. 1992. Analogia fidei. In *The Theology of Karl Barth: Exposition and Interpretation.* San Francisco: Communio Books, Ignatius Press.

———. 1993. *My Work: In Retrospect.* San Francisco: Ignatius Press.

———. 2000. *Theo-logic: Theological Logical Theory.* San Francisco: Ignatius Press.

Wolanin, Adam. 1996. Trinitarian Foundation of Mission. In *Following Christ in Mission: A Foundational Course in Missiology.* Ed. Sebastian Karotrempel et al. Boston: Pauline.

World Council of Churches. 1982. *The Nature and Mission of the Church.*

World Council of Churches Department on Studies in Evangelism. 1967. *The Church for Others, and the Church for the World: A Quest for Structures for Missionary Congregations.* Geneva: World Council of Churches.

Wright, Christopher J.H. 2006. *The Mission of God.* Leicester, UK: IVP.

Hannes Wiher has an MD and PhD in medicine, and an MA and PhD in missiology. He has spent twenty-two years of missionary service in West Africa and serves as professor of missiology in Africa, Asia, and Europe, developing primarily missiology in the French-speaking world.

CHAPTER 10

PAUL'S ECCLESIAL MISSIOLOGY

Bertil Ekström

Mission is the fundamental reality of our Christian life. We are Christians because we have been called by God to work with him in the fulfilment of his purposes for humanity as a whole. Our life in this world is life in mission. Life has a purpose only to the extent that it has a missionary dimension. (Emilio Castro)[1]

Is Paul's missiology ecclesial? What is the relationship between church and mission in his writings? Does Paul include the church in his missiological thinking as indispensable for mission? Great effort has been made to separate the Apostle Paul's theology from his missionary practice and his mission activity from the established church. The letter to Romans has been read as being a theological treatise without relation to the concrete situation in which the apostle was or to whom he wrote the letter.[2] Ferdinand Hahn states that:

> Paul did not entertain a moment's doubt that the gospel must be preached in the whole world. In his letters this concern is expressed in a great variety of ways. His view of the mission is inseparable from his entire theological thought; it therefore leads us into almost all the problems of his theology.[3]

A strong emphasis has also been given to Paul's missionary team as a parachurch movement in mission, disconnected from the local churches that had sent him or that he had planted.[4] The fact that we do not have a clear "mission commission" by Paul in his letters, commanding the churches to evangelize and be missionaries, has also been used as an indication that he did not expect the churches to be directly involved in mission.

However, it seems to me that there was no dichotomy between church and mission in the ministry and teaching of the apostle Paul. He keeps the two concepts closely tied together

---

1   Emilio Castro, "Liberation, Development and Evangelism: Must We Choose in Mission?" in *Occasional Bulletin for Missionary Research* (1987), 87.

2   For further discussion see for example: P.T. O'Brien, *Gospel and Mission in the Writings of Paul* (Ada, MI: Baker Academic, 2000), x–xii; A.J. Hultgren, *Paul's Gospel and Mission* (Philadelphia: Fortress 1985), 125,145; Susann Liubinskas, "The Body of Christ in Mission: Paul's Ecclesiology and the Role of the Church in Mission" in *Missiology: An International Review*, 41 (4) (2013), 402–415.

3   Ferdinand Hahn, *Mission in the New Testament* (London: SCM, 1965), 97.

4   Robert J. Banks, *Paul's Idea of Community* (Peabody, MA: Hendrickson, 2009), 168–169.

and does not conceive of one without the other. In fact, for Paul his missionary team is also church. The problem may be our understanding of mission and of church, a lack of an ecclesial missiology that is coherent with Paul's teaching and action. Perhaps the great problem is that we tend to limit mission to "going abroad and evangelizing the heathen" instead of having an integral comprehension of mission with a holistic view of the gospel. Or, that we limit the church only to be the local community. Sometimes church becomes just an institution and not the living body of Christ with the manifold gifts and ministries. The expansion of the gospel to other places was the church in action as much as the growth and discipleship in the local community.

In this chapter we will mention some of the basic aspects of Paul's missiology based on his understanding of the church and of the role the church plays in God's mission. That does not exclude the possibility of God doing his mission without the church, but emphasizes how God has chosen the church as his primary agent for missionary outreach and works through the church for the purpose of his mission. Therefore Paul's missiology is ecclesial. The limitation of space in this chapter does not allow a deeper or more complete discussion.

Paul's Relationship to the Church

The missionary journey of Paul starts in the local church of Antioch and ends in the local church of Rome. The "vision from heaven," the result of his first encounter with Jesus Christ, was given when he was persecuting the church. It was in the community of disciples in Damascus that he took his first steps of discipleship and had his "missionary call" confirmed. It is difficult to conceive that the three years in the desert of Arabia and the time in Damascus would not include deep conversations about faith issues in a group of followers of Jesus. Unfortunately we do not know much about his spiritual journey and theological development during the years in his hometown Tarsus, but again, it would be unlike Paul not to debate and, together with others (in a local church community?), to continue to search for a better understanding of what the gospel of Jesus meant and how he should fulfil the missionary call he had received.

Paul is also trained in a multicultural church under the mentorship of Barnabas, and he becomes one of the church leaders in Antioch. This same church, led by the Spirit, sends him and Barnabas to spread the good news of salvation and plant new churches in other places.

It is important to remember that the letters Paul sent to churches and church leaders were written during his missionary journeys or in prison because of preaching the gospel. It would be strange if his own situation did not affect his theological reflection and the way he was writing to the churches. On the contrary, he mentions quite often his own struggles and challenges as well as his achievements in the effort to reach out to those who had not heard about Jesus. Paul was a "reflective practitioner" who could combine and harmonize his theology with his practice.

Paul's Missional Ecclesiology

There is, of course, a lot to be said about Paul's ecclesiology but that is not the main purpose here. Paul speaks about the local assembly as the church but also the global and universal community as the church. Here it is sufficient to say that Paul saw the church as God's mystery, the new humanity that united Jews and Gentiles, a multicultural community. John Stott commenting on Paul's letter to the Ephesians (v. 3:10), says:

> The first result to be expected from the preaching of "Christ's unsearchable riches" and "the mystery" would be the birth and growth of the church. Gentiles and Jews would embrace the gospel, be converted, and find themselves joint members of the family of God and the body of Christ. Indeed, this had already happened, as Paul was writing. He was not theorizing. "The mystery" was not an abstraction. It was taking concrete shape before people's eyes. And this new phenomenon, this new multiracial humanity, the wisdom of God was being displayed.[5]

For the church to really become multiracial and multicultural there was a clear need for preaching the gospel among other nations. The "mystery" would not be completed without the presence in the church of people from different cultural and racial backgrounds. (Compare Rev 7:9.)

Referring to Paul's letter to the Ephesians, Charles van Engen affirms that:

> A careful study of Ephesians from the perspective of a dynamic ecclesiology will reveal Paul's view of the missionary nature of the local congregation. Paul saw the local church as an organism which should continually grow in the missional expression of its essential nature in the world.[6]

Another important aspect of Paul's understanding of the church is his analogy of the church as being the body of Christ. When Paul uses the metaphor in texts such as Romans 12:4–8; 1 Corinthians 12:12–30 and Ephesians 4:4–16, the diversity of gifts, functions, and services in the community is clearly stated. Interestingly, people with the gifts and functions that are associated with evangelism and mission are also part of the body of Christ! The argument that Paul is speaking of individuals and not collectively of the church does not exclude the fact that these services are within the context of the local community. Even apostles and evangelists are part of the church and when acting according to their gifts and functions, they are acting as the church. Their ministry cannot be something parallel to the church since the body is one and all members are fully integrated in the same body.

When we start thinking of human structures, things could be seen differently. For practical reasons we divide our ministries into organizations and institutions. However, that does not seem to be Paul's concern. His emphasis lies on the unity that contains diversity and acts in mutuality.

---

5   John Stott, *God's New Society: The Message of Ephesians* (Downers. Grove: IVP, 1979), 123.
6   Charles Van Engen, *Mission on the Way* (Ada, MI: Baker Academic, 1996), 105.

Is There a Pauline "Great Commission"?

As we have already pointed out, it could be the narrow definition of mission that makes us believe that Paul did not see mission as an essential part of the life of the local church. Chris Wright affirms:

> Evangelism and teaching/discipling are together integral and essential parts of our mission. Paul told Timothy to "do the work of an evangelist," and also to teach sound doctrine, and to mentor others to teach others also. And he did not imply that one was more important than the other: they were all essential parts of the mission entrusted to Timothy. For Paul, mission included church nurture as much as church planting.[7]

The words of encouragement and recognition that Paul directs to the church in Thessalonica show his appreciation of the fact that they have spread the gospel to others in the region. He says that they have become his imitators and "a model to all the believers in Macedonia and Achaia. The Lord's message rang out from you" (1 Thess 1:6–8).

Paul seems to have had high expectations of the churches he founded, and others that he had some kind of relation to, that they should engage in evangelistic and missionary work. The two most evident examples are the churches in Philippi and Rome.

The Church in Philippi

Paul planted the church in Philippi during his second missionary journey (Acts 16:11–40). The first converts were Lydia (a businesswoman from Thyatira, in the province of Lydia), probably also the slave girl who had been released from an evil spirit, and a jailer and his family. The start of the church was marked both by miracles and persecution, a not uncommon combination as the result of preaching the gospel. The emergent church did meet in the house of Lydia who may also have been the first leader of the church. More than other churches, the church in Philippi became Paul's favorite community, and a strong partnership between the Philippians and the apostle developed. The letter is a declaration of love for the church and a clear expression of joy in the cooperation that they were committed to. The letter contains a series of terms, often using the prefix syn (= with, in company with, along with, together with) that show this close participation of the Philippians in Paul's ministry as well as an exhortation to be united as a church. Some examples are:

- 1:5   Partnership in the gospel—*koinonia*
- 1:7   Share God's grace with me—*syn-koinonia*
- 1:27   Stand firm in one spirit, contending as one man for the faith—*syn-athlountes*
- 2:2   Being like-minded, one in spirit—*syn-psichos*
- 2:18   Be glad and rejoice with me—*chairete e syn-chairete*
- 2:25   Fellow or coworker—*syn-ergon*
- 2:25   Fellow soldier—*sy(n)-stratioten*
- 4:3   Yokefellow (yoke—wooden bar that joined animals)—friend, companion, comrade—*sy(n)-zyge*—could also be a name *Sysgoz*

---

7   Christopher Wright, *The Mission of God's People* (Grand Rapids, MI: Zondervan, 2010), 284–285.

- *4.3*   Contended at my side—*sy(n)-llambanon*
- *4:3*   My fellow workers—*syn-ergon*
- *4:14*   Share in my troubles—*syn-koinonesanthes*
- *4:15*   The church shared with me in the matter of giving and receiving—*e-koinonesen*

The idea is not just that the church sends financial help to the apostle and someone to visit him from time to time, but that the church is fully engaged in cross-cultural ministry together with the apostle.

The Church in Rome

That is also the case with the church in Rome. Paul is not the founder of the church in Rome but desires that they engage in his missionary project to Spain. In Romans 15:23–24 Pauls writes:

> But now that there is no more place for me to work in these regions, and since I have been longing for many years to see you, I plan to do so when I go to Spain. I hope to visit you while passing through and to have you assist me on my journey there, after I have enjoyed your company for a while.[8]

A quick look at the text could give the impression that Paul is only asking for financial resources for his mission enterprise into the west of the Roman Empire. However, the word "assist" is *propempo* (from *pempo*—send) and has meanings such as send or help on one's way, escort, and accompany (as in Acts 20:38 and 21:5). John Murray, commenting on Romans 15:24, says that:

> He expects from the church at Rome a sending forth with commendation and blessing comparable to that experienced earlier at the hands of other churches. How close was the bond of fellowship between the churches and the apostle in the discharge of his apostolic commission.

And John Stott goes further in his understanding of the verb *propempo* affirming that:

> The verb translated assist (*propempo*) seems already to have become almost a technical Christian term for helping missionaries on their way. It undoubtedly meant more than good wishes and a valedictory prayer. In most cases it also involved supplying them with provisions and money (cf. Tit 3:16; 3 John 6f.), and in sometimes providing them as well with an escort to accompany them at least part of the way (cf. Acts 20:38; 21:5). Perhaps Paul hopes to establish an ongoing relationship with the Christians in Rome, so that they will continue to support him, as other churches have done previously.[9]

To be sent to Spain by the church in Rome meant partnership in the missionary project, not just good wishes on the journey. He sought after an association with him and a church fully engaged. Rome was of course very strategic for reaching Spain, not only because of

---

8   John Murray, *The Epistle to the Romans* (Grand Rapids, MI: Eerdmans, 1967), 217–218.
9   John Stott, *The Message of Romans* (Downers Grove, IL: IVP, 1994), 385.

its location but also due to the fact that Latin was the language used in Spain as in Rome. To form a missionary team from the church in Rome to follow him to Spain would have been a perfect strategy.

Paul's Ecclesial Missiology

Paul's missiology is clearly gospel-centric, Christocentric and kingdom-centric, but also church-centric, focusing on the role of the community of believers as responsible for reaching out with the good news of salvation. However, it is not just the missionary activity of the church that is important for Paul. It is also the identification of the church as the body of Christ with the diversity of gifts and ministries. All these ministries are part of the mission of the church and should benefit people locally and globally. The church embodies God's mystery of uniting Jews and Gentiles in a direct relationship with Christ, the firstborn of the new humanity (Rom 8:29, 30) and the head of the body (Eph 4:15).

Paul's mission starts in the church and happens in close relationship and cooperation with local churches with the aim to plant new churches that can reproduce (in a discipleship model) new churches. The churches are not just used instrumentally for his missionary enterprise, they are the senders and in a way owners of his mission to whom he is also accountable. He comes back to the sending church of Antioch after his missionary journeys and he has to respond to the apostles in Jerusalem about his teaching and activity (Acts 15). To the church in Corinth Paul writes that they are his letters of recommendation (2 Cor 3:1–3). Although being an "apostle of Christ Jesus by the will of God" (2 Cor 1:1), the commissioning and authority in his apostleship was all the time based and confirmed by local churches.

Ecclesial Missiology Versus Missional Ecclesiology

It seems to me that it is important to affirm both ecclesial missiology and missional ecclesiology. Ecclesiology needs to be missional. The missionary nature of the church is essential for its existence. The church has been sent into the world to proclaim the good news of salvation and to promote and defend the kingdom values, giving continuity to the mission of Jesus (John 20:21; Luke 4:18–19).

At the same time missiology needs to be ecclesial. Although God could have chosen to do mission completely without the involvement of the disciples, he decided to not do it without the church. He created the church with the main purpose to cooperate in his mission. So God's mission has a church and regardless of its ecclesial structures and institutions, the church as a whole needs to be included in our missiological thinking.

Conclusion

Andrew Kirk affirms about the *missio ecclesiae* (the mission of the church) that:

> Mission is so much at the heart of the church's life that, rather than think of it as one aspect of its existence, it is better to think of it as defining its essence. The church is by nature missionary to the extent that, if it ceases to be missionary, it has not just failed in one of its tasks, it has ceased being church. Thus, the church's self-understanding and sense of identity (its ecclesiology) is inherently bound up with its call to

share and live out the gospel of Jesus Christ to the ends of the earth and the end of time. Without a strong sense of vocation to its missionary work, the church cannot consider itself either catholic or apostolic.[10]

Is it possible to see in the apostle Paul both a missional ecclesiology and an ecclesial missiology? Yes, I think so. The church has a mission, a task and function to fulfil as sent by God to the world. The mission of God has also a church as the community that gathers those who believe in Jesus and become his followers. The dichotomy between church and mission seems unthinkable to Paul. A purely pragmatic approach to missionary activity could lead us astray from the centrality of the church in the New Testament teaching. The fact that in practice many times missionary enterprises "do better" without the established (and sometimes accommodated) church, is no proof of God's intention but rather our inability to understand that mission is the essence of its existence.

Questions for Reflection:

1. How has your church tradition seen the relationship between church and mission?
2. What structures have been formed in your context that have taken responsibility for the missionary task of the church? What has been the influence of outsourcing mission to specialized structures in your denomination/church? How much have they been seen as integral part of the church?
3. What hinders the church from being missional? What hinders mission from being ecclesial?

References

Banks, Robert J. 2009. *Paul's Idea of Community: The Early House Churches in Their Cultural Setting*, 3rd ed. Peabody, MA: Hendrickson Publishers.

Castro, Emilio. 1987. Liberation, Development and Evangelism: Must We Choose in Mission? In *Occasional Bulletin for Missionary Research*, July.

Hahn, Ferdinand. 1965. Mission in the New Testament. London: SCM Press.

Hultgren, A.J., 1985. *Paul's Gospel and Mission: The Outlook from His Letter to the Romans*. Philadelphia: Fortress.

Kärkkäinen, Veli-Matti. 2002. *An Introduction to Ecclesiology: Ecumenical, Historical, and Global Perspectives*. Downers Grove, IL: IVP.

Kirk, J. Andrew. 1999. *What Is Mission? Theological Explorations*. London: Danton, Longham and Todd.

Liubinskas, Susann. 2013. The Body of Christ in Mission: Paul's Ecclesiology and the Role of the Church in Mission. In *Missiology: An International Review*, 41 (4) 402–415.

---

10   Andrew J. Kirk, *What Is Mission? Theological Explorations* (London: Danton, Longham and Todd, 1999).

Murray, John. 1967. *The Epistle to the Romans.* London: Marshall, Morgan & Scott.

O'Brien, P.T. 2000. *Gospel and Mission in the Writings of Paul: An Exegetical and Theological Analysis.* Grand Rapids, MI: Baker Books.

Stott, John. 1979. *God's New Society: The Message of Ephesians.* Leicester: IVP.

———. 1994. *The Message of Romans.* Downers Grove, IL: IVP.

———. 2007. *The Living Church: Convictions of a Lifelong Pastor.* Downers Grove, IL: IVP.

Van Engen, Charles. 1996. *Mission on the Way: Issues in Mission Theology.* Grand Rapids, MI: Baker Books.

Wright, Christopher J.H. 2010. *The Mission of God's People: A Biblical Theology of the Church's Mission.* Grand Rapids, MI: Zondervan.

Bertil Ekström (MTh, PhD) was born in Sweden and grew up in Brazil. Married to Alzira, the couple has four children and four grandchildren. An ordained Baptist pastor, Bertil has been involved in the mission movements of Brazil and Latin America for many years. Currently he is the director of the Mission Institute in Örebro, Sweden, and the executive director of the WEA Mission Commissions.

CHAPTER 11

THE FUTURE SHAPES THE PRESENT

Eschatology as Motivation for Mission

Rose Dowsett

"Christ shall come again, in great glory, to judge the living and the dead." This statement, or one like it, is embodied in all the ancient Creeds from the early centuries of the church, and remains an article of faith for Christians of all main traditions to the present day.

It is right that such a statement should be included in the summary of Christian faith that the Creeds represent because the New Testament has a great deal to say on the subject. The Lord Jesus Christ himself spoke frequently about his return one day in the future, though he also said that even he, in his earthly life, did not know when that would be (Matt 24:36). Shortly before his ascension he emphasizes again that, "It is not for you to know the times or dates the Father has set by his own authority" (Acts 1:7).

So, the date and many details remain hidden from us, but the sure fact of Christ's return is to shape the way we live, since we never know when it will take place, and he warns us to be ready. Christ's return is not an optional extra part of the gospel story but an essential part of it. While the cross and resurrection achieved completed salvation, God's total and final eternal purposes for the whole creation await the Son's return.

How does this great truth intersect with gospel, church, and mission? And how and why should it motivate us in our understanding and practice of mission?

Making Sense of Our Broken World

In every culture, people are troubled by the brokenness of our world. There is a profound realization that life ought to be different, that people do bad things as well as good, that sickness and war and death are horrible. Most religions and philosophies attempt to find ways of dealing with these, for example by sacrifices to the gods and spirits found in some places, or by resigned acceptance and efforts to become detached from it all in others, or by faith in science to solve it all in others again. Protest from the heart against all that hurts and harms is universal.

The Christian gospel not only explains the reason for the world's brokenness but also presents God's explanation of where all that brokenness stems from and his solution in dealing with sin decisively in the life, death, resurrection, and ascension of Jesus Christ. Yet, that is not the end of the story, for we still live in a fallen world; but the triumph of the gospel is that there will one day be a new and perfect world, where sin and suffering and brokenness are completely banished and the whole creation will once more be as the Creator initially made it. It is the return of Christ and all that happens then that will bring about this final triumphant transformation.

Christians, more than anybody else, are to be people of sure hope, and as we engage in mission we will be eager to point to all that God has done, is doing, and will do to restore the whole creation to its perfect state. At the heart of it, around the throne of God, will be a perfected humanity, engaged in beautiful worship, and in a context where all that makes life here and now painful will be decisively banished. The gospel enables us to live in the present, and to face the future, even death, with hope and with a quiet heart. Who would not want to share that with a hurting world?

The Awesome Reality of Judgment

When Christ returns, there will be a final and universal judgment. For those who have trusted in the mercy of God alone and acknowledged Christ as the only Savior, there will be great joy in his presence. For those who have deliberately rejected Christ, or been content to live very wickedly, there is the prospect of terrible judgment, and final and total exclusion from God's presence. Christians reach different conclusions as to exactly what that exclusion will look like—immediate destruction, eternal conscious separation, or various other possibilities: the Scriptures use different pictures, all seeking to describe the humanly indescribable, but all agree that the judgment of the unbeliever will be terrible and that we are to urge people to "flee the wrath to come" by turning to Christ for shelter and deliverance.

Just as different Christians interpret the details of the judgment passages differently, so also there are different understandings of the fate of those who have never heard the gospel. On the one hand, Romans 1 teaches that the created world around us and the conscience implanted within human beings as creatures made in the image of God are enough to make us aware that there is one sovereign Creator God, to whom we owe allegiance and from whom we need mercy. Those who choose to ignore these evidences of the one true God are thereby condemned through their own choice. At the same time, "shall not the God of all the world do right?" Hebrews 11 records those in Old Testament days who never heard of Jesus but who were men and women of faith, limited though their access to the truth about God was, and tells us that God accepted them in his grace. What is clear is that whether before or after Christ's earthly ministry and whether or not there is personal conscious trust in him, the only grounds on which anybody can be reconciled with God is through Christ's death and resurrection.

Since that is the case, and since it is not clear that following the revelation of Christ the Hebrews 11 pattern still holds, one pressing motivation for proclaiming the truth as it is in Jesus is to urge men and women and children to repent and believe while they may. We cannot be sure that they will have another opportunity, nor can we presume on the mercy of God embracing all people regardless of how they have lived their lives. Much of the modern world does not believe in judgment; but the Scriptures teach it clearly, and it will be terrible. If we profess to love people, we will urge them to believe and to seek sanctuary in the Lord Jesus; and we will pray urgently that the Holy Spirit will in his mercy create new life.

Reaching the unreached is urgent because nobody will escape final judgment.

The Glory of God

Glory is an essential element of the nature of God and cannot be diminished by human unbelief. At the same time, unbelief hides or ignores God's glory. God's people are to be jealous for God's rightful reputation and to be committed to urging others to recognize God's glory, for it is then that people will worship him. That worship belongs to him by right. We cannot add to God's glory, which is already absolute, but as the church engages in her mission we declare that glory and draw others into giving God all the glory that is due him.

God's glory will be fully seen once again when Christ returns, and within the context of the new heavens and earth. The Book of Revelation is full of images that express what it will be like for the glory of God to shine out through every dimension of creation. See for instance Revelation 21:1–22:6. This is frequently the subject of Old Testament prophecy too. So, for instance, the Psalmist links the declaring of the glory of God with the nations streaming to share in worship (e.g., Ps 19, 93, 95, 98), and Isaiah 56:6–8 describes what God will do for them. The Psalms, Isaiah, and other books point to the wonderful nature of the new heavens and earth to come (e.g., Isa 11:1–9). Habakkuk 2:14 promises "the earth will be filled with the knowledge of the glory of the Lord, as the waters cover the sea."

So, one key motivation for mission is the longing to see men and women and children of all nations bringing to God the worship that is his due and marveling at his glory. The calling of the church is to join in the mission of God, whose intention is that there should be people of every nation and tribe and tongue at home in the new creation, joyfully engaged in worship. As we contemplate what is yet to come, it energizes us for the present.

The Lordship of Christ

Just as nothing can diminish the fact of the glory of God, so also nothing can diminish the fact of the Lordship of Christ. He is already Lord of lords and King of kings. Yet sadly the case remains that many people do not recognize Christ for who he is and do not therefore live under his lordship and authority. The Scripture tells us that when he returns it will be in great glory and in a manner where "every eye shall see him" and recognize his identity.

Christians live in the overlap of the present world and of the world to come: the "now and not yet" paradox of the kingdom of God. Those who declare by life and lip that "Jesus Christ is Lord" already bear witness to the truth that the king has come, and that they are citizens of heaven. Part of the church's mission is to show in community the transformed relationships, priorities, values, and loyalties that are an embodiment of being citizens of the kingdom of God in this world, in anticipation of consummation in the world to come. So the Lord Jesus could teach that the kingdom of God had already come through his incarnation, but that nonetheless his disciples should pray "may your kingdom come on earth as it is in heaven" as something not yet fully realized in this life.

Since Pentecost there have been representatives of an ever-widening number of people groups who have come to recognize Jesus as Lord. In the latter part of the twentieth century in particular, the church became established more globally than ever before, and for that we praise God with great joy. At the same time there remain today billions of people who have never heard the gospel and have no understanding that the Christ of whom they are ignorant is Lord of the universe. In addition, countless millions, maybe billions, may have heard the gospel but have chosen to refuse to put themselves under Christ's authority. These facts, and the offence to God, are deeply grieving to Christian people and serve as a strong motivation for mission.

Reflections on the Timetable

Both Matthew (Matt 24:14) and Mark (13:10) quote Jesus as saying that the gospel must be preached to all nations "and then the end will come." Some people understand 2 Peter 3:11–12 ("You ought to live holy and godly lives as you look forward to the day of God and speed its coming"), taken together with the Matthew and Mark verses, to mean that we can "hasten" the Lord's return by ensuring that every unreached people group is reached with the message of the Lordship of Christ. This is a strong motivation for those who understand the text in this way, as an expression of their longing for the Lord to return, to focus all energy on pioneering among the unreached, as speedily as possible.

Over the centuries there have been many speculations about the imminence of the Lord's return, often with predictions relating to a particular date. Sometimes these predictions have been associated with what has been seen to be a particularly significant date, for example, the years 1000 and 2000 AD/CE. Sometimes they have been based on what has been perceived to be an acceleration in extensive natural disasters, war, and persecution, seen to be fulfillment of the various prophecies that such events would herald the end of the world (see for example, Matt 24: 4–14). The Lord urges his disciples to live as if he is coming back at any time, ready to respond, but also as an incentive to godly living and urgent testimony. At the same time he also makes it clear that nobody knows exactly when he will return, despite the signs, and that we should be very wary of predicting dates.

Martin Luther once famously said that if he thought the Lord was coming back the next day he would urge all around him to repent and to seek the grace and mercy of God, and at the same time he would plant an acorn—which would not grow to maturity as an oak tree for a hundred years—as a statement of investment in the future should he be mistaken about the Lord returning. This illustrates well the tension believers are to live under: being ready should the Lord return today but also engaging in the kind of service that might not bear fruit for a long time. It also illustrates well the two realities: we are citizens of time and this world, and simultaneously citizens of heaven and eternity. We do not find it easy to understand how time and eternity intersect.

And How About the Millennium?

Different parts of the Christian family have reached different conclusions about how to interpret the thousand years (the millennium) of Revelation 20. We should perhaps be cautious about constructing whole theological systems on a passage of prophecy and vision, a genre of writing that is always notoriously difficult to interpret. For some people this chapter is to be understood entirely literally; for others it is part of the pictorial, visionary language that the Apostle John uses in his struggle to describe so much that is beyond and outside present human experience, and is not to be understood literally.

How does this divergence of views affect mission? For some, following the dispensational understanding of Scripture popularized by Scofield through his annotated Bible, and for some contemporary premillennialists, this world can only get worse and worse until the Lord returns and investing effort in anything other than "winning souls for Christ" has no place in mission. There is pessimism about the world, and almost everything about all cultures of the world is so tainted that believers need to withdraw from as much as possible. Worse, trying to ameliorate human suffering or to engage in ecological issues, for instance, may even delay the Lord's return. This has not always been so: some of the great missionary pioneers of the nineteenth century were premillennialist, but were also thoroughly holistic in their practice of mission, engaging in widespread medical, educational, and mercy ministries alongside their preaching and church planting. Often premillennialists focus strongly on the restoration of the State of Israel and on the ingathering of the Jewish nation. This not only affects involvement in world politics, especially by the USA where dispensational and premillennial teaching is especially strong, but also can obscure the church, as opposed to Israel, as the post-Pentecost people of God. Some parts of this multifaceted and quite diverse community can be highly doctrinaire about eschatological details, for instance, the timetable around the so-called rapture. But, undoubtedly, premillennialism has inspired much dedicated and urgent mission, with particular attention to pioneering amongst those who have never heard of Christ.

Postmillennialists historically believed that the world would get better and better, and that the millennium, a golden age on earth where the world would be Christian and the church universal, would follow on seamlessly. This was especially popular in the nineteenth century in the light of industrial and other progress, and fed both into and out of evolutionary progress thinking. Here, mission was often understood as "Christianization" and "civilization," enabling nations hitherto outside the Christian sphere to be brought into the realm of Christendom. This position has been undermined by the vicious wars of the twentieth century, the cruelty of Marxism and Maoism, the condemnation of imperialism, and the technologies that have made inescapable the appalling suffering of much of the world. Further, the twentieth century saw the resurgence of all major faiths, not just the extension of Christianity. Nonetheless, some parts of the global church owe their beginning under God to postmillennial mission.

Both Augustine, whose influence lasted for many centuries, and the Protestant Reformers of the sixteenth century, were amillennialist, as are many in the Reformed tradition today. This does not mean a rejection of the fact of the millennium but a belief that Christ on the cross and through his resurrection has already decisively won the battle over Satan and death; that Christ taught both that the kingdom was already inaugurated with his first coming and that it is simultaneously "already" and "not yet": both present and future; and that we already live in the "last days." The present world, every inch of it, already belongs to Christ, whether or not people understand his ownership. That ownership extends to all of creation, not just to human beings. Mission must pay attention to every dimension of life, and every part of creation. This is more than "winning souls," although of course that is a totally indispensable part of authentic mission. Much mission, both past and present, has had this holistic understanding of mission, reflecting God's love for all that he has made and all that he lovingly sustains, and over which human beings are still called to be caretakers on his behalf.

Conclusion

While the different understandings of the millennium and of the events around the Lord's return may continue, let us celebrate that these may all inspire God's people to engage in God's mission. The Lord's return is sure, it will be glorious, and will mark the culmination of all that God has planned for people and for creation. The very final words in our Bible say:

> He who testifies to these things says, "Yes, I am coming soon." Amen. Come, Lord Jesus. The grace of the Lord Jesus be with God's people. Amen. (Rev 22:20–21)

Questions for Reflection:

1. What are the motivations for mission mentioned by Dowsett and how important are they for your church and mission context?

2. The author affirms that "reaching the unreached is urgent, because nobody will escape final judgment." Do you agree with that statement? How does that affect your understanding of mission?

3. In what way has eschatology influenced your church/denomination/mission organization in terms of mission?

Rose Dowsett, now retired, has with her husband Dick been a member of OMF International since 1969. She has served with the Mission Commission since 1998, especially through the Global Missiology Task Force.

Part Two

CONTEMPORARY MISSIOLOGICAL ISSUES

CHAPTER 12

MISSION AND ECCLESIOLOGY—WHY?

Birger Nygaard

One of the greatest tragedies in theological education has been the separation (to their mutual impoverishment) of ecclesiology from missiology. This separation has resulted on the one hand, in a missionless church and, on the other, in a churchless mission. (Eddie Gibbs)[1]

The modern missionary movement: Where do we come from? And who are we today? We are indeed part of a glorious heritage, often looking to William Carey as the father who spearheaded this great new move of Protestant overseas mission. The spiritual ferment around Carey and his time called thousands of missionaries from the old Christian churches into mission to the ends of the earth. Our concept of the word "mission" both in the church and culture at large is still heavily referring to this heritage.

The Edinburgh conference in 1910 took an inventory of the missionary movement 120 years down the road. It could document great accomplishments in several countries throughout the world. Mission leaders at that conference set ambitious new goals for the new century under the motto "The evangelization of the world in this generation." In spite of all the mishaps and divergences of the twentieth century, the movement continued to produce significant fruit, not least the rather unexpected development of Africa as the new Christian continent. It is fair to say that even up to today, the basic vision and energy of this movement has been a very important contributor to the development of the Protestant world church as we know it today. At both the conference in Lausanne in 1974 as well as in Cape Town 2010, the vision of going to those where there is not yet a church has been a compelling message, which prolongs the life of this more than two hundred-year-old movement and its structures (parachurch/voluntary mission organizations, overseas missionaries, fund raising, etc.). To a certain degree the movement is enthused by the eschatological language of "completing the task in order to pave way for the return of Christ" (cf. Matt 24:14).

The historical truth is that this movement has yielded tremendous fruit. At the same time we should acknowledge the significant contributions of the Pentecostal movement and of

---

1   Eddie Gibbs, *Leadership Next* (Downers Grove: IVP, 2005).

mission movements within other Christian world communities. Surely God has honored the faith and dedication of the thousands of missionaries who gave their life to ministry in often very difficult circumstances. However, this significant movement has rested on rather skimpy or unformulated theology in a number of regards. Its strength has been the centrality of preaching the gospel to the ends of the earth. But when it comes to theological reflections on issues like church, sacraments, social order, etc., the movement has by and large adhered to the traditions of each denomination. Many of these traditions did not have a well-formulated theology of the relationship of church and mission. Thus it has been usual to see a most unfortunate split between *ecclesiology* and *missiology*. The mission movement formulated its own concepts of what mission is. Meanwhile, the denominations continued church as usual, borrowed some missiology from the mission movement, but did not really integrate missiology into its overall theology. The result has been thin theological underpinnings for mission and absence of missiological dynamics in theology. This has been nothing less than a tragedy to both church and mission.

Over the last generation we have seen this dynamic being challenged due to a number of factors. The abolition of the colonial age proved that part of the modern Protestant mission movement did not fare well without the colonial system. The stable structures of mission organizations proved to have their limitations, many of them fading as the nineteenth century voluntary society dynamics are being replaced with other organizational forms in the information and network society. A new realization is now becoming clear: the basic eschatological vision of "reaching all the world for Christ in our generation" as a one-directional, progressive process is being replaced with a new realization that the whole world is to be evangelized in every generation—and that as such we will never "finish the task." In the old churches in the West this is now becoming an all-encompassing reality that really changes the rules of the game. Mission is not just something far away. We even call on missionaries from far away to help us with the task on our doorstep. Even the relatively new churches in the global South face the same as institutionalization and secularization leads to nominal Christianity without committed discipleship.

These new realities make obvious the complex and integrated relationship between mission and church. Today a significant and broadening number of theologians, pastors, missionaries, ordinary young Christians, etc., try to come to grips with the new situation through reflection on ecclesiology and mission. Not because of a new and curious interest in some marginal theological discipline, but because they see systems, which they thought were God-given and everlasting, disintegrate. They begin to realize that some of the presuppositions commonly held in the past about church and mission may be insufficient and actually leave the church very vulnerable when culture changes.

Missional Ecclesiology

The term "missional church" emerged in North America in response to the increasing sense of dislocation of the church from contemporary culture.[2] It raises basic questions on what

---

2   Darrell L. Guder, ed., *Missional Church: A Vision for the Sending of the Church in North America* (Grand Rapids: Eerdmans, 1998).

church is, i.e., on ecclesiology. A *missional ecclesiology* seeks to reformulate the framework for mission. It can bring about new vision, language, involvement, and forms of mission appropriate for our day. As such it should be interpreted as part of the continuous process of understanding our calling, which we can observe throughout church history.

In evangelical circles *ecclesiology* has traditionally been a fairly unimportant part of systematic theology, which students of theology are briefly introduced to in a couple of lectures on the unchangeable "marks of the church." When it comes to practical theology and mission, however, there is no end to the ongoing reflection and innovation, especially among those involved in cross-cultural mission. The church growth school and other inventive streams have contributed greatly to equipping missionaries, drawing on sociology, anthropology, communications, leadership, marketing, and other disciplines.

The group of thinkers behind the original *Missional Church* book intended to bridge this catastrophic gap. Once they commenced on this journey they found that the new missional understanding of church deeply affects our entire notion of church as well as our perception of mission. The book offers a significant reinterpretation of the call and role of the church in North America. It is harsh in its critique of a church that has become hostage to its culture, offering whatever religious goods and services that society demands, often at the expense of faithfulness to the gospel of the kingdom. It then lays out a number of missional features of the church, i.e., the reality of the church as God's called and sent people.

The *Missional Church* book was well received and became widely read, even beyond North America. Of course the understanding of the church as agent in mission is not new. But the cultural critique, innovative theological approach, together with the pressing need to find valid ways to be church in a post-Christian setting spurred a lot of new debate. The term "missional" was quickly adopted by all kinds of groups. It serves as a helpful variant to the terms "mission" and "missionary," which many don't like to use today because of colonial baggage attached. Through this broad adoption of the word *missional*, the specific and qualified meaning given to the word has diluted. Today the relationship between church and mission and the missional nature of the church has become a widespread theme in many circles in the West. Old mainline churches, for whom mission in the stable Christendom period was an interest of the committed few only, are eagerly struggling to gain a functional understanding of mission theology and praxis. The state of decline in these churches has suddenly made "mission" relevant. Some of this new interest takes the form of a marketing mentality without much theological reflection: "getting back customers in order to be able to perpetuate the institution." Although we are now using missional terminology, we still have a long way to go in internalizing what it really looks like.

The radical nature of the present societal changes deeply impacts nearly everything. New generations of Christians in the West are dealing with basic life and faith issues in an existential quest to find authentic forms of Christian community and mission that do not separate them from their given culture, but rather empower them to be missionally present in contemporary youth culture (emerging churches) and among those of older generations who have abandoned Christian faith. Much genuine innovation in church today may come from groups that do not first have to disentangle themselves from an outlived church culture. Hopefully older generations of church people will be humble enough to learn from these new generations as they are in better touch with contemporary culture than those of us who are steeped in our beloved old ways of being church.

Missional Ecclesiology and the Global Missionary Movement

Many of those involved in cross-cultural mission, either from a sending home-base or missionaries in field service, are not wholly comfortable with this focus on missional churches. They often find that the discussion is focused on the local setting only and does not have much to offer that will undergird and strengthen the cross-cultural global missionary movement, which has been so important to the spread of Christianity over the last two hundred years. The critique is legitimate as at the outset there can be a danger that the reinterpretation of the mission agenda tends to focus locally, simply because that is where it all organically begins: with a local community of believers as the primary agents in mission in their own community, the first locus of mission. If the local fellowship of believers is not truly missional in its very being, there is little hope that it can create anything of missional value in global mission. A truly sound missional rethinking of church will, however, not stop locally but will heed to the Great Commission, which mandates us to make disciples of Christ *wherever* we go.

We are now challenged to learn and see how forms and meanings of local churches and missionary movements are being transformed by new missional understandings and practices. In missional church terminology, the church does not "have a mission," which it supports with money and prayer and the sending of missionaries. Rather, the local church and each of its members are by their very nature sent by God as signs of the kingdom to their community. The sent-ness of the church is the focal point of all that the church is and does. This sent-ness is not limited to pioneering cross-cultural mission. It is to be understood in a holistic *missio Dei* perspective involving all walks of life. In that perspective the cross-cultural missionary is not more a missionary than the local school teacher or nurse, who are to give witness to the gospel and be signs of the kingdom wherever they are. At first glance that may sound as a scandalous denigration of the traditional cross-cultural missionary. How can we ever get anybody to support the important work of mission organizations on the basis of such an understanding of mission? But the new missional emphasis is first of all a strong call to discipleship with missionary focus: a plea that "Christianization" is so much more than superficial adoption of a set of religious truths and adherence to a religious institution. Christian living is to be all-encompassing in the life of every Christ-follower. From the New Testament we know of the missionary potential of just twelve disciples.

If we work through the likely consequences of a sound missional ecclesiology and spirituality, we will see that we are indeed moving mission to the center of church instead of making it an issue for those specifically committed or interested. Missional ecclesiology has the potential to open up promising new dimensions of missionary empowerment and engagement more adequate for a postcolonial, post-Christendom, multicultural and multireligious world.

What are some of the possible implications of a missional ecclesiology to the contemporary church and its mission?

Only missional churches will have durability in a multicultural and multireligious world. The Christendom form of Christianity could be sustained in relatively stable monocultural Christian societies with formal or informal alliances between church and state political power. In such societies significant traditions in church and culture coincided. With the emergence of much more complex societies due to globalization, urbanization, migration, multireligiosity, and other cultural phenomena, Christian churches will either have to become deliberately missional—or eventually die. For a long time we have seen the decline in old Europe. But growing nominal Christianity in Africa demonstrates that this is not a Western phenomenon only. Churches in Asian settings have always been a minority amid a plurality of religions. What can the rest of us learn from this Asian experience?

New sending structures in a globalized world. William Carey called for "means of conversion of the heathens." This enquiry resulted in many of the missionary structures that have served world mission so well over the last couple of hundred years. Today it is obvious that a number of these structures are coming to an end as their basis or effectiveness declines. Volunteerism as we knew it in the nineteenth and twentieth century is changing. Bureaucratic mission structures are having a hard time in the age of the network and in a world where moving people around the world is not really the challenge any longer. This is a hard lesson to learn for the old mission organizations as James Engel reminded us fifteen years ago.[3] That does not mean that mission organizations are not needed today. But their role is changing.

For a long time we have realized that most traditional mission structures and models are not fit for mission to many of the most challenging parts of the world. "Missionaries" do not easily get a visa to Saudi Arabia or China. But Christian businessmen and Filipino housemaids do! They are there in large numbers already. Yet they need to be able to integrate effectively their Christian witness with what they are doing professionally. For years we have focused on various forms of tentmaking ministry and business as mission; but it seems that these mission models are still weak and do not at all replace the traditional sending models. Why? Is it because the traditional missionary movement holds on to the old ideal? Or is it because a well-developed missional DNA of local churches is so rare? You do not become a missionary by going anywhere in the world. You become a missionary through the long process of spiritual formation taking place where you grow up and live your life. If such missional DNA becomes common among the majority of Christians, instead of the small minority of special "missionaries," an unprecedented mission force is birthed. Just imagine the multitude of faith encounters possible in our world with the present level of cross-cultural travelling and workplace interaction between Christians and not yet Christians! Millions of opportunities have been missed because mission conceptually has been outsourced to the "professional missionaries."

---

3   James F. Engel and William A. Dyrness, *Changing the Mind of Missions: Where Have We Gone Wrong?* (Downers Grove: IVP, 2000).

Fresh expressions of church. Missional church perspectives will not only affect the vision for and structure of cross-cultural mission. First of all it will have deep impact on what we find important in the local church. A missional approach to church life will make quite a number of present church activities redundant because it is difficult to see and explain their bearings on the kingdom of God, the life of church members, or the local community. They may not harm anyone; but Christians with a clear missional focus will have better things to do with their lives than taking part in various forms of church entertainment. They are enthused by seeing the gospel making a difference in the real-life struggles of their peers at school or work. As the missional nature of the church becomes a key focus, we should expect to see fresh expressions of church become widespread. Not changes for the sake of change and innovation, but because missional questions will constantly critique what we are doing and seek to find more meaningful ways to exhibit the love of Christ in any particular setting. The continued reformation of the church becomes the norm, not the exception.[4]

The Great Commission: Christian discipleship. The vision of a missional church cannot be realized without the people of God desiring to continually grow in personal and communal Christian discipleship. In the modern era the missionary movement has to a high degree been driven by quantity. A missional perspective is very clear that we will never see any worthwhile quantity without the qualities of committed discipleship. Conversion is so much more than a sudden decision at an evangelistic meeting. It is about entering into the life-long process of listening to Jesus, the master telling his followers about life in the kingdom. The Great Commission is primarily about discipleship and faithfulness to the teachings of Jesus. Missional churches are not propagators of "cheap grace." Because the church itself is the primary medium of the message, the church itself has to reflect its master and his message in all possible ways.

Faith for a New World

This is a time of new ferment as fresh elements towards a renewed vision for mission comes together. Some of these elements may not look like mission the way it used to be. Other elements may be fairly traditional in outward structure, but thoroughly renewed in their conceptual vision and dynamic. This is a time to come together as a truly global church in discernment of where the Spirit will take us.

Questions for Reflection:

1. Nygaard affirms that "it has been usual to see a most unfortunate split between ecclesiology and missiology. The result has been thin theological underpinnings for mission and absence of missiological dynamics in theology." Do you agree? How much have you seen of that in your own church and mission context? How can this split be reverted according to the author?

---

4   See Darrell Guder, *The Continuing Conversion of the Church* (Grand Rapids: Eerdmans, 2000).

2. In what ways has the terminology of missional churches helped to refocus the role of the church in mission? How has that affected your own church community and denomination?

3. What does the author mean by "the new missional emphasis is first of all a strong call to discipleship with missionary focus"? How does that change our perception of who is a missionary?

References

Engel, James F., and William A. Dyrness. 2000. *Changing the Mind of Missions: Where Have We Gone Wrong?* Downers Grove: IVP.

Gibbs, Eddie. 2005. *Leadership Next.* Downers Grove: IVP.

Guder, Darrell, ed. 1998. *Missional Church: A Vision for the Sending of the Church in North America.* Grand Rapids: Eerdmans.

————. 2000. *The Continuing Conversion of the Church.* Grand Rapids: Eerdmans.

Birger Nygaard from Denmark works with the Council of International Relations of the Evangelical Lutheran Church in Denmark—with responsibility for facilitating involvement of parishes in mission locally and globally. He is trained in theology from the University of Aarhus and in intercultural communication at Fuller Seminary, USA. He has previously worked with global mission organizations and as the general secretary of The Danish Mission Council and of The International Association of Mission Studies.

CHAPTER 13

A TRULY MISSIONAL CHURCH

From Church-Centered Mission to Kingdom-Centered Mission

Warren Beattie

An interest in contextual theology creates the constant tendency to ask how "context" shapes every discussion. As I read and interact with the materials about missional church, it is clear that much of it relates to specific contexts within Europe and North America. The more I explore the discussion around missional church, the more it has struck me that there is a very important question that remains to be answered: what exactly is the *scope* of mission in relation to the missional church?

Two Interactions with Missional Church Themes

Two interactions have particularly stimulated my curiosity about this issue of *scope*. The first incident occurred in Singapore at a conference for mission leaders working in Asia. The group was reflecting on the theme of missional church. In a presentation, one particular writer was described as one of the most important missiologists writing today about missional church. The name was unfamiliar, but a little research on the internet revealed that the author had written a book about young people who were beyond the reach of the church in the United States.[1] Compared to the two billion people of East Asia, where the mission leaders worked, the young and unchurched in any one country represent a small subset of people, and in a world of some seven billion people it is not a very high percentage at all.[2] If our horizons in mission and missiology are limited to one country (however large), we must be challenged as to whether that fully reflects a biblical view of mission.

---

1 The library where I teach has three books by the missiologist in question which we use regularly—for their stated contexts they are very helpful!

2 This is not to say, of course, that the missional church discussion is not important for North American churches, and the recent overview "mapping trends" indicates both the Euro-North American context and clarifies the etymology of "missional" at a functional and a theological level: Craig Van Gelder and Dwight J. Zscheile, eds., *The Missional Church in Perspective* (Grand Rapids, MI: Baker, 2011), 41–65.

The second "pause for thought" came as I looked more closely at one prominent book called *Introducing the Missional Church*.[3] In this discussion of missional church, the authors try to clarify their position by showing what missional church is *not*: "Missional church is not a label to describe churches that emphasize cross-cultural mission."[4]

To some extent, I welcome and endorse Roxburgh and Boren's willingness to give expression to their context and to claim, to define, and to limit it. The reasons for specifying what missional church is *not* arises precisely because "missional church has become a label used to describe practically everything a church does."[5] On the other hand, such an understanding does raise questions about the character of mission in relation to the missional church.

The Scope of Missional Church

These two interactions prompt deeper questions about the scope of mission in the missional church debate. For example, in the Canadian context it is stated that a missional church network "has been created to help leaders from churches and neighborhoods find a path towards hope for the church in a changing context."[6] Implicit in these discussions is a focus on the neighborhood around and beyond the church.

Missional Church: A Church Engaging with the Neighborhood

For many, missional church thinking underlines the church's concern with the neighborhoods around it and the church's needs to reconnect with local people. Since these people are not going to come through the doors of the church, there is a need to reimagine and reconceive church in terms of those very people who are beyond the church.

The rationale for European and North American churches to review these issues is ably summarized in terms of the history of trends and ideas by van Gelder and Zscheile. Indeed, they go on to explore the meaning of missional and note two strands within the missional church movement that would seem to have a wider and more traditional understanding of mission. The first strand defines missional as "Great Commission Obedience" and this group "consistently viewed missional as primarily concerning the church's task of obeying the Great Commission through engaging changed local contexts."[7]

The second strand defines missional as "being sent out to carry out God's mission" and two papers are quoted whose themes stress similar horizons—they talk about the local church needing to "go" in mission rather than expecting others to "come"—but the focus still appears to be local.

In a more telling quotation, we read:

> The Great Commandment and the Great Commission move us to engage the world in evangelism, compassion, and justice … The church is sent into the world to par-

---

3   Alan Roxburgh and M. Scott Boren, *Introducing the Missional Church* (Grand Rapids, MI: Baker, 2009).
4   Roxburgh and Boren, *Introducing*, 31.
5   Ibid., 31.
6   Forge Missional Church Network, 2012.
7   Van Gelder and Zscheile, *The Missional Church*, 72.

ticipate with God in this ministry of love and reconciliation … In the 20th century we were a sending church … sending missionaries around the world. But in the 21st century we must be a sent church, because the mission field is all round us—right here in North America.[8]

What would strike the reader who is curious about the scope of mission in the missional church movement is this—that even in these two perspectives, missional here ultimately connects the church essentially to the local culture.

Missional Church: A Church Engaging with the World?

We are left with the strange impression that at the end of the twenty-first century, at the moment in history when the world is, by many accounts, at its most global or globalized—where the internet, TV, film, the media, and the tourist industry take us to every corner of the globe—the church's focus on mission is the world in our neighborhood, the world on our doorstep. Now, in one sense, this is partly true of the experience of Europe and North America. However, we need to explore that concept and query whether "the world" is actually on our doorstep in any real sense.

Is "the world" or the "mission field" really in Vancouver or Toronto? Is it in Seattle or Los Angeles? Is it in Glasgow or London? Certainly, we have more people from places like China in these communities than previously—but there are more than one billion Chinese people and most of them are not in our neighborhoods—a huge proportion are in China! If the reader cares to consult the *Atlas of Global Christianity* they will find that the majority of believers in Chinese religions and in Hinduism are tied geographically and statistically in a quite remarkable way to two particular nation-states—neither of which is in Europe or North America.[9]

If we want to do justice to the scope of mission in the biblical sense, then we need to be careful about keeping a broad concept of mission firmly in place as we clarify our concepts of being missional church—it seems to me that in our thinking and in our horizons, we need to go beyond the neighborhood.

A Truly Missional Church: From Church-Centered Mission to Kingdom-Centered Mission

The title of this chapter reflects a helpful resource in the "theology of the kingdom" that has to do with *scope* and which can help us to have a more balanced perspective on the church's mission.

---

8   Van Gelder and Zscheile, *The Missional Church*, 73.
9   Todd Johnson and Kenneth Ross, *Atlas of Global Christianity* (Edinburgh: Edinburgh University Press, 2010), 12–13, 16–17.

There are hints in the missional church literature that the theme of the kingdom can help to broaden horizons.[10] Ringma, for example, notes the importance of kingdom in relation to his vision of missional church:

> [There is] a renewed theological vision of the church in mission … around Jesus' proclamation of the good news of the kingdom. Missional churches seek to respond to God's invitation to join him in his mission in and for the world, as a sign … as a servant … as a foretaste."[11]

We need to recover a more robust view of mission—one that moves from putting the church at the center to one that puts the kingdom of God at the center.[12] This is not because the church is not important (or cannot be universal), but because there appears to be a tendency in missional church circles to reduce our horizons down at a practical level—the church becomes the local church and mission becomes mission to the neighborhood.

There are pointers to a wider scope for mission in the literature of both mission and church.

Kingdom Concerns stresses the way in which a kingdom horizon broadens our understanding of mission: "We need a wider vision which will take in the whole horizon of God's dealing with mankind and its world."[13] He sees the theology of the kingdom as critical for this. These thoughts are echoed in *Exploring Ecclesiology*, where the authors suggest that "the church in the world must look beyond itself, to a God bigger than the earth and bigger than the present."[14] We need to recover a grander vision of the kingdom of God— a more global and a more eschatological vision. Personally, I find Ephesians 3 reminds us of the scope of mission in relation to the church's role—which looks forward to the vision in Revelation, epitomized in Revelation 5, of the coming of God's kingdom—characterized as it is, by the presence of the redeemed from within the global community.

The Kingdom of God Across Time: The Temporal Dimensions

In Ephesians, Paul looks at the role of the church against the backdrop of God's reign and his eternal purposes. Using the language of "the mystery of Christ" we are told that this mystery was not made known in other generations but is now revealed. We could describe this process as the unfolding of the reign and kingdom of God across time: God has been working his purpose out that across time people will be brought into a new community.

---

10   See Van Gelder and Zshceile, *The Missional Church*, 7ff., 27ff., 53ff. and 72–73 for existing discussions on the kingdom in relation to missional church but note that though theologically sophisticated, the focus generally relates to the church in the neighborhood.

11   Next Reformation, "Missional." http://nextreformation.com/?p=2897, 2013.

12   For books that connect mission to the kingdom in a wholistic manner, see Andrew Kirk, *What Is Mission? Theological Explorations* (London: Darton, Longman and Todd, 1999), especially chapter 2; Andrew Walls and Cathy Ross, *Mission in the 21st Century* (London: Darton, Longman and Todd, 2008), especially Section 1 Part 1.

13   Ken Gnanakan, *Kingdom Concerns: A Theology of Mission Today* (Leicester: IVP, 1993).

14   Brad Harper and Paul Louis Metzger, *Exploring Ecclesiology: An Evangelical and Ecumenical Introduction* (Grand Rapids, MI: Brazos Press, 2009), 47. They have a helpful discussion relating the church to the kingdom of God in terms of how it "models the kingdom"—describing the church as "the doorway to the kingdom," "the witness to the kingdom," "the instrument of the kingdom," and the church as "an eschatological community" (53 ff.).

As we think about the mission of the church, we need to remember that this task is still unfolding.

The Kingdom of God Across Space: The Cosmic Dimensions

The second thing that Paul stresses is that God is working his purpose out on a geographical scale as well. Here, Paul steps back, and his canvas is different from what we might imagine—he envisages the rulers and authorities in the heavenly realms as watching the unfolding of the mission of God. It is a canvas that takes in the cosmos, and having established the scope of the watching world, Paul emphasizes again that this took place according to God's eternal purpose.

Such is Paul's canvas for mission: temporally, from before creation on the one hand until the eternal rolling up of the end of time; geographically, not just the physical globe that we know from space and imagine in our mind's eye, rather God's concern, according to Ephesians 3, is for the cosmos. This is a very important thought for us as we think about the church's mission—is it mission to the world or mission to the neighborhood?

Conclusion

At the end of his earthly ministry, in Acts 1:7–8, Jesus gives us this sketch of the scope of mission: from Jerusalem to Judea and Samaria and to the ends of the earth—from the neighborhood, to the nation, and then on to the world.

It seems to me that this represents a challenge to missional church thinking—we need to see the scope of mission as not just reaching out to the neighborhood but to continue to reach out to the world with the mercy and grace of God. It is right and proper to be concerned with the *church* because local communities of Christians are the foundation and core of God's work in the world; it is also appropriate to stress the *missional* character of the church. The church's task, however, is both to build communities of the kingdom, and to represent the kingdom to the whole of society and to the world as we present "good news" to others.

In this chapter, I am arguing for a robust understanding of the scope of mission: a missional church should not just be concerned with local contexts and neighborhoods, but it should reflect a church that looks out to "the ends of the earth." A missional church should empower and connect to local people, but it also needs to be a church that partners with the global church. We need to recover a healthy understanding of missional in relation to the local and the global, to the neighborhood but also to the world. A truly missional church has to move on from a neighborhood and church-centered view of mission to a kingdom-centered view of mission.

Questions for Reflection:

1.   Beattie says that "if we want to do justice to the scope of mission in the biblical sense, then we need to be careful about keeping a broad concept of mission firmly in place as we clarify our concepts of being missional church." Do you agree with him? Why is this affirmation necessary?

2. What is the danger that the author sees in much of the current missional church thinking?

3. What does the author mean by "going from church-centered mission to kingdom-centered mission?" Do you agree that there is a need for this move in our understanding of mission?

References

Forge Missional Training Network. 2013. AXIOM: An Introduction to Missional Church. http://www.forgecanada.ca/axiom-an-introduction-to-missional-church/Accessed November 29, 2013.

Gnanakan, Ken. 1993. *Kingdom Concerns: A Theology of Mission Today.* Leicester: IVP.

Guder, Darrell L. and Lois Barrett. 1998. *Missional Church: A Vision for the Sending of the Church in North America.* The Gospel and Our Culture Series. Grand Rapids: Eerdmans.

Harper, Brad and Paul Louis Metzger. 2009. *Exploring Ecclesiology: An Evangelical and Ecumenical Introduction.* Grand Rapids, MI: Brazos Press.

Johnson, Todd M. and Kenneth R. Ross. 2010. *Atlas of Global Christianity.* Edinburgh: Edinburgh University Press.

Kirk, J. Andrew. 1999. *What Is Mission? Theological Explorations.* London: Darton, Longman and Todd.

Next Reformation. 2013. Missional. http://nextreformation.com/?p=2897. Accessed December 2, 2013.

Roxburgh, Alan J. and M. Scott Boren. 2009. *Introducing the Missional Church.* Grand Rapids, MI: Baker.

Roxburgh, Alan and Fred Romanuk. 2006. *The Missional Leader: Equipping Your Church to Reach a Changing World.* N.Y.: Jossey-Bass.

Van Gelder, Craig and Dwight J. Zscheile (eds.) 2011. *The Missional Church in Perspective.* Grand Rapids, MI: Baker.

Walls, Andrew and Cathy Ross. 2008. *Mission in the Twenty-first Century: Exploring the Five Marks of Global Mission.* London: Darton, Longman and Todd.

Rev. Dr. Warren R. Beattie is the MA Program Leader and Tutor in Contextual Theology, Research, and Arts with Mission at All Nations Christian College, Herts, UK; prior to this he was Director for Mission Research with OMF International in Asia and editor of the journal *Mission Round Table.* This is his third contribution to the *Globalization of Mission* series.

CHAPTER 14

THE MISSION-SHAPED CHURCH IN GLOBAL SOUTH PERSPECTIVE

Trends and Challenges

Bertil Ekström

The mission-shaped church is a church that crosses borders and barriers, regardless of cultural, linguistic, social, generational, or religious boundaries. In other words, it is a borderless church that exists to serve the community independent of whether people attend the church or not.

The discussion about the relationship between the church and its missional or missionary nature is of course old. From a global perspective, the discussion takes different approaches depending on the local and national context. Issues that may be relevant in Sweden and in Europe may not be the ones that are the most important in Africa, Asia, and Latin America. This obviously results in a very limited picture of the church and mission reality around the globe. And if you detect here a bias towards Latin America, it could be explained by the fact that I have lived there for more than forty years.

The Problem with the Words Mission, Missions, and Missional

Mission has been understood primarily, and many times only, as the sending of people and resources to heathen lands. It is often designated as missions (plural in English), and is very much understood this way in North American missiology. Spanish and Portuguese have appropriated the same meanings, with little difference between mission (singular) and missions (plural). In Swedish, as in many other languages, the words don't have that distinction. The use of the term missions (in the plural) for the sending activity of the church, particularly in evangelical circles but not exclusively, has certainly affected our understanding of mission (in the singular) and often reduced it to what the church does. This confusion, or let's say, partial understanding of what mission is about, has also led to mission becoming something secondary to both church-life and theology.

I am not going to develop here the terms *missio Dei* and *missio ecclesia* more than to say that the mission of God is bigger and broader than the mission of the church. In a brief historical review of the mission concept, David Bosch confirms that for centuries mission has been understood in a variety of ways. He says that:

> Sometimes it was interpreted primarily in soteriological terms: as saving individuals from eternal damnation. Or it was understood in cultural terms: as introducing people from the East and the South to the blessings and privileges of the Christian West. Often it was perceived in ecclesiastical categories: as the expansion of the church. Sometimes it was defined salvation-historically: as the process by which the world would be transformed into the kingdom of God.[1]

Karl Barth was one of the first theologians to define mission as an activity of God himself and he had a decisive influence on the discussions that followed from the 1930s onwards. There is no doubt that the ecumenical movement was the first to develop more deeply the concept of *missio Dei*. Eastern Orthodox, evangelicals, and Roman Catholics have followed and also adopted the terminology, sometimes with a slightly different understanding of the term.[2]

In an attempt to summarize his concept of mission, Bosch states that:

> Mission is not primarily an activity of the church, but an attribute of God. God is a missionary God. Mission is the movement from God to the world; the church is viewed as an instrument for that mission. To participate in mission is to participate in the movement of God's love toward people, since God is a fountain of sending love.[3]

Emilio Castro, the Uruguayan ecumenical leader, affirms that:

> Mission is the fundamental reality of our Christian life. We are Christians because we have been called by God to work with him in the fulfilment of his purposes for humanity as a whole. Our life in this world is life in mission. Life has a purpose only to the extent that it has a missionary dimension.[4]

Leslie Newbigin, in his seminal book *The Open Secret*, a book that gave impulse to a lot of rethinking regarding mission, states that mission is "the proclamation of the kingdom, the presence of the kingdom, and the anticipation of the kingdom."[5] What is clear from Newbigin's missiology is this holistic understanding of mission that has its roots in the kingdom concept of the Scriptures. It has both a temporal and an eternal time-aspect, as well as the necessary combination of proclamation and presence, words, and deeds.

---

1   David Bosch, *Transforming Mission: Paradigm Shifts in Theology of Mission* (Maryknoll, NY: Orbis, 1993), 389.
2   Cf. Bosch, *Transforming Mission*, 391.
3   Bosch, *Transforming Mission,* 390.
4   Emilio Castro, "Liberation, Development and Evangelism: Must We Choose in Mission?," *Occasional Bulletin for Missionary Research* (July 1978), 87, (Quoted by Andrew Kirk, *What is Mission? Theological Explorations* (London: Darton, Longman, Todd, 1999), 31.
5   Leslie Newbigin, *The Open Secret* (Grand Rapids, MI: Eerdmans, 1978), 72.

The theme of the kingdom of God has been discussed, among others, by Latin American theologians and defended by some of them at conferences such as the Lausanne Congress on World Evangelisation in 1974. The development of a kingdom missiology in Latin America was to large extent a Protestant and evangelical response to Liberation Theology that focused almost exclusively on political and social transformation. There were of course Protestant theologians involved in Liberation Theology as well, such as the Brazilian Presbyterian Rubem Alves and the Argentinian Methodist Jose Míguez Bonino. However, a holistic approach to mission, including the different dimensions of the gospel, is, according to my understanding, better represented in Latin America by The Latin American Theological Fraternity and theologians such as Orlando Costas, Samuel Escobar, Rene Padilla, and Emilio Nunez.

Similar developments in theological and missiological thinking have occurred also in other continents, both in ecumenical and in evangelical spheres.

From an evangelical perspective, Chris Wright's definition of mission represents well what is currently accepted in evangelical circles. He says that:

> Fundamentally, our mission (if it is biblically informed and validated) means our committed participation as God's people, at God's invitation and command, in God's own mission within the history of God's world for the redemption of God's creation.[6]

According to that definition, Wright would use the term "missional" as "simply an adjective denoting something that is related to or characterized by mission, or has the qualities, attributes, or dynamics of mission."[7]

The reason why I feel the need to mention this discussion is that the global South has been influenced by the way we have described and motivated our missionary enterprise from the West. The receiving churches in Africa, Asia, and Latin America, the traditional mission fields as we have called them, have learned perhaps more from practice than from teaching that mission is an expensive, complementary thing that only experts from the West are able to do. The local life of the church, the engagement in society, the proclamation of the good news through word and action in the neighborhood was not defined as mission. The emphasis was also on human efforts that demanded all kind of resources, and being poor was not affordable for the emerging churches.

What Characterizes a Mission-Shaped or a Missional Church?

The first answer could be that a "mission-shaped" church is a church that follows the example of Jesus Christ. Ross Hastings defines the "mission-shaped" church as follows:

---

6   Christopher Wright, *The Mission of God: Unlocking the Bible's Grand Narrative* (Downers Grove, IL: IVP, 2006), 22–23.

7   Wright, *The Mission of God*, 24.

Churches, because they are communities of the presence of the risen Christ, the sent One who has now sent them will be "missional" or "mission-shaped" churches. They will not be shallow, dumbed-down churches in order to be missional, because their very essence is their connectedness in intimacy with the risen missional Christ, who was sent that we might be sent in him. Churches are by identity missional because they are conjoined to the sent Christ and because they are thereby grounded in the nature of the missional triune God.[8]

Frost and Hirsch define the missional church as "a sent church, a going church, a movement of God through his people, sent to bring healing to a broken world."[9]

A Relevant Church for Today

The key question is not in the first place that of terminology, of course, but how the church can be relevant in our days. What kind of church contributes to the advance of God's missionary agenda in the diverse contexts that we live in?

Two voices from Latin America underscore the challenge for relevance:

Rene Padilla says:

> The church is not the kingdom of God, but it is the visible result of the kingdom. The church still carries the signs of the historical presence of the kingdom, the signs of the "not yet" that impact the present age.[10]

Orlando Costas expresses his frustration because he does not see the church more active in representing the kingdom, in spite of its growth in Latin America. He affirms:

> The issue seems to me to be not whether the church is growing, but whether it is authentically engaged in the mission of the triune God in its concrete sociohistorical situations. It is a matter of efficacious participation in the on-going life-struggles of society in a total witnessing engagement, which, more than a program or a method, is a lifestyle. For when this happens, the church is turned upside-down. It becomes a living organism, a dynamic training and research center, and an effective team that is capable of leading multitudes to Jesus Christ. In such circumstances, the church is turned inside-out; its structures are put at the service of the kingdom and its missionary practice is transformed into a comprehensive endeavour, where the gospel is shared in depth and out of the depths of human life.[11]

Why this frustration and desire for correction from Costas? Let's take a brief look at mission history.

---

8   Ross Hastings, *Missional God, Missional Church: Hope for Re-evangelizing the West* (Downers Grove, IL: IVP, 2012), 140–141.

9   Michael Frost and Alan Hirsch, *The Shaping of Things to Come: Innovation and Mission for the 21st Century Church* (Peabody, MA: Hendrickson, 2003), 18.

10   Rene Padilla, *Guds Rike och Kyrkans Uppdrag (Mission Between the Times: Essays on the Kingdom)* (Örebro: Libris, 1988), 33.

11   Orlando Costas, *Christ Outside the Gate* (Maryknoll, NY: Orbis Books: 1982), 54.

What Has Influenced the Development of the Church Concept Globally? Some Factors

What kind of churches were those planted by Western missionaries? Often missionaries came with an understanding that the new churches should focus on their neighborhood, at the most on the nation, but not to cross borders or go to other cultures. The "mission" vision of the missionaries was many times just for their own move to other nations but not for the newly planted church to become mission-minded in the sense of crossing cultural borders.

The paradox was that they planted "missional" churches very much in the way Leslie New-bigin and others have defined it in later times. Unfortunately, the holistic view of the gospel was not always present, and the emphasis was basically on "saving souls for eternity," particularly as a response to preaching. However, in practice, very few missionaries would limit their ministry to "saving souls." Most of them, if not all, would also engage in social action, community development, and some even in political issues. The church was the church of the neighborhood, at least before the enormous invasion of new denominations and the never-ending division of churches. Integral mission or holistic ministry were not terms used at that time, and "missional church" would probably only be understood as the church founded by missionaries.

Having said that, it is important to recognize that the strong emphasis of the Bible teaching in most churches was the salvation of the soul and the hope for an eternity in heaven. This teaching formed generations of believers and of church leaders who did not engage in political, economic, and social issues in society.

The dichotomy between spiritual and secular, between the holy church and the sinful world, between soul and body characterized more and more the growing churches in the global South. We all know that it was not just there; we had also in the West very much the same problem.

Particularly in church traditions were the separation between state and church was a key doctrine, the alienation from the society outside the church was a fact. But again, it was not exclusively in the so-called "free-churches" that this happened. Also in state church traditions with just a pragmatic division of roles or an expressed agreement with the political powers to not interfere in the arena of the other, there was a clear separation between the religious and the secular realms.

One example in Latin America was that Liberation Theology was started primarily by Roman Catholic theologians and activists but it was not the official view of the Catholic Church. Several of the Liberation Theology theologians were ex-communicated, like Leonardo Boff. The church had an agreement with the military governments to not engage in politics, and in compensation the governments would continue supporting the church, giving all kind of concessions. And it was basically the same situation for the "free-churches."

In the 1970s we start to see in the global South a new awareness of the reason for the existence of the church and a redefinition of its mission. It was a reaction from being mere objects or passive spectators to what foreign missionaries had done in social action and thus becoming agents of transformation. But it was also a reaction against oppression and injustice from foreign colonial powers and from national undemocratic governments.

The Change of Gravity

As we all are aware of, the gravity or the epicenter of the Christian church has moved south- and eastwards. What is "normal" Christianity today may not be the Western style or tradition anymore. Philip Jenkins discusses this in his book *The Next Christendom*, and he says that:

> If in fact the bulk of the Christian population is going to be living in Africa, Asia, or Latin America, then practices that now prevail in those areas will become ever more common across the globe. This is especially likely when those distinctive religious patterns are transplanted northward, either by migration, or by actual missions to the old imperial powers, to what were once the core nations of world Christianity.[12]

I do not think that the West, and particularly Europe, should see this as a threat but as hope for the future. It is very much a "mission-shaped" church in Africa, Asia, and Latin America that is sending out people across the globe. However, I think that the West needs to be open for the movements that are coming from outside and not dismiss them as just old-fashioned and immature models. As we search for relevant models, fresh expressions of church in our distinct contexts, I would suggest that we include some of the church expressions that come from outside.

What Characterizes a Missional Church in the Global South? Examples from Three Continents

The Church in Ghana

According to church leaders in Ghana, the fact that the theological heritage was not clearly cross-cultural did not hinder the theology of being holistic.[13] In most cases theology of mission is therefore integral, including both gospel proclamation aiming for conversion to the Christian faith and social concern, seen in educational, health, and community development projects. Even Pentecostal and charismatic movements, known for their aggressive evangelism, operate social institutions, professional training, workshops, and relief work. Three of the four major hospitals in Accra are owned by Pentecostal/charismatic agencies, two of them belong to the Church of Pentecost and one belongs to the Assemblies of God.[14]

In more recent years, this integral mission has been largely influenced by theologians such as Kwame Bediako and other scholars at the Akrofi-Christaller Centre outside Accra. Other

---

12   Philip Jenkins, *The Next Christendom: The Coming of Global Christianity* (Oxford: Oxford University Press, 2002), 107–108.

13   Cephas Omenyo, "A Comparative Analysis of the Development Intervention of Protestant and Charismatic/Pentecostal Organisations in Ghana," *Svensk Missions Tidskrift – SMT* (2006), 10,11.

14   Omenyo, "A Comparative Analysis," 20.

Ghanaian thinkers have contributed to the development of a holistic approach to mission through the Christian Council of Ghana and other associations. Mission statements of local churches, denominations, and mission organizations show a basic theological understanding of expansion and of social inclusion although not all have a more systematic and formalized theology of mission.

Christian Churches and Mission in India

Despite the National Christian Council's involvement and influence in drawing up the Indian Constitution, political involvement has not been the forte of churches in India. Traditionally, the tendency has been for silence and non-participation in political debate. The voluntary associations formed by Christian churches and related organizations have dealt almost exclusively with education and social relief work without challenging the political and economic structures contributing to poverty and marginalization.

Historically, there were two main reasons for this, apart from Roman Catholics and Protestants being minority groups. These were the policy of political neutrality inherited from foreign mission organizations, and the theology of separation from worldly matters, focusing almost exclusively on a future heaven. Certainly this attitude towards politics favored the missionising work in many places, particularly where Hindu authorities were antagonistic to Christian activities.

In recent years, however, there has been a change of opinion regarding Christian involvement in political issues. For example, the Indian Mission Association (IMA) devoted an issue of its magazine *Indian Missions* to the theme of "Politics and Christians," encouraging evangelical believers to participate in the national political scene and advocating that Christians assume their responsibility for civil society.[15]

Manokaran, a church leader in India, affirms that "politics are definitely an important aspect of a Christian's life" and that "Christians have no right to criticise the government in which they do not want to be involved."[16]

Questioning how much the Christian church is impacting society in general in India, Joseph D'Souza, Director of Operation Mobilisation in India, said some years ago that

> The church has been a bystander, seen as on the periphery of Indian society rather than an integral part ... There has not been a sustained Indian expression of the reality of Jesus at the practical level during the last fifty years.[17]

However, in a leaflet on interfaith dialogue published by the Evangelical Fellowship of India (EFI), the holistic aspect of the Christian message is strongly emphasized as the best way of building bridges amongst the local culture and people of other religious confessions. The appreciation shown, particularly by Hindus, towards Christian groups and NGOs working

---

15   *Indian Missions*, October–December, 2002

16   J.N. Manokaran, "Should Christians Be Engaged in Politics?" in *Indian Missions*, 2002, 16.

17   Quoted by K. Rajendran, *Which Way Forward Indian Missions? A Critique of Twenty-five Years 1972–1997* (Bangalore, India: SAIACS Press, 1998), 39.

amongst the marginalized (for example in the fields of health and education) is fitting recognition of the vital role played by such voluntary associations, despite the rather frequent conflicts between these Christians and Hindus. EFI recommends, therefore, that Christian churches act more decisively, creating opportunities and structures for holistic ministry.[18]

Fortaleza, Brazil

Jorge, one of my colleagues and friends in Fortaleza, in northeast Brazil, could be a good example of how to develop a local church to be missional. Born in a poor region of the country he had a personal experience with Jesus Christ when he was a teenager and soon felt called to be a full-time minister. After theological studies he came to this small congregation in the slum area of Dois Irmãos (Two brothers) in the outskirts of Fortaleza. He realized soon that preaching the gospel and making disciples of Jesus would not be successful without considering the entire situation of people in the neighborhood.

There were no schools in the area and he started first a preschool in the backyard of the church and alphabetization courses for adults. The school started to grow and today they offer quality education from preschool to secondary, with support from local authorities. Being a community of poor people, many of them without permanent jobs and living in subhuman conditions, a program was also started, with help from those the south of Brazil, to build and renovate houses, provide clean water, and improve the sanitary system, giving people jobs and better living standards.

The former slum area Dois Irmãos is not the same anymore. The church continues with a holistic ministry, preaching the gospel of salvation and transformation, praying for healing and for God's help, and acting in different areas of community development, following the example of Jesus Christ and echoing his words in Luke 4:18–19.

Conclusion

I believe that the challenge for the Christian churches in Africa, Asia, and Latin America is partly different from that in the West. The challenge for these churches, as I see it, is not so much of isolation from people outside the church but more of overcoming the dichotomy between spiritual and secular and to engage more directly in the daily struggle for better living standards for all. Unfortunately the West has exported divisions and they have learned how to multiple these divisions even more. So, although the churches are growing fast, they do not have the influence in society as they could because of a lack of unity. Our church-box labels such as ecumenicals, evangelicals, and Pentecostals are just nonsense in many of these countries. But internationally it seems that we require alignment to these different traditions and historical divisions.

In the global South, there is not so much a lack of creative models of services and liturgy in order to attract people to the churches. Sunday services may be well frequented but most of church life happens during the week in the local neighborhoods and in the daily contact

---

18   Evangelical Fellowship of India, *Statement of Perceptions of Christianity by People of Other Faiths and Our Response*, leaflet published December 4, 2002.

with friends and colleagues. Relationships, solidarity, and collective action are strengths in many of these cultures.

New models of being church emerge sometimes within established churches and many times as new church plants parallel to existing ecclesiastical structures. The Church Planting Movement in north India with thousands of new local congregations, using new believers as church planters, is one good example. The youth movements that are very much globalized with a local flavor challenge also the established traditions in most of these nations.

In the urban settings the tendency is of increasing pluralism and secularization. Therefore the missional emphasis and the fresh expressions that we have seen in the UK and in some other European countries may also be important in the big cities in the global South. But I think also that the West need to learn from the growing churches in the South. Sometimes we look for models and methods that will take us closer to unchurched people while Nigerians, Brazilians, and Filipinos establish relationships in a very natural way and they could show us how to do it.

In his book *The Gospel in a Pluralistic Society*, Leslie Newbigin describes the Christian congregation as hermeneutic of the gospel, giving continuation to the way Jesus accomplished his mission on the earth.[19]

In conclusion I think we need to come back to the key questions: what is the church and how can the church be relevant for people today? Is the church just a vending machine where you insert your coins and your personal problems are solved? Or is it a borderless community of disciples of Jesus that keep the different dimensions of the gospel together and live out the values and the blessings of the kingdom in their own society and beyond cultural, linguistic, geographical, generational, and religious boundaries? I believe that is a "mission-shaped" church.

Questions for Reflection:

1. In what way were churches planted in the global South influenced by the mission organizations and respective denominations that started them? Mention some concrete examples from your own church and mission context.
2. How would you describe a "mission-shaped" church? Are there general characteristics of missional churches valid for all cultural contexts?
3. Reflect on examples of contextualized and relevant church models of missional churches in your own society. What do they have in common? What could and should be improved and developed in order to be truly missional?

---

19   Leslie Newbigin, *A Word in Season: Perspectives on Christian World Missions* (Grand Rapids, MI: Eerdmans, 1994), 227–232.

References

Allen, Roland. 1962. *The Spontaneous Expansion of the Church.* Grand Rapids, MI: Eerdmans.

Belcher, Jim. 2009. *Deep Church: A Third Way Beyond Emerging and Traditional.* Downers Grove, IL: IVP.

Blauw, Johannes. 1962. *The Missionary Nature of the Church.* Grand Rapids, MI: Eerdmans.

Bosch, David. 1993. *Transforming Mission: Paradigm Shifts in Theology of Mission.* Maryknoll, NY: Orbis.

Castro, Emilio. 1978. Liberation, Development and Evangelism: Must We Choose in Mission? *Occasional Bulletin for Missionary Research* (July), 87.

Cook, Matthew, Rob Haskell, Ruth Julian and Natee Tanchanpongs, eds. 2010. *Local Theology for the Global Church: Principles for an Evangelical Approach to Contextualization.* Pasadena, CA: William Carey.

Drane, John. 2001. *McDonaldization of the Church: Spirituality, Creativity and the Future of the Church.* London: Darton, Longman and Todd.

Frost, Michael, and Alan Hirsch. 2003. *The Shaping of Things to Come: Innovation and Mission for the 21st Century Church.* Peabody, MA: Hendrickson.

Fuellenbach, John. 2002. *Church: Community for the Kingdom.* Maryknoll, NY: Orbis.

Hedlund, Roger. 1991. *The Mission of the Church in the World.* Grand Rapids, MI: Baker.

Indian Missions. 2002. *Journal of the Indian Mission Association,* October–December.

Jenkins, Philip. 2002. *The Next Christendom: The Coming of Global Christianity.* Oxford: University Press.

Kirk, Andrew. 1999. *What Is Mission? Theological Explorations.* London: Darton, Longman, Todd.

Lundy, David. 2005. *Borderless Church: Shaping the Church for the Twenty-first Century.* Milton Keynes, UK: Authentic.

Manokaran, J.N. 2002. Should Christians be Engaged in Politics? *Indian Missions* 2002:16.

Miley, George. 2003. *Loving the Church—Blessing the Nations: Pursuing the Role of Local Churches in Global Mission.* Waynesboro, GA: Gabriel Publishing.

Newbigin, Lesslie. 1978. *The Open Secret.* Grand Rapids, MI: Eerdmans.

———. 1994. *A Word in Season: Perspectives on Christian World Missions.* Grand Rapids, MI: Eerdmans.

———. 2000. *The Gospel in a Pluralistic Society.* London: SPCK.

Nikolajsen, Jeppe Bach, ed. 2012. *Missional Kirke: En Introduktion.* Fredericia, DK: Lohse.

Omenyo, Cephas N. 2006. A Comparative Analysis of the Development Intervention of Protestant and Charismatic/Pentecostal Organisations in Ghana. *Svensk Missions Tidskrift.* 94(1): 10–11.

Padilla, Rene. 1988. *Guds Rike och Kyrkans Uppdrag* (*Mission Between the Times: Essays on the Kingdom*). Örebro: Libris.

Rajendran, K. 1998. *Which Way Forward Indian Missions? A Critique of Twenty-five Years 1972–1997*. Bangalore: SAIACS Press.

Ruiz, David D. 2006. *La Transformación de la Iglesia: Un Llamado al Retorno a la Esencia Genética de la Iglesia*. Guatemala: COMIBAM.

Stackhouse, John G., ed. 2003. *Evangelical Ecclesiology: Reality or Illusion?* Grand Rapids, MI: Baker.

Svensk Missions Tidskrift. 2004. Missional Church—Missional Religion. 92(4).

Van Engen, Charles. 1991. *God's Missionary People: Rethinking the Purpose of the Local Church*. Grand Rapids, MI: Baker.

Van Gelder, Craig. 2000. *The Essence of the Church: A Community Created by the Spirit*. Grand Rapids, MI: Baker.

Van Gelder, Craig, and Dwight Zscheile. 2011. *The Missional Church in Perspective: Mapping Trends and Shaping the Conversation*. Grand Rapids, MI: Baker.

Wright, Christopher. 2006. *The Mission of God: Unlocking the Bible's Grand Narrative*. Downers Grove, IL: IVP.

———. 2010. *The Mission of God's People: A Theology of the Church's Mission*. Grand Rapids, MI: Zondervan.

Yamamori, Tetsunao, and Rene Padilla, eds. 2004. *The Local Church, Agent of Transformation*. Buenos Aires: Kairos.

Bertil Ekström (MTh, PhD) was born in Sweden and grew up in Brazil. Married to Alzira, the couple has four children and four grandchildren. An ordained Baptist pastor, Bertil has been involved in the mission movements of Brazil and Latin America for many years. Currently he is the director of the Mission Institute in Örebro, Sweden, and the executive director of the WEA Mission Commissions.

CHAPTER 15

THE CHURCH AS A TRANSFORMING COMMUNITY

Richard Tiplady

We can observe two countervailing trends across churches in Europe at the moment.

The first is the perceived marginalization of the Christian faith in our culture and society. Widely felt and often commented upon, this extends beyond the neoatheist attacks on religion and declining church attendance figures to redefinitions of marriage and the exclusion of the expression of Christian faith in the workplace.

Yet at the same time, evangelical Christians are increasingly rediscovering the socially transformative impact of the gospel. This seems to be motivated by more than a simple desire to retain some kind of Christian presence or influence in society. There is an increasing recognition that the gospel is not only about personal salvation, but it has a social and communal aspect as well. This coincides with an opportunity, described by historian Tony Judt as "the collapse of the postwar welfare settlement" (wherein, across Europe, welfare states established after the Second World War are proving financially unsustainable and governments are seeking partners across civil society to deliver and support social safety nets).

In my former role as the director of a church-planting mission agency, I described our work as founding "communities of personal and social transformation," places where people find personal transformation (forgiveness, healing, reconciliation, and so on) but in so doing also become part of communities working for the wider transformation of their locality and beyond.

I have identified four different ways that Christians have sought to define the work of the church in social transformation, each of which can draw on biblical precedents.

Compassion / Care for Those in Need
(Luke 10:25–37)

This approach draws its inspiration from stories like the parable of the Good Samaritan, a clear illustration of how one should "love your neighbor as yourself" (Luke 10:27).

There are strong Old Testament precedents for this, with injunctions such as not harvesting to the very edge of your field and not taking a second harvest of olives and grapes, leaving them instead for the socially vulnerable (the foreigner, the fatherless, and the widow) (Deut 24:19–21). We see this principle operating in stories like Ruth, chapter 2. We also see it reflected in the story of the rich young ruler (Luke 18:18–25), who is unwilling to obey Jesus' instruction to sell all he has and give it to the poor, leaving him to lament that it is "easier for a camel to go through the eye of a needle than for a rich man to enter heaven" (v25). However else we choose to interpret this story, Jesus seems to see our ability (or not) to give away our wealth for the sake of the needy as an indicator of spiritual health.

My experience is that, on balance, Christians are quite good at this, willing to step in and help those in need. But compassion fatigue or scepticism about real need can so easily set in. And while the stories of the Good Samaritan and the Rich Young Ruler stand as powerful indictments of our self-excused indifference, a deeper question is raised—is it just a Band-Aid or sticking plaster, dealing with symptoms rather than causes? In effect, rather than being good Samaritans helping those who have been mugged, maybe we should install traffic police on the Jericho Road?

Transforming the Structures of Society
(Matt 5:13)

The idea of the church as the "salt of the earth," which is interpreted as having a preservative or purifying function, has a long history in Reformed theology and has been perhaps expressed most clearly in Europe in those countries with Reformed national churches, such as Scotland and the Netherlands. The famous Scottish Reformer John Knox introduced universal primary education in every parish in the country, overseen by the local church, in order to ensure that everyone could read the Bible for themselves. The socially-transformative wider impacts of this initiative made Scotland one of the most educated and prosperous countries in Europe and a leader in the UK's Industrial Revolution. Dutch theologian Abraham Kuyper, who was Prime Minister of his country from 1901–1905, famously declared, "There is not a square inch in the whole domain of our human existence over which Christ, who is Lord over all, does not cry 'Mine'!"

This is an idea that is growing in influence again, perhaps as a reaction to secularizing tendencies that would push Christian faith to the margins of society. It is based on the Old Testament idea of "shalom" (peace, or wholeness). Life as God intends it is a good life, enjoyed in relationship with him, with other people, and with his gifts in creation. It is what Jesus intended in his promise of "life to the full" (John 10:10). It should however not be understood as a prosperity gospel. We see clearly in the Bible that not all wealth is obtained by God's blessing (Amos, Isaiah, Micah) and not all suffering is the result of disobedience or sin (Job, Jeremiah, Jesus).

This has also been defined as "doing the will of God in the political sphere," and we should applaud and support those Christians who enter local and national politics with a motivation to serve and improve their societies. But it is not only about political activity undertaken by Christians; it is also about political activity inspired by Christian principles. This is perhaps most clearly articulated by the poet and writer TS Eliot, in whose 1939 essay *The Idea of a Christian Society* we read; "What the rulers believed would be less important than the beliefs to which they would be obliged to conform. A skeptical or indifferent statesman working in a Christian frame might be more effective than a devout statesman obliged to conform to a secular frame." We see these principles operating in recent initiatives led by Christians such as the Jubilee 2000/Drop The Debt campaigns, the Make Poverty History campaign (which hold politicians accountable to the Millennium Development Goals) and the Stop The Traffik campaign.

Such political initiative does not have to be simply "top down" or national in scope, but can include community development processes which seek to harness the resources and initiative inherent in poorer communities, rather than simply relying on outside help. Christian development agency Tearfund works to empower churches in this regard, as they are so often the main or only form of civil society in their communities.

This approach emphasizes the lordship of Christ over all the structures of society, and the church as his agent in expressing this lordship. It releases Christians for transformative work in whatever place they find themselves. But it can dissolve into a power struggle against those of different political and social values. And we should heed the words of Paul, for "the weapons we fight with are not the weapons of this world" (2 Cor 10:4).

An Alternative Community / An Example to the World
(Matthew 5:14)

Christians are comfortable with the idea that Jesus is the light of the world (John 8:12). What is rather more challenging is the fact that he also described his followers as such, and as a city on a hill, one which cannot be hidden. This is a solemn challenge, and one in which our lives together as his disciples matter a great deal, which is probably why it gets so much attention in the New Testament (e.g. John 17; Acts; Rom; 1 Cor; Gal; Eph). We should also pause to note that Jesus said "you are," not "you might be."

The desire for transformative social impact is laudable, but our world is deeply fallen, corrupt, and under the influence of the evil one. It exhibits a brokenness that strongly resists being "fixed." Utopian dreams often fall far short and become oppressive themselves.

In such a context, the church is an alternative community. We bear witness by who we are, not by what we do. There is a strong Anabaptist heritage to this idea, although it goes back to the early church itself, wherein the early Christians shared all their possessions and sold property in order to give to those in need (Acts 2:44–45). The North African theologian Tertullian wrote about Christians thus: "See how they love one another, and how ready they are to die for one another" (Apology 39.7), and the last pagan Roman emperor Julian the Apostate (who ruled from AD 361–363) wrote to the high priest of Roman paganism to complain, "These impious Galileans not only feed their own poor, but ours also!"

The main idea is that rather than trying to change the world through effort, one tries to influence it by showing an alternative. Often pacifist and non-violent, it tries to live by the Sermon on the Mount. It focuses on the cross of Christ and on weakness and suffering (e.g., 2 Cor). And it is a powerfully influential approach, as shown by the worldwide impact of just four people—Mohandas Gandhi, Martin Luther King, Mother Teresa, and Nelson Mandela.

But the focus on community purity can easily degenerate into petty legalism, as the subsequent history of many early Anabaptist communities demonstrates. Jesus said the same when he criticized the Pharisees for tithing their dill and cumin while neglecting the weightier matters of the Law, such as justice, mercy, and faithfulness (Matt 23:23). Perhaps this broken, fallen, corrupt, and resistant world needs a more radical approach to change?

Overturning Unjust and Oppressive Structures
(Luke 1:46–55, especially 51–53)

This final approach appears at first glance to be similar to the Reformed/transformative approach. But it is more radical and more confrontational; not transforming but overturning, not renewing but replacing. Of the four, it tends to be the least appealing to evangelicals, who tend to be socially conservative, but it has clear biblical support and so is a challenge to all who claim to accept biblical authority.

Mary's song has strong Old Testament precedents, with the people crying out to God and the prophets railing against exploitation and oppression, all of them expecting God's intervention on behalf of the poor, whether in Psalms 73, 85, and 86 or prophetic passages like Isaiah 1:18–25. The same emotion lies behind Mary's song, with the Jewish people under Roman rule, the most powerful empire of the known world. Having previously been under Babylonian, Persian, and Greek rule for 500 of the previous 600 years (with only glimpses of freedom), they were longing for God to intervene and deliver them.

How does this affect us in Europe today? Perhaps less than it used to, although one does not have to go far back into history to find parallels. Robert Tressell's novel *The Ragged Trousered Philanthropists*, which recounts the woes of exploited workers during the laissez-faire capitalism of early twentieth-century Edwardian England, was one of the most widely-read books by British soldiers during the Second World War, and is credited with playing a powerful role in postwar demands for a universal welfare state. Neither should the Christian socialist foundations of the UK's Labour Party be overlooked. Perhaps the closest parallels today lie in unequal global trading relationships?

Issues of injustice and exploitation can be complex, hard to understand and hard to decide what to do for the best. The challenge to the church is to keep the Old Testament prophets (and Mary's song) in mind, and to have the courage to challenge and confront similar injustices today. As the German theologian and martyr Dietrich Bonhoeffer wrote, "We are not simply to bandage the wounds of victims caught beneath the wheels of injustice. We are to drive a spoke into the wheel itself."

Conclusion

I began by describing churches as "communities of personal and social transformation," which empower individuals to seek or work for transformation in their workplaces, neighborhoods, and families, with churches as bodies doing the same in their towns, nations, and worldwide. As we have seen, there are different ways of doing this—showing compassion and caring for those in need, working to transform politics and community life, demonstrating an alternative community, and confronting and overturning injustice. All four approaches have strengths and all four approaches have weaknesses. All four also have biblical support. All four should therefore be in evidence in the mission of the church today.

Questions for Reflection:

1. Tiplady describes four different "ways that Christians have sought to define the work of the church in social transformation." Which ones have you seen being applied to your context? What has been the main biblical/theological motivation for using a specific way of engaging in social transformation?

2. The author affirms that all four ways "should be in evidence in the mission of the church today." Do you agree and how would that be possible in your country, city, and neighborhood?

Richard Tiplady is the Principal of the Scottish School of Christian Mission (previously known as International Christian College). He is passionate about finding ways to respond to the missionary challenge of the West and has served in leadership roles in mission for many years. He has written extensively on the changing nature of world mission and is keen to invest his energies in developing creative and innovative leaders in mission. He is married to Irene, who works in a mental health project in one of the most deprived council estates in Scotland, and they have one son, Jamie, who is a computer game designer.

CHAPTER 16

THE MISSIONAL DISCIPLE

David D. Ruiz M. and Rita Rimkiene

In this chapter we attempt to draw a picture of a missional disciple. As those who belong to the so called periphery of the church, we are looking at discipleship from our experience, and our fresh reading of the Word is from our particular context. It seems strange to talk about "what does it mean to be a disciple?" as if we are asking "what does it mean to be a Christian?" There should not be any difference between the two.

Unfortunately, over the last decades much of the church has focused on evangelistic programs and has forgotten that to raise a mature Christian it is not enough to see his/her conversion. Conversion is an initial decision for a lifetime committed to the next stage—discipleship. Sadly, the concept of discipleship from Jesus' time—inviting disciples to take a walk with the Master and to share all of life with him—has been narrowed down to church programs. Jesus' ministry shows what a missional disciple lifestyle looks like, but somehow it got lost in translation. Thus, we came to an age of relearning the Great Commission call to discipleship.

A Personal Testimony

My concept of church was drawn by a missionary couple that came to my city in the early 1990s. Their lifestyle was filled with love, grace, forgiveness, and mercy. Since I did not speak English and it took a while for them to learn Lithuanian, my eyes were my guides in understanding Christian faith. Their lifestyle was enough for me to make the most important decision of my life.

Unfortunately, when I moved to the UK I saw more passivity and flaws in the church than warmth and acceptance. The church that took the gospel around the world had lost its understanding and lacked imagination for what it meant to be disciples of Christ. It was clear that the church's main focus was on their clergy, their programs, and their buildings. The employed professional Christian staff were the driving force of the church and the rest were spectators. Listening to local Christians, one understood that the church was the building, and if you were not there during the week then you were not "doing" church.

How did Christians forget that being in a church building does not make us disciples of Christ? We turned Jesus into a figure of worship, not an example to follow. Such life makes us religious followers of Christ, sadly, not disciples. The story of Nicodemus in John 3 reminds us that being religious is not enough to follow Christ.

It is naive to believe that discipleship courses or evangelistic programs will draw non-Christians into church. It is worth noting, too, that these programs speak only to Christians because of the exclusive evangelical language that the world has never come across. It pains to say that we have many converts but few disciples. Our understanding of being a Christian is based on conversion. Did Jesus leave his disciples on their own? Evangelism is a starting point of Christian faith, which eventually leads to conversion, but the core of a mature Christian faith is rooted in discipleship. And the Great Commission calling is, "Therefore, go and make disciples of all nations" (Matt 28:19). When we talk about mission we hear "go and evangelize." Sadly, "churches are successful in converting people but unsuccessful in forming Christians into disciples."[1] Paul and Peter urged all followers of Christ, "This suffering is all part of what God has called you to. Christ, who suffered for you, is your example. Follow in his steps" (1 Pet 2:21).

Follow in His Steps

I am a mother of two daughters. I know that the only way they will see Christ living in me is by my invitation to them to walk with me. At first, I will hold their hands until they make a commitment and then, step by step, I will let them take their own walk. It is a time-consuming journey. Since we live together, they have a chance to observe my life with Christ, meet all those strangers that come to our home, hear conversations, and see God changing people's hearts and lives. The theologian, Howard Snyder, said that there is a difference between "church people" and "kingdom people":

> Kingdom people seek first the kingdom of God and its justice; church people often put the church work above concerns of justice, mercy, and truth. Church people think about how to get people into the church; kingdom people think about how to get the church into the world. Church people worry that the world might change the church; kingdom people work to see the church change the world.[2]

It is hard to understand why Christians spend day after day in the church building, complaining about secularism taking over the world. The only answer to this can be that most Christians choose a safer way to give their time and energy and remain within the church walls, which eventually leads to the stagnation of faith. Christian faith calls us to live out justice, mercy, forgiveness, and grace in everyday life. Without these, Christian faith is nothing but the theory of what God's kingdom is like or could be. The gospels are full of examples of missional lifestyle of discipleship. There is no need to explain what "missional" means, but there is a great need for Christians to dig deeper into the concept of discipleship. Michael Frost observes:

> When Jesus is just true light from true light, ethereal and otherworldly, we are only ever called to adore him. But when he is true human, one who loved and healed, who

---

1   Robert Webber, *Ancient-Future Evangelism: Making Your Church a Faith-Forming Community* (Ada, MI: Baker Books, 2003), 43.

2   M. Frost, *The Road to Missional: Journey to the Center of the Church* (Ada, MI: Baker Books, 2011), 80.

served and taught, who suffered and died and rose again, he becomes one we can follow.[3]

Jesus' life was the greatest example. He took his twelve disciples on a life journey. He allowed them to be part of his life, ask questions, eat with him, see him weep and rejoice, perform miracles, cast out demons, and much more. Instead of practicing our faith on Sunday morning among our Christian friends, we are commanded to take our faith outside the church walls and open our homes to our neighbors, friends, and family.

> Social networking in a post-Christian world will primarily happen where people eat together in houses of Christians and in neighborhood communities where faith is shared. Eating has always played a central role in the Christian faith.[4]

We underestimate the power of hospitality. Homes provide a platform for on-going relationships. At first people come as strangers, then slowly grow into friends by spending time together, sharing life stories, and taking a journey of trust and openness. During this time we listen, open up and learn about one another. Christian lives become transparent for people to see living hope in us—the hope that is preached on Sundays, but forgotten outside the church building. This hope lives in Christian homes.

There is no need to create and search for new discipleship programs. The nature of discipleship is revealed through Jesus' relationship with his disciples (Matt 10:24–25). Jesus' ministry was relational and intentional and thus, "building relationships is a kingdom way of working, for the kingdom is relational by nature."[5]

The Church and Discipleship

We say that the church in our times is facing an identity crisis; it is growing farther from its original image as presented in the Bible. The same is true when we think about the meaning of discipleship. In essence, every Christian must be a disciple, as exemplified in Acts 11:26: "The disciples were called Christians first at Antioch;" but, that is not the reality today. As Dallas Willard said, "It is almost universally conceded today that you can be a Christian without being a disciple."[6]

The Great Commission of Jesus Christ was given to Christians, not to institutions. When he said, "Therefore go and make disciples," Jesus was teaching us that discipleship is not a program but a lifestyle. He wants us to be a disciple all the time and everywhere but he was also asking us to be involved in making disciples on a daily basis as we do whatever calling the Lord has given to us.

---

3   M. Frost, *Exiles: Living Missionally in a Post-Christian Culture* (Peabody, MA: Hendrickson Publishers, 2006), 32.

4   Webber, *Ancient-Future*, 58.

5   M. Moynagh with P. Harrold, *Church for Every Context: An Introduction to Theology and Practice* (London: SCM Press, 2012), 422.

6   Dallas Willard, *The Divine Conspiracy: Rediscovering Our Hidden Life in God* (London: HarperCollins, 1998), 309.

We say that most of the church is going in the opposite direction from the Bible mandate. We have transformed an experience of life with Jesus into programs, calendars, budgets, buildings, titles, logos, and egos. The calling of Christ to be his disciples is as simple and as challenging as Paul describes in Colossians 2:6, "Walk in Him:" to follow in his steps on a daily basis, to imitate Christ, to represent Christ, and to introduce Christ every time, everywhere, and to everyone.

The Character of a Missional Disciple:

As Bosch properly said, "Being a disciple of Jesus does not signify that one has, as it were, arrived … The call to constant vigilance is certainly intended as warning against any possibility of self-exaltation, but also as motivation to an eager engagement in mission."[7] Following Jesus is a daily commitment of those that are called disciples. Matthew 16:24 presents for us a threefold picture of what we can call a missional disciple.

A missional disciple of Jesus must deny himself; this is the first perspective of the portrait of a disciple. Every disciple is called to die to a life ruled by his feelings, his own thoughts, and especially by his own desires. Jesus is inviting his followers to become part of those who, forgetting themselves, decided to submit their whole experience of life under the lordship of Jesus. "The appeal is not to gloom but to discipleship."[8] This appeal is to transform our character because discipleship to the real committed Christian must mean to "be what his Master wants him to be."

A missional disciple of Jesus must take up his cross; this is the second perspective of the portrait of a disciple and presents a call for every disciple to be obedient whatever the consequences and whatever the cost. This appeal is to transform the disciples' way of living by a radical transformation of their daily lives. The disciple of Jesus Christ must "do what his Master wants him to do." It is a matter of obedience; as Harvey pointed out: "For Matthew, obedience is the key quality in a disciple who is in mission. This theme may be seen throughout Matthew's gospel."[9]

A missional disciple of Jesus must follow him; this is the third perspective of the portrait of a disciple. It presents a call for every disciple to follow Jesus with total focus. This appeal is to commit our life to Jesus' will, to follow him wherever his will is leading us, whether he gives us a geographical calling—sending us to a place to serve him and continue the dynamic process to establish the church—or a call to a particular profession that challenges us to be tested and presented as his committed follower in the marketplace. The disciple of Jesus Christ must "go wherever his Master wants him to go." That includes anywhere on earth and whatever may be involved.

---

7   David Bosch, *Transforming Mission: Paradigm Shifts in Theology of Mission* (Maryknoll, NY: Orbis Books, 1991), 76.

8   Bosch, *Transforming Mission*, 257.

9   John Harvey, "Mission in Matthew," in *Mission in the New Testament: An Evangelical Approach,* ed. Williams J. Larkin Jr. and Joel F. Williams (New York: Orbis Books, 1998).

Discipleship is presented not as a program on a church's board or bulletin; it is shown in the life of Christians. The Great Commission could possibly be restated in this way: "As you live a Christ-like life invite others to follow you, to identify themselves as Christ followers, and to commit to become more and more like Christ all the time, everywhere, and to make his name known among all nations."

Conclusion

Jesus' church is formed by missional disciples: ordinary people in a constant process to be more like their Master's model, committed to deny themselves in order to "be what their Master wants them to be." Missional disciples are ready to take up their cross every day in a clear commitment to "do what their Master wants them to do." The are Christians who are ready to follow him and to "go wherever their Master wants them to go," including the ends of the earth at whatever the cost. A missional disciple will follow Christ by emulating his lifestyle.

How we think shapes how we act. Our vision of church must not stem from an institutional paradigm with its attention to buildings, clergy, programs, and so on. It must derive from the Great Commission, the practice of the New Testament church, and even historical examples of the church at its missional best.[10]

Missional disciples will always seek opportunities to build relationships and take a lifetime walk, where both parties will experience the grace and faithfulness of God. "It is the Spirit of Christ within each of us that gives rise to a missional 'discipleship' [author's word] lifestyle."[11] The life of a disciple is a journey marked with suffering and the grace of Christ, being willing, obedient, and ready to follow in the footsteps of his Master.

Questions for Reflection:

1. How has discipleship been defined in your church and mission context? How has that affected the way mission has been done?
2. What are, according to your experience, the best ways of making disciples in your cultural context?
3. Do you agree with the authors about the character of a missional disciple? How can we grow in our Christian life in order to be the disciples that Jesus deserves and wants us to be?

References

Bosch, David J. 1983. The Structure of Mission: An Exposition of Matthew 28:16–20. In *Exploring Church Growth*. Ed. Wilbert R. Shenk. Grand Rapids: Eerdmans.

---

10   Moynagh and Harrold, *Church for Every Context*, 419.
11   Frost, *Exiles*, 29.

———. 1991. *Transforming Mission: Paradigm Shifts in Theology of Mission*. New York: Orbis Books.

Crosby, Michael H. 2000. *"Do You Love Me?": Jesus Questions the Church*. New York: Orbis Books.

Culver, Robert D. 1968. What Is the Church's Commission? *Bibliotheca Sacra* Vol. 125 (July).

Frost, M. 2006. *Exiles: Living Missionally in a Post-Christian Culture*. Massachussets: Hendrickson Publishers.

———. 2011. *The Road to Missional: Journey to the Center of the Church*. Michigan: Baker Books.

Krentz, Edgar. 2006. Make Disciples: Matthew on Evangelism. *Currents in Theology and Mission* 33/1 (February).

Moynagh, M. and Harrold, P. 2012. *Church for Every Context: An Introduction to Theology and Practice*. London: SCM Press.

Stanton, Graham N. 1992. *A Gospel for a New People: Studies in Matthew*. Edinburgh: T&T Clark.

Webber, Robert, E. 2003. *Ancient-Future Evangelism: Making Your Church a Faith-Forming Community*. Michigan: Baker Books.

Willard, Dallas. 1998. *The Divine Conspiracy: Rediscovering Our Hidden Life in God*. London: Harper Collins.

Rita Rimkiene was born and raised in Lithuania. In 2004, together with her husband Vidas and daughter Rugile (a second daughter Ugne was born in 2013), Rita moved to Gloucester, UK to study at Redcliffe College, where she completed a MA in Global Issues and Contemporary Mission. In 2010 she joined European Christian Mission and began making friends with Polish neighbors. God brought to their doorstep families, singles, and widows. They describe their ministry as simple: "We proclaim God's love in our neighborhood by inviting people to discover who God is through hospitality and sharing life together."

David D. Ruiz M. is from Guatemala and holds a MA in Mission Studies from All Nations, UK. Married to Dora Amalia and father of three children, David has worked as a pastor and executive director of COMIBAM (The Ibero American Mission Cooperation). Currently he is an Associate Director of the WEA Mission Commission and Vice President for Global Ministries of Camino Global.

CHURCH AND AGENCY RELATIONSHIP

Tom Hayes and Decio de Carvalho

From the Perspective of a Church

Tom Hayes

A healthy human body is capable of a wide array of incredible accomplishments. Some of those accomplishments are physical in nature, such as climbing mountains or competing in triathlons. Other achievements are more cognitive in nature, such as solving complex mathematical problems or memorizing entire books. However, when a body is unhealthy, whether ravaged by a disease or an apathetic approach to diet and exercise, the body loses some of its capabilities.

It is with this in mind that I approach the question of the relationship between the local church and mission agencies, and how they can work together. The relationships between these entities can be related to the idea of healthy or unhealthy bodies. Unfortunately, there are many examples of unhealthy relationships between local churches and mission agencies. First however, it is beneficial to concentrate on the unique roles of both church and agency. These roles, when understood and embraced, can bring about a relationship that, like a healthy body, can accomplish incredible things. These accomplishments would not be limited to feats of strength or wisdom but are achievements that will help to usher in the kingdom of God.

It is this idea of the kingdom of God that should compel churches and agencies to work together. Ushering in the kingdom of God on the earth as Jesus prayed for in Matthew 6:10 is the goal of both church and agency, because that should be the goal of all followers of Christ. This work of ushering in the kingdom is such an immense work that the only means by which it can be accomplished is for God to provide all the resources necessary. That means God will call and equip individuals, provide all the funds needed, and set a vision so large that the churches and agencies must continue to seek him for any success. The key point here though is that God has spread these resources throughout his followers. Some of those resources are found in the local church and some resources are found in the agencies. The implications of this is that there will need to be a dynamic, healthy relationship forged between churches and agencies for the purpose of establishing the kingdom.

With that as a backdrop, here is a closer look at the unique roles of both the local church and mission agencies with a few thoughts for how they should interact at the conclusion.

The Unique Roles of the Church

- *The church sends out their own members for engagement with God's mission.* This could be short or mid-term involvement, but best when regularly sending out members to long-term service. Within the church, there should be a missionary development ministry of some variety. There will be aspects of preparing individuals for cross-cultural ministry than can only be developed by the agency chosen by the missionary. However, the procesggs of yielding oneself to a missionary call can be difficult to navigate and is more of a spiritual journey than a step by step process. This journey should begin within the confines of a loving local church. The local church must then continue deep relationships with these missionaries as they serve overseas because the church holds a unique position in keeping the missionaries on the field. The church, which should have an existing long and deep relationship with the missionary, will uniquely be positioned to encourage and support a missionary while on the field. The "career" term of a missionary seems to be getting shorter. The local church should be part of the mechanism of preparing well and keeping a missionary on the field long term. A strong relationship with their missionaries can limit the decreasing length of career service for a missionary.

- *The church provides events, resources, and opportunities locally that contribute to a greater knowledge of God's mission.* Many of those who sit in the pews each Sunday morning are unaware of God's plan to establish his kingdom. This is not by design, but many followers of Christ have settled for a shallow, self-centered belief in God. The local church should educate and challenge their church body to respond wholeheartedly to the call to join God in his mission. This cannot be reduced to simply increasing head knowledge though; there must be efforts to also engage the heart of believers.

- *There should be regular, substantial, and generous use of the resources God has placed within the local church body for the advancement of God's global kingdom.* It is vital that the local church support works that do not simply enlarge their own ministries, but equip those outside their church body to participate in God's mission. The two most significant resources found within every church are finances and prayer. A church's financial resources are not their own, as they do not belong to the individual believer either. God in heaven is who blesses individuals and churches with financial resources, and they should be used according to his purposes. They should also not be given begrudgingly but with a joyful heart. The church should also mobilize their members to fight battles unaware through the miracle of prayer. Prayer is the means for *every single believer* to be engaged in the work of God globally. There is no credible excuse for the lack of prayer exhibited in most churches for the global work of God.

- *In the prayer of Jesus found in John 17, it is telling that he prays for his believers to be unified.* In his prescient knowledge of the future he knew that his followers would at times be petty, unforgiving, and small-minded to the point of disunity. The local church serves as many things, but it is definitely an example to the world around it for how Christ followers should act. Each local church should exhibit to other churches their commitment to God's mission, not as a comparison, but as a means to join together for an example of the unity found within the body of Christ. This unity will speak volumes to those outside the church within their own communities as well as exhibiting worldwide the harmony found within Christ followers.

- *There should always be an attempt to learn from and join with organizations such as mission agencies, the World Evangelical Alliance, and the Lausanne Movement to better equip the local church to understand global and cultural trends.* A local church is by nature—local. However, a local church can access additional information by partnering with these other types of organizations to provide the wisdom needed to minister well cross-culturally.

The Unique Roles of the Mission Agency

- *The mission agency provides strategic insight and the infrastructure needed to reach out cross-culturally.* The focus of each agency varies as some focus on unreached peoples, others concentrate on a particular region or language, and others are actively serving wherever they are able. In any of these agencies though, the agency's capacity to network, build relationships, and provide plans to reach people will always be higher than a local church.

- *Once a church has adequately prepared a missionary, and if they choose to utilize a mission agency to deploy the missionary to the field, the agency will assume responsibility for the missionary's journey toward serving cross-culturally.* The agency will continue to equip, they will manage services, and care for the missionaries as they serve throughout the world. The home offices of many mission agencies are filled with those who previously served on the field and hold a unique perspective on how a missionary feels and acts through every aspect of ministry. There is a specialized relationship that can be forged through these common experiences. These agencies think every day about how to best serve and encourage those on the field to reach the nations. A local church should look to the agency to best provide these services.

- *One of the most important functions of mission agencies is to employ mission specialists that increase knowledge, advance strategies, and build networks needed for both church and agency.* Generally speaking, a local church will not be a position to employ the types of mission specialists as those found within an agency. These specialists are who can and should shape mission trends and practices.

How Do They Serve Together?

It should first be stated that not only are all believers called to be participating in God's mission, they should also fully acknowledge that he will provide the vision, move people's hearts to join with him, and provide all the resources needed to fulfill this mission. Those resources are not housed exclusively within the local church or the agency. The church and agency must work together to see God's kingdom expand. However, there seem to be two regular issues: 1) the church has often times abdicated her responsibility to reach globally and 2) the agencies have too quickly abandoned the local church and her slow moving ways.

First: the local church is called to reach the nations. It is always extremely disappointing to see a local church that has focused inwardly and is not actively seeking to be used either locally or globally to exhibit God to those who do not yet believe. It is also not enough to only reach locally; God has exhibited throughout Scripture that his heart is for people from all nations, which should also be the burden of the local church.

Second: the agencies are good at what they do. Often times it will be quicker for the agencies to expedite the process of sending missionaries when the local church is not involved. However, that will lead to issues in the future between the church/missionary and the church/ mission agency. It is better to build stronger relationships with churches at the risk of delaying the process of the sending of a few missionaries for the hope of sending many more together in the future.

When each church and agency rightly recognizes their own primary abilities and strengths, they will joyfully embrace the other entity, which has what they lack. There must be open dialogue between the church and agency to better understand their unique roles and the relationship between them.

Just like the human body that is capable of special achievements, when the relationship between a church and agency is healthy, incredible accomplishments can be made for the glory of Christ and his work in this world.

From the Perspective of an Agency

Decio de Carvalho

And you Philippians yourselves know that in the beginning of the gospel, when I left Mace-donia, no church entered into partnership with me in giving and receiving, except you only. Even in Thessalonica you sent me help for my needs once and again. (Phil 4:15–16)

Growing up as the son of a pastor, I never noticed a clear dividing line or a reason to con-sider mission agencies as so distinct and separate from the church. Granted, I had limited contact with well-structured and well-established mission agencies, but the concept was not unfamiliar.

During a period of five years, as a family, we were sent to a region of the country where there were few churches, and the need to firmly establish the incipient ones as well as form new churches was huge. We were sent by a mission arm of the denomination. Later on as the director of the national office of an international mission, it was my natural conviction to remain deeply involved in my local church and to facilitate the ministry in such a way that it would be intrinsically connected with it.

In between, I had the privilege of being sent to serve in mission for several years. In those days the opportunity to send young adults for a period of mission work was very new to the church environment in the region. Yet even with shortfalls and limitations, there was a positive response; there would be wonderful fruit in the years to come, though not without a share of heartache and failure.

So what can I say about the church-mission agency relationship? The word that comes to my mind is collaboration. In Philippians 4 verses 15 and 16, the Apostle Paul uses precisely that concept when he is about to finish his letter to the believers in Philippi. He dedicates an important part in his letter to them, expressing his appreciation and recognizing their sac-rificial support for the ministry that he and his team were carrying out, and teaching about good use of God's resources.

The word used here is "koinoneo" meaning "to have communion with," "to partake." It is the same word used in Hebrews 2:14, which points to a family relationship type of partner-ship, and in 1 Peter 4:13, which goes much further and describes a partnership that involves trials and suffering together. It clearly implies that the believers in Philippi had made a commitment to Paul and to the work that he was doing, and they wanted to be a part of it, to partner with, to collaborate. It is important to remember at this point that Paul was originally sent, along with Barnabas, by the church in Antioch. Such strong support from a different church is a wonderful demonstration of collaboration and partnership in mission.

That is where I come from when I think of the church-mission agency relationship. Now, I realize the text is far from referring to our current concept of mission agency, and that there have been discussions, consultations, and books written about this subject. Often the focus is on dealing with one question: Should mission agencies even exist, and are they biblical? The purpose of this text is not to deal with that question, but allow me to point to a couple of examples of written material that look into it.

In an article published in the January 1998 edition of the *Mission Frontiers Magazine*, with the title "The Sender: Local Church and Mission Agency," author Jack Chapin, himself a pastor for over twenty-three years in three different churches, contends that for over two centuries churches and mission agencies worked together with mutual respect. He concludes his introduction of the topic with these words:

> Yet in the last two decades there has been an increasing crescendo of dissatisfaction over this time-honored and efficient arrangement of responsibilities. Some have felt, and not without some justification, that mission agencies have become too aloof and too independent, an entity unto themselves, ignoring the church—except for finances.[1]

Chapin then goes on to offer a detailed study of the biblical basis for the mission agency, strongly anchored in the first verses of Acts chapter 13. At the end of his article, he expressed his perspective on the issue with these words:

> Let us then labor together under the Lordship of Christ until the task is finished and our Lord returns. We shall then give account of ourselves to Him Who Is The Ultimate Sender.

Considering the question from a practical perspective, which is my intent, I quote another text. The Lausanne Movement dedicated great effort to discussion on the topic and an ample amount of the underlying issues. The Commission on Cooperation eventually published an edition of the *Lausanne Occasional Papers* (LOP: 24) with the title "Cooperating in World Evangelization: A Handbook on Church/Parachurch Relationships." It is an extensive document, but very practical and clear.

At the introduction to the contents of this guide, we find this description and a foundational statement connecting the topic to the Lausanne Covenant:

> It is true that in Philippians 1, Paul refers to envy and rivalry between different gospel-preaching groups and declares that even in this situation he rejoices. Yet this fact is to be understood as a symptom of Paul's humble Christ-centeredness, and not as an excuse for rivalry. What made him rejoice was that Christ was being preached, not that some of the preachers had ulterior motives (Phil 1:15–18).

It is this New Testament emphasis on "striving side by side for the faith of the gospel" which lies behind paragraph 7 of the Lausanne Covenant, which is entitled "Cooperation in Evangelism." It reads:

---

1   Jack Chapin, "The Sender: Local Church and Mission Agency: What Is the Best Relationship?" *Mission Frontiers*, Jan–Feb, 1998.

We affirm that the church's visible unity in truth is God's purpose. Evangelism also summons us to unity, because our oneness strengthens our witness, just as our disunity undermines our gospel of reconciliation. We recognize, however, that organizational unity may take many forms and does not necessarily forward evangelism. Yet we who share the same biblical faith should be closely united in fellowship, work, and witness. We confess that our testimony has sometimes been marred by sinful individualism and needless duplication. We pledge ourselves to seek a deeper unity in truth, worship, holiness, and mission. We urge the development of regional and functional cooperation for the furtherance of the church's mission, for strategic planning, for mutual encouragement, and for the sharing of resources and experience (John 17:21,23; Eph 4:3, 4; John 13:35; Phil 1:27; John 17:11–23).

At the conclusion of one of the many work sessions, the group came up with a long list of hindrances to good cooperation between churches and mission agencies and between different mission agencies, which they reduced to this very helpful short list of categories:

(i) Dogmatism about non-essentials and differing scriptural interpretations (matters of theology, conviction, terminology, tolerance).

(ii) The threat of conflicting authorities (matters of validity, mandate, accountability, fear).

(iii) The harmfulness of strained relationships (matters of attitude, prejudice, personality, fellowship).

(iv) The rivalry between ministries (matters of goals, duplication, specialization, umbrellas).

(v) The suspicion about finances (matters of fund-raising, publicity, overhead, overseas aid).

The paper goes on to discuss these categories at length, offering some very practical material for consideration.

There is ample material to study on this topic. An excellent list was published in the bibliography of a paper written by Philip James Leage, titled *The Mission Agency: An Investigation into Its Legitimacy and Its Future*. If you would like to explore the question and the various related topics, please refer to these materials.[2]

Changing Scenario
We have all perceived the change in this recent period. One of the truths about this new global mission scenario is that local churches want to be more involved, if not directly at the field level at least having an active contact with and some level of involvement in the ministries they help resource, either by giving money or supporting a missionary.

---

2   Phil Leage, *The Mission Agency: An Investigation into Its Legitimacy and Its Future*, diss., University of Gloucestershire. England.

This represents new or simply more areas of potential relationship challenges to work through. The tendency seems to be to move away or drop the partnership in mission concept altogether. This is a subject for another discussion, and there is valuable material about it. Considering these changes, in the above mentioned paper Leage offers some recommendations to mission agencies, calling on them to embrace the change, add flexibility in local church partnership, and to operate with a servant heart.

Fundamental Issue

A fundamental issue that may be the cause for much of the difficulty in the church-mission agency relationship in these recent times is how mission agencies deal with the home church of a candidate and with the churches they connect with. This was very clear to me while serving as a sending agency leader, and I was committed to figuring out how to do it right. Let me share some things I learned in the process, which I summarize into three areas of the mission process.

1. *Value the local church mission initiative.* Mobilize in such a way that will reinforce and build the church and its mission vision. In the effort to share the vision and particular ministry that God has given to the mission agency, the agency may neglect the fact that many of the churches they visit in order to mobilize prayer and financial support and to find new mission candidates may already have a mission program, and perhaps the church already has years of work and effort invested into a certain country, region, or ministry. Asking the church for this information before a visit, recognizing it, and looking for ways to build upon their experience is a very important first step. And once missionaries are sent, the mission agency should stay well connected with the home church, sending field reports, expressing appreciation for their continued support or checking with the church if there is an issue with the support, and discussing difficulties the missionary may be facing. I learned this the hard way, having failed to do it right at first.

2. *Value a simple but thorough screening and equipping process.* Look to the home church, both the pastor and his wider leadership group, to provide the best and most reliable profile of any mission candidate. You can look to others for medical, psychological, and physical evaluations later, but the home church leaders will be able to give the mission agency their most important information. Mission training and equipping, whatever the overall established requirements of the agency have been, should be adjusted to the individual as much as possible, based on the information gained during this process. Standard training for all has been a huge mistake, particularly in this day of such varied opportunities in the mission field. This essential value has been ignored in many cases, resulting in dramatic difficulties later on, for the missionary, the church, the mission agency and even many in the mission field. This one I realized early enough, and followed carefully.

3. *Value the individual, the missionary himself or herself, above projects and strategies.* Most of the ministry that mission agencies carry out is related to a plan or project. It is important to have an overall vision and mission and to prepare for the work at the field level by considering the whats, wheres, and hows. However, the value of the person

must be placed above these, and each one's gifts, talents, experiences, training, and ideas should all play a very important part in deciding how to best place him or her into the plan. It is important that the new missionary be prepared to adapt to various aspects of field ministry life or an organization's broader vision, mission, and goals, but adjustments to the project should also be possible to respect the individual, or a very intentional effort should be made to place new missionaries where they fit best and can make the most use of the abilities and gifts God has given them. This will go a long way in the church-mission agency relationship because the church is interested in seeing the energy of the missionary and the resources they have assigned to this venture being used in a fruitful and God honoring way. I am convinced this is an ongoing challenge for every mission agency, small and large, in any region of the world.

Practical Church–Mission Agency Partnership

If this partnership in mission between the church and the mission agency is going to happen, it must become a practical and dynamic process. The idea that we can put all of the aspects of this relationship into a memorandum or document and everything will be fine and will work out well is wrong. It is good to have a document, but many things will change over time so there must be a willingness to adjust and reformulate the agreements, without becoming unhappy and uncomfortable about each other.

This has been one of the biggest challenges I have observed in many of the church–mission agency partnerships, and it also applies to mission agency–mission agency partnerships. Either the church is not willing to let some changes be made to the initial plan they had agreed to for a particular missionary, or the mission agency is set on what they had planned and will not make adjustments after the missionary has been in the field for a while and it is obvious that there is a need to change things.

Clearly in this relationship there are different roles that may best be performed by the home church and those that the mission agency can handle very well, and most mission agencies will already have considered this aspect. This is a very important aspect to discuss with a church and perhaps review and revisit together every other year or so. There are various suggested lists to start with, if you need ideas on this. In his article, Chapin offers one.

Conclusion

When Jesus gave his command to go and make disciples among all the peoples of the world, he addressed the disciples both individually and collectively. Today we must respond both individually and collectively to complete the task. The church, mission agencies—and to add a bit more flavor—missionaries, mission leaders, and pastors have all received this command, and all have the responsibility to find ways to do it, together.

Chapin concludes his article with this call to partnership between the church and mission agencies:

> "As the Father has sent Me," Jesus said, "So send I you"(John 20:21)." The Holy Spirit said, "Separate to me Barnabas and Saul"(Acts 13:2). GOD IS THE ULTIMATE

SENDER. The church and mission agency are under His Lordship to get the job done together, respecting HIS specific calling to each. How tragic if in the midst of a dispute over control, the missionary never gets sent! Or if sent ill-advisedly he or she is severely handicapped in their ministry![3]

Questions for Reflection:

1. How could your church partner better with mission agencies?
2. How could your mission agency partner better with churches from which your cross-cultural missionaries come?
3. What changes have you seen, from both the mission agency's perspective and from the local church's perspective, in relation to this partnership? What has been gained? What has been lost?

References

Chapin, Jack. 1998. The Sender: Local Church and Mission Agency: What is the best relationship? In *Mission Frontiers*, Jan–Feb 1998.

Leage, Phil. The Mission Agency: An Investigation into Its Legitimacy and Its Future. Dissertation submitted in partial fulfilment of the requirements for a BA(Hons) degree in Theology with the University of Gloucestershire, England.

Decio de Carvalho is Brazilian and joined OM in 1979. He first served on the OM Ship Doulos for four years and then as director of Operation Mobilization in Brazil for the next ten years. With his wife Elba and three children, he worked in Central Asia for seven years. In 2001 they moved to Puerto Rico, Elba's native land, and Decio served as Director of RE-COMI, the Puerto Rico Missions Network. In November of 2009 he was appointed Executive Director of COMIBAM, the Cooperación Misionera Iberoamericana (Ibero American Mission Alliance). He is a member of the La Cumbre Christian and Missionary Alliance Church in San Juan, Puerto Rico.

Tom Hayes serves as the Executive Vice President of International Ministries for Insight for Living Ministries. He has been involved in international ministry efforts for many years helping to equip the Western church to be involved globally, regularly traveling to and speaking in countries around the world. Tom and his wife Katie are blessed with two sons.

---

3   Chapin, "The Sender."

CHAPTER 18

MOVEMENTS OF THE SPIRIT

Church Planting and the Church in Mission

Jim Memory

For the best part of fifteen years I was a church planter in Spain with the European Christian Mission (ECM). Europe is considered by many as the most resistant continent to the gospel. I have certainly experienced that resistance but I have also experienced surprising movements of God's Spirit. As a result I have come to understand that mission in general, and church planting in particular, is first and foremost about "joining in with the Spirit."[1]

This chapter asks a simple question: does our thinking about church planting, church planting movements, and missional church take into account that fundamental insight? As we consider the church in mission today, and specifically the genesis of new Christian communities, are we being sufficiently sensitive to the movements of the Spirit?

The Spirit and the Church in Mission

The understanding of church and mission has been transformed over the last few decades by the concept of *missio Dei*—the realization that mission is not merely an activity of the church but rather the result of God's initiative.

As Bosch put it,

> Mission (is) understood as being derived from the very nature of God. It (is) thus put in the context of the doctrine of the Trinity, not of ecclesiology or soteriology. The classical doctrine of the *missio Dei* as God the Father sending the Son, and God the Father and the Son sending the Spirit (is) expanded to include yet another "movement"; Father, Son, and Holy Spirit sending the church into the world.[2]

Jesus' words, "As the Father has sent me, I am sending you" (John 20:21) are a call to his disciples in every age to participate in this Trinitarian missional "movement" from God to the world with the Spirit of God rather than the church as the chief protagonist. Through

---

1   Kirsteen Kim, *Joining in with the Spirit* (London: Epworth Press, 2009).
2   David Bosch, *Transforming Mission* (Maryknoll, NY: Orbis, 1991), 390.

participating in what God is doing through his Spirit, the church fulfils its purpose in God's mission.

Unsurprisingly, this has led to a fundamental reappraisal of the role of the church in mission. As Guder puts it, "we have begun to see that the church of Jesus Christ is not the purpose or goal of the gospel, but rather its instrument and witness" (1998:5). It is in this context that any evaluation of contemporary church planting must take place.

Church Planting

Though the expression *church planting* has been around for less than a century it is evidently not a new idea. Every church was "planted" at some time or another. Whatever the process or strategy or nomenclature, whenever and wherever people have become Jesus followers throughout the last 2,000 years, new Christian communities have been established. If forming part of a Christian community is a normal part of following Jesus, then church planting is a normal part of Christian mission.

Church planting is a topic that tends to polarize people, particularly in Europe. On one side there are those who consider it to be divisive and unnecessary, working against unity and our common testimony in Christ. On the other are those who see church planting as a biblical mandate and "the single most effective evangelistic methodology under heaven."[3]

Churches are planted for all sorts of motives, not all of them honorable, but far away from these heated debates in the churches of the West the movement of God's Spirit has established new Christian communities in Africa, Asia, and Latin America at an extraordinary rate.[4]

And yet as we shall see, much of what is written about church planting, missional church, and even church planting movements is by missiologists from Europe and North America. Their approach is generally analytical and strategic rather than an exercise in spiritual discernment.

Traditional Church Planting

Church planters are activists and pragmatists more often than not. They tend to write "how to" manuals setting out the stages of the church planting process and the challenges that each phase presents. There are a few notable exceptions where theological considerations are to the fore, but the vast majority of church planting titles are analytical and practical.[5]

Key considerations in the early stages tend to be the location of the plant, the demographics of the community, the methodology or model that is to be used. They then turn to consider

---

3   Peter Wagner, *Church Planting for a Greater Harvest* (Ventura, CA: Regal Books, 1990), 5.
4   Stuart Murray, *Planting Churches: A Framework for Practitioners* (Carlisle: Paternoster, 2008), 19–46.
5   David Shenk and Ervin Stutzman, *Creating Communities of the Kingdom* (Scottdale: Herald Press, 1988); Stuart Murray, *Church Planting: Laying Foundations* (Carlisle: Paternoster, 1998); see e.g., David Hesselgrave, *Planting Churches Cross-Culturally* (Grand Rapids, MI: Baker Books, 1980); Johan Lukasse, *Churches with Roots* (Eastbourne: Monarch, 1990); M. Robinson and S. Christine, *Planting Tomorrow's Churches Today* (Eastbourne: Monarch, 1992); Murray, *Planting Churches*.

the making of contacts and evangelism, discipleship, developing leaders, the structure of the new congregation, and finally its reproduction.

Even the recent *Global Church Planting* has a similar structure.[6] After a brief theological treatment, the authors quickly turn to strategic considerations and then to a detailed treatment of the developmental phases, which takes up nearly half of the book. The authors are to be commended for the inclusion of many excellent global case studies to illustrate their points, but overall the impression is of yet another "how to" manual. Is church planting in the world today, as the subtitle suggests, simply a matter of adopting "best practices for multiplication"? Or do we need a more radical reappraisal of church and mission that relocates and redefines church planting as fundamentally not about strategy but about participating in a movement of the Spirit?

Church Planting Movements

It was over one hundred years ago that Roland Allen first suggested that the missionary strategies of his time, rather than helping, were actually hindering the reproduction of churches. His revolutionary books *Missionary Methods: St. Paul's or Ours?* and its sequel, *The Spontaneous Expansion of the Church and the Causes Which Hinder It*, shone a light on the chronic dependency in much of the mission work of his day and contrasted it with Paul who had a "profound belief and trust in the Holy Spirit indwelling his converts and the church of which they are members."[7] The explosive growth of Christianity in the global South in the postcolonial period has shown that Allen was right.

With dramatic speed and vitality, indigenous church planting movements in many countries of the world are establishing churches at a rate that many of us struggle to comprehend. A movement that began in one restricted access country in Asia in November 2000 has resulted in 1.7 million baptisms and the planting of over 150,000 churches.[8] Even in secular Europe migrant churches have enjoyed spectacular growth with the Redeemed Christian Church of God, seeing over 700 churches planted over the last thirty years in the UK alone.

The Global Research Department of the International Mission Board have established three criteria to assess Church Planting Movements (CPMs). To be recognized as a CPM there must be:

- A 25% annual growth rate in total churches for the past two years
- A 50% annual growth rate in new churches for the past two years
- Field-based affirmation that a CPM is emerging

Despite these very challenging criteria, by the end of 2008 over 200 CPMs had been identified globally.[9]

---

6   Craig Ott and Gene Wilson, *Global Church Planting* (Grand Rapids, MI: Baker Academic, 2011).
7   Roland Allen, *Missionary Methods: St Paul's or Ours* (Cambridge: World Dominion Press, 1962), vii.
8   David Garrison, "Church Planting Movement FAQS," *Mission Frontiers*, 33:1 (2011), 10–11.
9   Ibid.

It is, of course, hugely encouraging to read stories of church planting movements around the world, but once again we might ask whether the reduction of CPMs to a list of ten elements is not taming the movement of God's Spirit by means of analysis.[10] Can a strategy of facilitating CPMs jump-start movements of the Spirit? And will all movements of God's Spirit be the same? History would tell us otherwise I suggest.

Missional Movements

The origins of the contemporary missional movement can be traced back to Lesslie Newbigin. Newbiggin argued that changes have taken place in contemporary Western culture over the past seventy years which mean that there is a completely new context for the church in mission. This context, which some have labelled post-Christendom, requires more than better church-planting practices.[11] It requires a completely fresh reimagining of church and mission for the West.

Responding to Newbigin's challenge, the Gospel and Our Culture Network in the USA published *Missional Church: A Vision for the Sending of the Church in North America*.[12] Such was the impact of the book that the word missional has passed into common usage, but more significantly the book set in motion a wave of other titles which worked out its implications.

In their excellent review of the trajectories of the missional conversation since 1998, van Gelder and Zschiele set out the six arguments of missional church:[13]

1. The church in (the West) is now located within a dramatically changed context.
2. The good news of the gospel announced by Jesus as the reign of God needs to shape the identity of the missional church.
3. The missional church with its identity rooted in the reign of God must live as an alternative community in the world.
4. The missional church needs to understand that the Holy Spirit cultivates communities that represent the reign of God.
5. The missional church is to be led by missional leadership that focuses on equipping all of God's people for mission.
6. The missional church needs to develop missional structures for shaping its life and ministry as well as missional connectedness within the larger church.

---

10   David Garrison's research identified ten common elements in all CPMs and this encouraged the IMB to realign the vision and strategy of all of their missionaries to the facilitation of CPMs around the world (*Church Planting Movements* (Richmond, VA: International Missions Board 1999), 7, 33–36): 1. Prayer, 2. Abundant gospel sowing, 3. Intentional church planting, 4. Scriptural authority, 5. Local leadership, 6. Lay leadership, 7. Cell or house churches, 8. Churches planting churches, 9. Rapid reproduction, 10. Healthy churches.

11   Michael Frost and Alan Hirsch, *The Shaping of Things to Come* (Peabody, MA: Hendrickson, 2003); Stuart Murray, *Post-Christendom: Church and Mission in a Strange New World* (Carlisle: Paternoster, 2004).

12   Darrell Guder and Lois Barrett, eds., *Missional Church: A Vision for the Sending of the Church in North America* (Grand Rapids, MI: Eerdmans, 1998).

13   Craig Van Gelder and Dwight Zscheile, *Missional Church in Perspective* (Grand Rapids, MI: Baker Academic, 2011), 49–52.

This is all part of the necessary reimagination of the church in mission for the West and is to be welcomed. However, just as with CPMs, the acceptance of these propositions, or alternative expressions such as Hirsch's missional DNA, are no recipe for success.[14] The movement of the Spirit cannot be bound, even by the postmodern language of missional church.

Movements of the Spirit: Reflections on Church Planting Today

Space will simply not allow me to engage in a broad theological and missiological reflection on the role of the Spirit in God's mission. I will limit myself to the implications for church planting of understanding mission as joining in with the Spirit.

What the Spirit Is Doing Is Bigger than the Church (and Church Planting)

Church planters tend to see establishing churches as the goal of mission. The planting of churches increases the number of instruments that the Spirit of God has at his disposal, but it is no guarantee of effectiveness. In fact, as my own research has proved, church planters rarely measure their effectiveness in any other way than numbers of converts and churches planted, as if these were the only criteria that matter.[15] Roxburgh cautions us about what he calls the "ecclesiocentric obsession," where the success of our church (or church plant) becomes our focus rather than God's mission.[16] Understanding that the Spirit (and not the church) is the true protagonist of mission keeps us from such reductionism.

The Spirit's Work in Context

If we recognize that the Spirit of God is present and active in mission in the world and that the church's role is to participate in this missional movement, then we will attend to our local context. Contextual church planting will not seek to establish congregations that exist in isolation from a "godless" culture. Rather, "it will seek to form new Christian communities in which the Spirit's work in context is fused with the Spirit's work in the church."[17] Unfortunately, as Roland Allen showed, the desire for control over daughter congregations has frequently inhibited spontaneous multiplication. The discovery of dozens of contextual church planting movements around the world demonstrates just how powerful it is when the Spirit's work in context and in the church are combined. And of course this finds its

---

14   Hirsch argues that the following six elements of missional DNA (mDNA) or Apostolic Genius are always present in Jesus movements: Jesus is Lord, Disciple-making, Missional-incarnational impulse, Apostolic environment, Organic systems, Communitas not community. Alan Hirsch, *The Forgotten Ways: Reactivating the Missional Church* (Grand Rapids, MI: Baker Books, 2006).

15   J. Memory, "Effective Church Planting in Europe," *Vista* 6, 1–3, (2011) Accessed 18th Feb 2014 (http://europeanmission.files.wordpress.com/2011/08/vista-issue-6-july-2011-final.pdf); J. Memory, "How Can Me Measure the Effectiveness of Church Planting?" in E. Van de Poll and J. Appleton, eds., *Church Planting in Europe* (Eugene: Wipf & Stock, 2015), 193–215.

16   Alan Roxburgh, *Missional: Joining God in the Neighborhood* (Grand Rapids, MI: Baker Books, 2011), 48.

17   Michael Moynagh, *Church for Every Context* (London: SCM Press, 2012), 133.

echo in the "missional-incarnational" language of many missional church authors.[18] Mission is thus understood as "joining God in the neighborhood."[19]

The Uncontrollable Spirit

The Spirit of God is not subject to human control. As Jesus himself said, "The wind blows wherever it pleases" (John 3:8). And the Spirit's missional movement is no different. It is unpredictable. It is not subject to strategic analysis.

Yet, as highlighted above, most books on church planting break down the planting process into simple stages or principles that will lead to success. Garrison's attempt to discern the elements of church planting movements can easily become a ten-step plan while Hirsch's six elements of missional DNA could pose the same dangers for the missional movement.[20]

Church planters, students of church planting movements, and missional church thinkers must resist the temptation to reverse-engineer the movement of God's spirit in mission.

The Migrant Spirit

Since the Day of Pentecost the work of the Spirit of God has been evident in the dissemination of the gospel as peoples have migrated around the world. The Modern Missionary Movement was inextricably linked to the Great European Migration.[21] And over the past century the reversal of migration patterns have brought countless millions of Africans, Asians, and Latin Americans to Europe and North America leading to the planting of thousands of churches, many of them in countries where native churches are in decline.

Church planters must cooperate with the Holy Spirit in this too, both in engaging and supporting the leaders of these new churches in formerly Christian homelands, and in recognizing the presence of many who, in other times, were inaccessible to all but the most intrepid of missionaries but who are now living next door to us.

The Uniting Spirit

> We may have recognized the missionary context of the local church but we have not yet understood that in mission we are linked into the worldwide movement of the Spirit, and therefore with other churches worldwide.[22]

Church planting need not be divisive, provided that planters take account of what the Spirit is already doing through other Christian communities. My own experience in Cordoba, Spain, where missionaries and churches from across the denominations work together in planting new churches has borne this out. Collaborative church planting is not easy but it is a powerful testimony to the movement of the Spirit both to the church and to the world.[23]

---

18   Hirsch, *The Forgotten Ways*; Michael Frost, *The Road to Missional* (Grand Rapids, MI: Baker Books, 2011).
19   Roxburgh, *Missional*.
20   Hirsch, *The Forgotten Ways*.
21   Andrew Walls, "Christian Mission in a Five-hundred-year Context," in Andrew Walls and Cathy Ross, eds. *Mission in the Twenty-First Century* (London: Darton, Longman and Todd, 2008).
22   Kim, *Joining in with the Spirit*, 283.
23   J. Memory, "Collaborative Church Planting in Córdoba, Spain," in E. Van de Poll and J. Appleton, eds., *Church Planting in Europe* (Eugene: Wipf & Stock, 2015), 254–262.

Conclusion

As you do not know the path of the wind, or how the body is formed in a mother's womb, so you cannot understand the work of God, the Maker of all things (Ecc 11:5).

God's mission is beyond our comprehension and yet God invites the church to join in. If mission is defined as "finding out where the Holy Spirit is at work and joining in" then "discernment is the first act of mission."[24]

This chapter has sought to evaluate contemporary church planting in the light of a single fundamental insight: that the Spirit of God, not the church, is the chief protagonist of mission. Church planters, students of church planting movements, and missional church practitioners must balance their actions and strategic thinking with sincere reflection as to the movements of the Spirit in our day. As two missional church writers have rightly put it:

We need to develop skills of reading the winds of the Spirit, testing the waters of the culture, and running with the currents of God's call so that we are not lost on the journey.[25]

Questions for Reflection:

1. Memory asks if we take into account the fundamental insight that church planting is, first and foremost, about "joining in with the Spirit"? What would be your answer to his question? What have you seen from your experience that could confirm that affirmation?

2. Do you agree that the Spirit of God, not the church, is the chief protagonist of mission?

3. The author challenges us to "a more radical reappraisal of church and mission that relocates and redefines church planting as fundamentally not about strategy but about participating in a movement of the Spirit." Do you see that need as well? What would then be the implications for church planting?

References

Allen, Roland. 1962. *Missionary Methods: St Paul's or Ours*. Cambridge: World Dominion Press.

————. 2006. *The Spontaneous Expansion of the Church*. Cambridge: Lutterworth Press.

---

24   James Dunn, "The Christ and the Spirit: Collected Essays," vol. 2 *Pneumatology* (Edinburgh: T & T Clark, 1998), 72.

25   Alan Roxburgh and M. Scott Boren, *Introducing the Missional Church* (Grand Rapids, MI: Baker Books, 2009), 25.

Bosch, David. 1991. *Transforming Mission: Paradigm Shifts in Theology of Mission*. Maryknoll, NY: Orbis.

Dunn, James D. G. 1998. *The Christ and the Spirit: Collected Essays,* vol. 2. Pneumatology. Edinburgh: T. and T. Clark.

Frost, Michael. 2011. *The Road to Missional*. Grand Rapids, MI: Baker Books.

Frost, Michael, and Alan Hirsch. 2003. *The Shaping of Things to Come*. Peabody, MA: Hendrickson.

Garrison, David. 1999. *Church Planting Movements*. Richmond, VA: International Missions Board.

———. 2011. Church Planting Movement FAQS. *Mission Frontiers,* 33(2).

Guder, Darrell, and Lois Barrett, eds. 1998. *Missional Church: A Vision for the Sending of the Church in North America*. Grand Rapids, MI: Eerdmans.

Hesselgrave, David. 1980. *Planting Churches Cross-Culturally*. Grand Rapids, MI: Baker Books.

Hirsch, Alan. 2006. *The Forgotten Ways: Reactivating the Missional Church*. Grand Rapids, MI: Baker Books.

Kim, Kirsteen. 2009. *Joining in with the Spirit*. London: Epworth Press.

Lukasse, Johan. 1990. *Churches with Roots*. Eastbourne, UK: Monarch.

Memory, James. 2011. Effective Church Planting in Europe. *Vista,* 6: 1–3. Accessed February 18, 2014. http://europeanmission.files.wordpress.com/2011/08/vista-issue-6-july-2011-final.pdf.

———. 2015. Collaborative Church Planting in Córdoba, Spain. In *Church Planting in Europe*. Eds. E. Van de Poll and J. Appleton. Eugene: Wipf & Stock.

———. 2015. How Can We Measure the Effectiveness of Church Planting? In *Church Planting in Europe*. Ed. E. Van de Poll and J. Appleton. Eugene: Wipf & Stock.

Moynagh, Michael. 2012. *Church for Every Context*. London: SCM Press.

Murray, Stuart. 1998. *Church Planting: Laying Foundations*. Carlisle: Paternoster.

———. 2004. *Post-Christendom: Church and Mission in a Strange New World*. Carlisle: Paternoster.

———. 2008. *Planting Churches: A Framework for Practitioners*. Carlisle: Paternoster.

Ott, Craig, and Gene Wilson. 2011. *Global Church Planting*. Grand Rapids, MI: Baker Academic.

Robinson, M., and S. Christine. 1992. *Planting Tomorrow's Churches Today*. Eastbourne, UK: Monarch.

Roxburgh, Alan J. 2011. *Missional: Joining God in the Neighborhood*. Grand Rapids, MI: Baker Books.

Roxburgh, Alan J., and M. Scott Boren. 2009. *Introducing the Missional Church.* Grand Rapids, MI: Baker Books.

Shenk, David W., and Ervin R. Stutzman. 1988. *Creating Communities of the Kingdom.* Scottdale, PA: Herald Press.

Van Gelder, Craig, and Dwight Zscheile. 2011. *Missional Church in Perspective.* Grand Rapids, MI: Baker Academic.

Wagner, Peter. 1990. *Church Planting for a Greater Harvest.* Ventura, CA: Regal Books.

Walls, Andrew. 2008. Christian Mission in a Five-Hundred-Year Context. In *Mission in the Twenty-First Century.* Ed. A. Walls and C. Ross London: Darton, Longman and Todd.

Jim Memory is Lecturer in European Mission at Redcliffe College in Gloucester, UK and coeditor of *Vista*, Redcliffe's quarterly bulletin of research-based information on mission in Europe. He was a church planter in southern Spain for fourteen years and is a member of the International Leadership Team of the European Christian Mission.

CHAPTER 19

INDIGENOUS CHURCHES

ETHNIC AND MULTICULTURAL

Samuel Cueva

Since the 1980s and the beginning of the twenty-first century, there have been increasing changes in different ways and levels of doing Christian mission. There are new initiatives that show the dynamic changes of a "church in mission." One of these changes is the propagation of more indigenous initiatives that emerge from the church's mission activity with models of ethnic and multicultural churches. This paper will discuss the historical background of indigenous churches and the impact of ethnic and multicultural churches as well as their main characteristics from a missiological perspective.

Historical and Theoretical Foundation

To understand the mission-phenomenon of indigenous churches it is vital to clarify the historical background and its theoretical foundation. Accommodation or adaptation have been used as similar concepts to the term indigenization.[1] Today, "contextualization" has become the new concept for indigenization, but in a broader sense this term includes sociocultural, economic, and political viewpoints.[2] Because culture is a dynamic process, ethnic groups have been damaged consciously or unconsciously by the evangelization of Christendom. During the period of evangelization in Latin America, more than 800 languages and cultures disappeared within Christendom, so this requires us to exercise care in promoting change to indigenous groups. It must come from within, not from without.

Historically, "indigenous" church is commonly thought to be one that meets the "three selfs" mission theory of mission developed by Henry Van and Rufus Anderson during the nineteenth century Christian mission. In addition to self-support, self-propagation, and self-governing, in the 1990s David Bosch added the need of self-theologizing, and in 2003 I proposed the need of a self-missiology.[3] The three self mission theory was empowered

---

1   David Bosch, *Transforming Mission: Paradigm Shifts in Theology of Mission* (Maryknoll, NY: Orbis Books, 1991), 447–448.
2   Tom van der Meer, "Accommodation/Adaptation," in *Dictionary of Mission Theology*, John Corrie (Nottingham: IVP, 2007), 2.
3   See Samuel Cueva, "From the Local Mission to a Global Mission," MA Dissertation (University of Birmingham, United Kingdom, 2003); Bosch, *Transforming Mission*, 451–452.

by Roland Allen, an Anglican British missionary to North China. His book *The Spontaneous Expansion of the Church* provides key issues and principles of an indigenous church which somehow can still be applied to the twenty-first century mission.[4]

The term "indigenous" refers in mission to churches that reflect the cultural distinctive of their ethno linguistic group.[5] Therefore, the missionary effort to establish indigenous churches is an effort to plant churches that fit naturally into their environment and to avoid planting churches that replicate Western patterns.[6] An indigenous church is sometimes characterized by a self hymnology, a self lay people, and a self contextual theology, or ethno theology. Symbols, worship, leadership, prayer, and healing are also its characteristics.

An important practitioner of indigenization within the Assemblies of God is Melvin Hodges, a missionary who worked in El Salvador. He started to put in practice the indigenous church concept, and from his experience he permeated his denomination with this mission theory. As a result, between the 1980s and 2000, Assemblies of God has grown from 110,098 churches to 187,392 in Latin America.[7]

In his book *Missionary Methods: St Paul's or Ours?*, Roland Allen tries to explain the importance of mission strategy developed by the apostle Paul for planting indigenous churches. Allen suggests that Paul's principles in founding churches have five key principles which are as follows:

1. Teaching must be understandable.
2. Organization must be understood and maintained.
3. Finances must be administrated free of any foreign influence.
4. Mutual responsibility must be inculcated.
5. Authority must be given freely and immediately.[8]

With this explanation in mind, I understand that the presence of indigenous churches is expressed in a form of ethnic and multicultural churches. These models are signs of the capability of the gospel to be translatable to every culture by intentional missiology or through diaspora[9] or migration,[10] which are tools for mission. Accordingly, Samuel Escobar

---

4   Roland Allen, *The Spontaneous Expansion of the Church* (Cambridge: Lutterworth Press, 2006, first published 1927).

5   Scott Moreau, ed., *Evangelical Dictionary of World Missions*, Grand Rapids, MI: Baker Books, 2000), 483; Bosch, *Transforming Mission*, 448–449.

6   Bosch, *Transforming Mission*, 483.

7   Melvin Hodges, *The Indigenous Church* (Springfield: Gospel Publishing House, 2009, first published 1953), 14.

8   Roland Allen, *Missionary Methods: St Paul's or Ours?* (Grand Rapids, MI, Eerdmans, 1962, first published 1912), 151.

9   See further: Enoch Wan, ed. *Diaspora Missiology: Theory, Methodology, and Practice* (Portland: Institute of Diaspora Studies, 2011). Wan and other specialists have made a great contribution to the diaspora mission theology and its application.

10   See further: Concejo Evangélico de Madrid and Seminario Teológico Bautista, eds., *Las Iglesias y la Migración* (Madrid: Rivadeneyra, SA, 2003), a study of churches and migration in the context of Spain.

explains that the Christian faith is a faith that was born to travel; it is a missionary faith by excellence.[11] Therefore, he states that:

> The nature of this religion in itself is an impulse to cross-cultural and geographical frontiers so that today it is not possible to understand the history of humanity without reference to the process of expansion of Christianity around the world.[12]

This missionary dynamism of ethnic or multicultural churches is not mission activity result of McGavran's theoretical missiology of "homogenous unit principle," where people can become Christians without crossing any racial, linguistic, or racial barrier.[13] It is rather models of God's dynamic tools he provides for the church's mission activity. To avoid distraction, I will provide models later in this article to show the impact of this mission activity, especially within the European context.

Theological and Missiological Understanding

Indigenous churches are also not what the missiological concept *panta ta ethne* describes in terms of sociological or ethnological categories[14] such as "the classes," tribes, lineages, and people of earth. *Panta ta ethne* of Matthew 28:19 is rather a theological meaning of salvation history that includes Jews and Gentiles—the whole world.[15] However, we do not deny the presence of our cultural ethnicity which must always be tested and judged by Scripture. Hence, indigenous churches happen as a result of the Holy Spirit at work in mission allowing the church to use complementary models for the fulfilment of the *missio Dei*. Ethnic and multicultural church models become signs of the mystery of the sovereign Lord.

The Bible provides a foundation for multicultural churches as described by the Christological teaching given in the gospels and the books of Acts and Ephesians. Multicultural churches fulfill Christ's Great Commission of Matthew 28:18–20; to proclaim the gospel to all nations is understood as worldwide mission. But we have to avoid the misconception that one verse holds the totality of Christ's mystery of mission.[16]

Defining an Ethnic and Multicultural Church

It is worthwhile clarifying that ethnic (apart from tribal mission) and multicultural churches operate mainly within the context of urban and mega cities such as Tokyo, Los Angeles, New York, London, Paris, Milan, Rome, Berlin, or Madrid.

---

11   Samuel Escobar, "Las Migraciones y la Misión de la Iglesia Cristiana," in *Las Iglesias y la Migración*, Consejo Evangélico de Madrid and Seminario Teológico Bautista, eds. (Madrid: Rivadeneyra, SA), 129–154.

12   Ibid., 129.

13   For the analysis of "Homogenous Units," see Wilbert Shenk, ed., *Exploring Church Growth* (Grand Rapids, MI: Eerdmans, 1983). See also Stott, "The Pasadena Statement on the Homogenous Unit Principle" (Lausanne Occasional Papers,1996), 56–68. Donald McGavran, *Understanding Church Growth* (Grand Rapids, MI: Eerdmans, 1970), 198.

14   Bosch, see the whole theological explanation in Shenk, *Exploring Church Growth*, 218–244.

15   Bosch in Shenk, *Exploring Church Growth*, 229, 234–235.

16   Bosch in Shenk, *Exploring Church Growth*, 241.

Max Weber's definition of an ethnic group remains as the most commonly used.[17] However, here we provide a more general definition: An ethnic group is a given community identified by particular characteristics such as culture, race, beliefs, values, geographical origin, history, costumes, institutions language, and tradition. Politically, ethnic groups lack sovereignty which makes them different from nation-states. Sociologically, ethnicity refers to a minority group within the country where these people live.[18] Accordingly, an ethnic church can be defined as a segment of people integrated or less integrated within a specific society. Integration into a society can be fast or slow.

Key elements of an ethnic church are the predominant influence of culture, language, and identity. Culture tends to be retained, language of origin is predominant, and identity lacks integration into a receiving culture. The Willowbank Report says the broad definition of culture is "the patterned ways in which people do things together."[19] Culture includes the beliefs, values, customs, and institutions that hold a society together. Hence, gospel and culture are always in dynamic tension within mission.

An ethnic church retains things such as forms of dress, a model of Holy Communion, church architecture, and standards of cultural morality. In other words an ethnic church is always in tension with issues of identity and tensions of inculturation within a different society of its origins. Inculturation expresses the dynamic and reciprocal relation between the gospel, church, and culture[20] and involves the entire context such as social, economic, political, religious, etc.[21] Hence, as Glenn Schwartz explains, this identity is what the group feels it needs to be faithful to its heritage, both theologically and culturally.[22]

A multicultural church is not easy to define. Scholars and practitioners have different views. However, here we provide Ken Davis' definition as the more understandable for our purpose.[23] For Davis, multicultural church is "a biblical community of believers who (1) intentionally recruit, recognize and embrace a diversity of peoples; (2) are committed to a racial reconciliation; and (3) are working out administrative structures that assure the continuation of both unity and diversity. Davis emphasizes the need of a pluralistic strategy for a multi-ethnic evangelism within a pluralistic society.

A multicultural, called also a multiethnic or international church is a group of culturally and ethnically diverse people who meet as one body. A multicultural church is characterized by the diversity of its congregation, which determines its mission, worship styles, and church

---

17   Max Weber, *The Ethnicity Reader: Nationalism, Multiculturalism and Migration* (Cambridge: Polity Press, 1997), 18–19.

18   Anthony Giddens, *Sociology* (Cambridge, Polity Press, 2009), 635.

19   John Stott, ed., *Making Christ Known* (Carlisle: Paternoster Press, 1996), 78.

20   See further Michael Pocock, Gailyn Van Rheenen and Douglas McConnell, *The Changing Face of World Missions* (Grand Rapids, MI: Baker Academic, 2005), 329.

21   Bosch, *Transforming Mission*, 453.

22   See further Glenn Schwartz, "Ethnic Churches and Identity in Missiological Perspective," *World Mission Associates*, February 4, 2003, revised, http://www.wmausa.org/page.aspx?id=83836.

23   Ken Davis, "Multicultural Church Planting Models," *The Journal of Ministry and Theology*, Spring, 115, http://www.bbc.edu/journal/volume7_1/Multicultural_Church-Davis.pdf.

culture. It requires developing a clear vision and mission that people are keen on following. Martin Lee provides three concepts for a better missiological understanding of ethnic and multicultural churches:[24]

1. Monoethnic: A church where the vast majority of members are from one ethnic grouping or a few similar ethnic groupings. There may also be a language element as well. Some may be formed due to actual or perceived racism.

2. Monocultural or homogenous: A church based around a particular uniting principle—be it class, age, language, upbringing, etc. This would include a white middle class church which would be unable to change to accept working class people—i.e., most of the white evangelical churches in southern England!!

3. Multicultural: A church where there are people of all backgrounds, cultures, classes, income levels, and ethnicities.

Main Characteristics and Issues

There are at least three characteristics that promote ethnic churches. The affinity of language, cultural identity, and residential concentration are important factors in producing the ethnic church phenomenon.[25] Therefore, the presence of ethnic minorities encourage the formation of ethnic churches.

In *Becoming a Multicultural Church*, Laurene Beth Bowers explains that "a multicultural church builds solidarity among the marginalized groups and confronts the power structure of the dominant group."[26] Thus, the distribution of power is crucial for a multicultural church. This implies that language for example, would be defined by the majority of the dominant ethnic group or by the country of adoption.

One of the issues to address within ethnic and multicultural churches is of power. When a congregation begins to look somewhat international or multicultural it is time to look at the mission structure and also the staff administration. One would begin slowly and gradually to introduce key leaders from various national and racial backgrounds into the various boards and committees. It would be possible to recruit and train lay-ministers from varied ethnic backgrounds to undertake various ministries and to collaborate in pulpit ministry. Being a multicultural church implies having people of other ethnicities move from just attending church to becoming integral collaborators of the church family. I understand there is a need to work even more on this aspect of power.

Ed Stetzer in his book *Planting New Churches* states that most growth in church planting in recent years has occurred among ethnic groups and he provides different ethnic church planting models the Nazarene Church has researched.[27]

---

24   Lee, electronic information sent to the author on 18th December 2013.

25   See the case of Latinos in America in "Changing Faiths: Latinos and the Transformation of American Religion (http://www.pewhispanic.org/2007/04/25/vi-the-ethnic-church/).

26   Laurene Beth Bowers, *Becoming a Multicultural Church* (Cleveland, OH: Pilgrim Press, 2006), 14.

27   Ed Stetzer, *Planting New Churches* (Nashville, TN: Broadman & Holman, 2003), 159–164.

In the UK, one of the biggest cultural divides is based on social class rather than ethnicity. In this way Martin Lee suggests the following characteristics:[28]

1. *Monoethnic.* Church structure, worship, and activities are based around the cultural norms of the predominant ethnic community. There is one language of operation and the leaders are all from the same ethnic group. It attracts its own and is unable to adapt to people of other ethnicities. People are never taken out of their comfort zones to address the breadth of God's people. People feel safe. New converts must conform to the predominant behaviors. There may be sensitivity to feelings of racism from the dominant people group if the group is from an ethnic minority. One predominant feature is that people are assimilated. The key issue is that it has a theological and ecclesiological flaw seeming to deny oneness in Christ as he has reconciled people for all ethnicities into one body, the church.

2. *Monocultural or homogenous.* This church has similar issues to a monoethnic church. There is one "language" of operation, but that might include dialect. Just try speaking Scause (from Liverpool) in a middle class Queen's English church. All the leaders again are from the same majority group. New converts come from the same group and must conform to the predominant behaviors. People again feel comfortable and safe, again with a string sense of belonging. The predominant feature is that people are assimilated. The key issue is that this also has a theological and ecclesiological flaw seeming to deny oneness and liberty of expression in Christ, and that Christ has reconciled people from all backgrounds and ethnicities and brought them into his church that the majority may not faithfully represent.

3. *Multicultural.* A church where there are people of all backgrounds, culture, social class, income levels, and ethnicities. It will be led by people from different social classes and ethnic backgrounds with a diverse leadership. The church will try to change if people from different backgrounds, cultures, ethnicity or language group come along. Worship will be in different styles, with acceptance of all those styles and even languages. People are "integrated" rather than assimilated. A key issue is that it may find it hard to attract outsiders as they tend to gravitate to their own culture. But because it is hard does not mean that we should not aim for it.

The Impact of Ethnic and Multicultural Churches

There are more than twenty Latino ethnic churches and more than thirty-two Brazilian churches in London. One of these is Congregación de Evangélicos en Londres, which has 250 Latin-American members led by the Colombian pastor Edgar Ibarguen; they rent the building of an Anglican church. Brazilian pastor Jackson Antonio leads Cathedral Revival Church, a Brazilian church where the Portuguese language is spoken. Kingsway International Christian Centre is a 12,000 member African church led by the Nigerian Matthew Ashimolowo.

The British Anglican Church All Souls Langham Place in London led by Hugh Palmer has a multicultural model. People from over 60 nationalities attend services. Palmer empowers

---

28   Lee, electronic information sent to the author on 18th December 2013.

a multiethnic staff to promote cultural diversity in its mission activity. They focus on the hundreds of students from different countries that come to study in British universities. The church has an intentional plan to include people from different nationalities in their mission activity. Palmer says:

> All Souls has some 60+ different nationalities. We define ourselves as an "international community" because in the light of the previous fact we are one. We are trying to reach a multicultural society because the West End of London is very multicultural. We have around 2,000 people worshiping with us on a Sunday.[29]

In Germany, the Baptist Union has statistics of 201 migrant churches worshiping on German soil; 16 of them are Latin American-speaking congregations.[30] Two models in Germany that provide clear signs of the non-Western movement in Europe include the Ghanaian Life Church in Dusseldorf and the Stadtmission Wanne Eickel—an international church led by Tomas Milk in Herne, which has 130 people from 25 different nationalities. Milk began an international church in 1998 within the denomination Evangelische Gesellschaft.[31]

While the second model has a team-leadership which includes people from Turkey, Paraguay, and Germany, the first has an international team led by Pastor Richard Aidoo[32] from Ghana. Aidoo founded New Life Church in 1989; 400 people attend church services every Sunday representing 38 different nationalities. Services are held in English, Spanish, French, Farsi (Iranian), and Kurdish-Sorani. One key characteristic is that all services are translated into German. These two models indicate what global missiology is all about, people married to persons from a different country of origin, sometimes speaking different languages, and ministry within a country that does not belong to the wife or the husband, allowing their children to thrive as "third culture kids," children who are bilingual or in some cases trilingual and who are influenced by at least three different cultures in their worldview. These are expressions of the new twenty-first century mission.

In Scandinavia, Smyrna International Church in Gothenburg is a multicultural church working under the umbrella of the Swedish Pentecostal church Smyrna Kyrkan, led by the senior pastor Urban Ringbäck. Pastor Mark Beckenham explains that services are provided in the English language for the English speaking community.[33] Founder-pastor Johannes Amritzer leads SOS Church in Stockholm, including more than 600 attendants from 55 different nationalities; English is the official language of communication.[34] In Belgium, Eddy Dela-

---

29   Hugh Palmer, electronic information from London to the author on 17th December 2013.

30   See further "Bund Internationale Mission in Deutschland," Evangelisch-Freikirchlicher Gemeinden in Deutschland-IMD- (http://www.baptisten.de/mission/mission-live/internationale-mission-in-deutschland/). See also, The Baptist Union (Bund Evangelisch-Freikirchlicher Gemeinden – BEFG (www.baptisten.de).

31   Tomas Milk, information by email sent to the author on 18th May 2011.

32   Richard Aidoo, information by email sent to the author on 10th May 2011.

33   See Smyrna International Church (http://smyrna.se/centrum/moetesplatser/smyrna-international).

34   Schelander, information provided to the author from Stockholm on 29th December 2013. See further: SOS Church (http://missionsos.org/)

meillieure, a former British missionary in Madrid, started an ethnic church within the Latino community in Ghent composed of some Belgians but mostly Latin Americans.[35]

Finally, Graceway Church in Kansas City practices a multicultual approach. Senior Pastor Jeff Adams has integrated a Latino community into the American church; they have more than 3,500 members, including a mix of white and black membership. There are more than 35 different nationalties. While the three largest blocks this church would be Anglo, African American, and Latino, no one group has a majority. Therefore, Graceway Church's multicultural approach is to have all groups involved in one church, interacting with each other as Christian brothers and sisters in most activities. This form of "multicultural" is now increasingly called being "*intercultural.*" Adams states,

> As to the future, I have seen many churches set out to be multiethnic and fail. Obviously, there are many ethnic churches in this country. However, what normally happens is that the grandparents never fully integrate, their children become perfectly bilingual, and then their children, the grandchildren of the immigrants, do not want to speak the original language. They love to maintain a cultural heritage, but become integrated into the general society. This seems not to be taken much into account by church planters in my opinion.[36]

Challenges and Conclusions

It seems to me that the new tendency for twenty-first century mission will fall in line with the presence of a more multicultural approach. However ethnic churches will not disappear as a mission model because there is an increasing resurgence of *ethne* in the world, and migration and diaspora will mobilize more people from one country to another. As Harvie Conn points out, the church plants churches in the homogenous units of Jerusalem, but the church cannot forget that its final ethnic attachment is with the New Jerusalem; he points out that not understanding the other controls the mission method.[37] Therefore, for a church in mission, unity in diversity has to be central in every mission model—ethnic or multicultural.

In the kingdom of God, all ethnic groups will not disappear. What counts is the universal presence of all *ethne*, worshiping the King Jesus.

Some conclusions I would like to suggest are as follows:

1. Most ethnic and multicultural churches struggle with cultural identity and the use of language. Language has become a tool of power because it influences opinion.
2. Most ethnic churches are united by ties of culture, language, and identity. These characteristics help them to have a common goal.
3. Most multicultural churches are a mix of different cultures which help them to be more versatile in communicating the gospel.

---

35 Delameillieure, electronic information sent to the author from Belgium on 22nd November 2013.
36 Adams, information sent by email to the author from Kansas City on 18th December 2013.
37 Shenk, *Exploring Church Growth*, 91.

4. It seems to me that multicultural churches are the way forward to empower mission for the twenty-first century. This can be seen within the different models shared.

Questions for Reflection:

1. Why is there a new tendency toward multicultural churches?
2. How do you make the distinction between ethnic and multicultural churches?
3. Why did indigenization not work in the past despite good mission theory?
4. How would you help to change from a monocultural church to a multicultural one?

References

Allen, Roland. 1962. *Missionary Methods: St Paul's or Ours?* Grand Rapids, MI: Eerdmans. (First published 1912.)

———. 2006. *The Spontaneous Expansion of the Church.* Cambridge: Lutterworth Press. (First published 1927.)

Bosch, David. 1991. *Transforming Mission: Paradigm Shifts in Theology of Mission.* Maryknoll, NY: Orbis Books.

Cueva, Samuel. 2003. From the Local Mission to a Global Mission. MA Dissertation, University of Birmingham, UK.

Davis, Ken. 2003. Multicultural Church Planting Models. *The Journal of Ministry and Theology,* Spring. http://www.bbc.edu/journal/volume7_1/Multicultural_Church-Davis.pdf.

Escobar, Samuel. 2003. Las Migraciones y la Misión de la Iglesia Cristiana. In *Las Iglesias y la Migración.* Ed. Consejo Evangélico de Madrid and Seminario Teológico Bautista. Madrid: Rivadeneyra.

Fédération Protestante de France. http://www.protestants.org/

Frost, Michael. 2006. *Exiles: Living Missionally in a Post-Christian Culture.* Peabody, MA: Hendrickson.

Giddens, Anthony. 2009. *Sociology.* Cambridge, UK: Polity Press.

Hodges, Melvin L. 2009. *The Indigenous Church.* Springfield, IL: Gospel Publishing House. (First published 1953.)

McGavran, Donald. 1970. *Understanding Church Growth.* Grand Rapids, MI: Eerdmans.

Moreau, A. Scott, ed. 2000. *Evangelical Dictionary of World Missions.* Grand Rapids, MI: Baker Books.

Pew Research. 2007. Spanish Trends Projects: Latinos in America. In *Changing Faiths: Latinos and the Transformation of American Religion.* http://www.pewhispanic.org/ 2007/ 04/25/vi-the-ethnic-church/.

Pocock, Michael, Gailyn Van Rheenen and Douglas McConnell. 2005. *The Changing Face of World Missions*. Grand Rapids, MI: Baker Academic.

Schwartz, Glenn. 2003.   Ethnic Churches and Identity in Missiological Perspective. *World Mission Associates*. February 4, 2003. http://www.wmausa.org/page.aspx?id=83836.

Shenk, Wilbert, ed. 1983. *Exploring Church Growth*. Grand Rapids, MI: Eerdmans.

Smyrna International Church. http://smyrna.se/centrum/moetesplatser/smyrna -international.

SOS Church. http://missionsos.org/.

Stetzer, Ed. 2003. *Planting New Churches*. Nashville, TN: Broadman & Holman Publisher.

Stott, John, ed. 1996. *Making Christ Known*. Carlisle: Paternoster Press.

van der Meer, Tom. 2007. Accommodation/Adaptation. In *Dictionary of Mission Theology*. John Corrie. Nottingham: IVP.

Wan, Enoch, ed. 2011. *Diaspora Missiology: Theory, Methodology, and Practice*. Portland, OR: Institute of Diaspora Studies.

Weber, Max. 1997. *The Ethnicity Reader: Nationalism, Multiculturalism and Migration*. Cambridge, UK: Polity Press.

Samuel Cueva (MA, Birmingham and PhD, University of Wales Trinity Saint David) is a Peruvian missiologist who promotes two-way mission bridges to every continent for the fulfillment of God's mission. A member of the Latin American Theological Fraternity and Vice Chairman of Global Connections Latin American Forum, UK, he has planted a Spanish-speaking church in London in collaboration with St. James's Church-Muswell Hill; his most recent publication is *Mission Partnership in Creative Tension* (Langham Monographs, 2015). He is married to Noemi, with two grown children, Noemi Delia and Claudia.

AFRICAN MONISM VERSUS WESTERN DUALISM

How the Church Responds to Local Realities

Moss Ntlha

The term African monism references a worldview that, while it shares a lot of similarities with other non-Western worldviews, has distinct points of difference with what is often referred to as Western dualism. It refers broadly to the idea that the traditional African worldview posits a monistic reality in which the sacred and the secular/material are indivisible; that the living, the dead (ancestral spirits), and the unborn share an inseparable unity and community; and that the human being is not a split personality of mind and body in a way that makes it possible to dichotomize between the two.

For its part, Western philosophy conceives of the world in dualistic terms, distinguishing between the world of the spirit and the world of matter. This is traceable to ancient Greek philosophy, notably Gnosticism, which held a dualism between matter and spirit. In ancient Greek thought, flesh and spirit were seen as antithetical, they represented the tangible and the intangible, the base and the lofty. While the Greeks may have laid the foundations of such dualism, it was later to be systematized in the sixteenth century by Rene Descartes, famously captured in the formulation "I think therefore I am." This laid the ground for the rationalism of modernity in which reason and spirit were cast in stark dichotomy.

Early Christianity, while still in its predominantly Jewish environment where a more integrated Hebraic worldview existed, was relatively protected from Gnostic influence. This was to change in the second century as the church and Christian missions spread outward where Greek culture and pagan philosophies were the order of the day.[1]

That said, it is important to preface the discussion on African monism by stating two caveats: First, the fact that Africa is a diverse continent with different countries, cultures, and peoples, each of which have a cultural uniqueness that makes any treatment of aspects of African culture a generalization at best. Secondly, modern day Africa is home to many self identified African dualists who, thanks to globalization and the role of media and Western

---

1   J. L. Hurlbut, *The Story of the Christian Church* (Grand Rapids, MI: Zondervan, 1970), 51.

education, have bought into the Western mode of separating the sacred and the secular. One can even happen upon African atheists who deny the existence of the transcendent Other.

For the purpose of this discussion, African monism is used in order to reference this important African cultural feature in relation to its Western dualistic opposite.

Culture Wars

Whenever different cultures meet and compete for space, a contest is inevitable as each culture strives to maintain itself or even dominate others. In contemporary times, the meeting of the two cultures, Western and African, was not a cordial and respectful encounter of equals, but an epochal clash, thanks to colonialism and the imperial expansion of Western powers. The clash meant the subjugation of Africans by Western powers. While on the face of it, colonialism was a military, political, and economic conquest of one group by another, the spiritual and cultural aspects of this conquest have been less obvious, if more enduring. Beneath the physical damage of conquest lay a more debilitating threat to the African sense of identity and personhood: the erosion of what gave meaning to the African's inner world.

For its part, Christian mission had an unfortunate historical association with colonialism in a way that made it complicit in the twin crimes of political subjugation and spiritual alienation. After the colonial conquests, the African sense of personhood lay buried beneath the imposing superstructure of empire.

How Churches in Africa Respond to Cultural Dualism Imposed by Western Mission

It can be said that Christian mission has historically led to a response to this clash of cultures in three phases: acquiescence, resistance, and proactive partnership in missions.

Tienou provides a helpful framework for the assessment of African Christian responses to this cultural clash. He identifies four stages as: Western condescension (stage 1), African reaction (stage 2), Challenging the reality of African philosophy (stage 3), and fourthly, a synthesis of stage 2 and stage 3, which is still to be.[2] In this paper, I will use Tienou's stage 1 and 2 as being characteristic of the first two phases of African response, with stage 3 being a proactive partnership in mission.

African Acquiescence

The first stage was simply African acquiescence to the hegemony of Western missions. Tienou places this stage historically as the period between 1800–1930.[3] It was a period in which Western missionaries sought to displace indigenous cultures with Western culture wherever they went. African Christians were made to feel that they had to be Europeans

---

2   S. Ngewa, M. Shaw and T. Tienou, eds., *Issues in African Christian Theology* (Nairobi: East African Educational Publishers, 1998), 40–45.

3   Tienou in Ngewa et al, *Issues in African Christian Theology,* 40.

in order to become proper Christians. Setiloane notes that: "For almost two centuries this (colonial) type of Christianity has been passed on to this continent. We have imbibed it all."[4]

In a parallel development with mission to American Indians by seventeenth century New England missionaries, Wilbert Shenk observes: "The missionaries felt compassion and responsibility for their converts. They gathered these new Christians into churches for nurture and discipline and set up programs to transform Christian Indians into English Puritans."[5]

The Second Phase: Resistance (1930–1970s)

It is not hard to see why Africans and other indigenous cultures will resist this colonial tendency. It is therefore the case that Africans, in their struggle for political liberation from Western powers, have sought to complete such political emancipation by reclaiming their own sense of identity and responding to existential questions that are important to their own religio-cultural worldview. Otherwise J. V. Taylor's observation will continue to haunt African missiology. He said:

> Christ has been presented as the answer to questions a white man would ask, the solution to the needs that Western man would feel, the Savior of the world of the European worldview, the object of adoration and prayer of historic Christendom … But if Christ were to appear as the answer to the questions that Africans are asking, what would he look like?[6]

This is why the following declaration by a conference of African evangelical theologians gathered in Seoul in 1982 is a welcome one. It says in part:

> Those of us in Africa will have to take seriously the traditional African worldview, the reality of the Spirit-world, the competing ideologies, the resurgence of Islam and the contemporary cultural, political, and religious struggles. Theology will have to explore ways of presenting the personal God and Jesus Christ as the only mediator between God and man.[7]

This declaration points to a growing African concern for an African theological effort that seeks to remedy colonial missionary errors for the purpose of the advancement of Christian missions.

There are pitfalls, however. These have arisen in the heat of resisting Western cultural and theological impositions. I will mention but two of these.

Firstly, such African theologians as Gabriel Setiloane, in resisting Western theological patronage, have felt the need to make the claim that the African conception of God, notably the Sotho/Tswana notion of Modimo, is superior, richer, and more powerful than the

---

4   K. Appiah-Kubi and S. Torres, eds., *African Theology en Route* (New York: Orbis Books, 1983), 61.

5   P. G. Hiebert, *Anthropological Reflections on Missiological Issues* (Grand Rapids, MI; Baker, 1994), 55.

6   Taylor in K. Bediako, *Jesus in Africa: The Christian Gospel in African History and Experience* (Akropong-Akuapem, Ghana: Regnum Africa, 20).

7   Ngewa et al, *Issues in African Christian Theology,* xiii.

Western notion of God. As a result, Setiloane wonders if it is necessary to convert devotees of African traditional religion to Christianity, or even for himself to remain in the Christian fold.

He writes: "The question as to why we are still in the Christian fold can be answered in different ways. For myself … I am like someone who has been bewitched, and I find it difficult to shake off the Christian witchcraft with which I have been captivated. I cannot say I necessarily like where I am."[8]

This glamorization of African culture points to the danger that African theology itself can fall into the same cultural imperialism that it accuses others of.

Secondly, the resurgence of the ancestor cult as African people reclaim the African traditional religion opens the way to syncretism. The religio-cultural worldview of Africans, as stated before, sees life as being a community of the living, the departed, and the yet to be born. This was given public expression in the glare of global media at the occasion of the death and mourning of Nelson Mandela. As the body of the global icon lay in state, repeatedly his next of kin would speak to the spirit of Mandela to announce key moments of his journey from the urban centers of Johannesburg and Pretoria where he lived and worked, to his burial place in rural Qunu. African traditional religionists made the case that Mandela's spirit would now join the spirits of his Tembu ancestors, from whence he would continue to be in communion with the Mandela clan.

The growth of the ancestor cult in the post-apartheid period is cause for concern, in particular the resurgence of sangomaism. The sangoma is an African medicine man or woman who serves as a traditional healer and is able to connect with African ancestors, mediating between the living and the dead. As part of the African Traditional Religion, the ancestor cult, and with it sangomaism, rides on the wave of African self-determination and the overthrow of the colonial and apartheid legacy. To adherents and sympathizers, it appears that to be free from the yoke of apartheid and colonial oppression is to be free to rediscover the ancient spiritualities of African antiquity. In this environment, the ancestor cult enjoys a privileged status as a politically correct means of relating to the "transcendent Other" in a way that affirms, and presumably remedies, the historic dispossession—spiritually, culturally, politically, and economically—of indigenous people.

Even in many churches, particularly in African Indigenous churches but increasingly other historic/mainline churches (Methodist, Anglican, Catholic, etc.), the idea that to be a sangoma is incompatible with what it means to be a minister of the gospel of Jesus Christ is by no means clear.

From the point of view of Christian mission in South Africa, and perhaps even further afield on the continent, it may well be the case that the ancestor cult in general,

---

8   Appiah-Kubi and Torres, eds., *African Theology en Route*, 61.

and sangomaism in particular, is one of the most important obstacles and strong-
holds of hindrance to the advance of Christian mission. It is an obstacle in two ways.
Firstly, as with Islam, which is also a dominant religious presence on the continent,
it has become increasingly aggressive in asserting and reclaiming its right to exist
in South Africa, in the spirit of African Renaissance. The South African constitution seeks intentionally to promote and protect the African heritage and worldview
that a presumably misguided Western cultural and religious order sought to destroy.
Secondly, it is often the case that many believers combine, in a syncretistic way, both
Christianity and the ancestor cult. The idea of Christian uniqueness is thereby lost in
the process.

Third Phase: Proactive Partnership in Mission

It would be remiss for African Christian theology to content itself merely with reacting to the errors of Western mission. Rather, the God who is the Subject of Mission
(*missio Dei*) invites the African Church to freely and joyfully contribute to world mission from her own vantage point, experience, and gifting. This can be most fruitfully
done in partnership between north, east, south, and west in the global community of
Christians.

Ariarajah, an advocate for a North-South dialogue in hermeneutics, refers with approval to Benezet Bujo who states that "we must acknowledge the fact that hermeneutics largely remains a Western philosophic tradition, and that this tradition is
increasingly challenged by non-Western philosophers."[9] Ariarajah follows Bujo in
making a number of hermeneutical observations, of which I will mention only three,
that are important in forging missional partnership in Africa and beyond. While these
may be generalizations, they nevertheless point to important dimensions of the hermeneutical diologue between North and South.

First, in classical (Western) hermeneutics, the aim is ultimately to understand oneself.
It is an individualistic enterprise. The non-Western hermeneutics has a communitar-
ian approach.

Second, classical hermeneutics is focussed on harmonization. Intercultural hermeneutics recognizes differentiation. The other as a stranger is to be done justice.

Third, classical hermeneutics is based on propositional understanding of truth; intercultural hermeneutics is based on existential understanding of truth.[10]

Accepting the dialogical and partnership nature of the church and Bujo's insights in
intercultural hermeneutics, it is possible to forge ahead with missional partnership
that responds to the spiritual needs of the unreached. African missiology can, with

---

9   S. Wesley Ariarajah, *Exchange: Journal of Missiological and Ecumenical Research*, 34.(2) (2005),
94.
10   Ariarajah, *Exchange*, 94.

confidence, proceed with the task of making Christ known in the context of Africa and beyond.

In this enterprise, the following will be important in helping the church in Africa to avoid some pitfalls with regard to syncretism:

The primacy of Scripture, as it is allowed to interrogate context. Contextualization has often erred in allowing the text and context equal rights in the determination of what is normative.

Dependence on the Spirit. Africa being a continent alive with spiritual realities of all sorts, it makes sense that the power of the Spirit be allowed full sway in mission. It is not coincidental that the churches that experience the most dramatic growth in Africa are African Independent churches and Pentecostal churches. It is because these churches connect with something essential in the religio-cultural world view of the African.

A commitment to the hermeneutical community, in which the blind spots of one are corrected by others. As Hiebert notes: "We need Christians from other cultures, for they often see how our cultural biases have distorted our interpretations of the Scriptures. This corporate nature of the church as a community of interpretation extends not only to the church in every culture, but also to the church in all ages."[11]

Conclusion

The African religio-cultural experience, in tension with the African context, is the crucible within which the church in Africa must work out its missiology. Having come from a period of colonial subjugation and the damage to African personhood that colonialism entails, the church in Africa has responded to Christian mission progressively from acquiescence, to resistance, and is now in a position to forge confident mission partnerships with others in hermeneutical community. The cultural categories of African monism versus Western dualism need no harmonization. This is because "difference" and "otherness" can be welcomed as necessary in the hermeneutic interaction of the church as a community of interpretation across cultures and ages.

Questions for Reflection:

1. What can we learn from mission and church history in Africa regarding the way the gospel came to the continent? In what ways was there a clash between Western dualism and African monism and what were the consequences for the African church?

2. How can the concept of African monism help us to understand a holistic gospel and an integral mission?

---

11   Hiebert, *Anthropological Reflections*, 91.

3. In what ways, according to Nthla, do ancestor cult and sangomaism constitute hindrances for the advance of the gospel in Africa? What would be the ways of avoiding syncretism, suggested by the author? How can the global mission community interact with those suggestions?

References

Appiah–Kubi K., and S. Torres, eds. 1983. *African Theology en Route.* New York: Orbis Books.

Ararijah, S. Wesley. 2005. Exchange: Journal of Missiological and Ecumenical Research. 34(2).

Bediako, K. 2000. *Jesus in Africa: The Christian Gospel in African History and Experience.* Oxford: Regnum.

Hiebert, P.G. 1994. *Anthropological Reflections on Missiological Issues.* Grand Rapids, MI; Baker.

Hulbut, J.L. 1970. *The Story of the Christian Church.* Grand Rapids, MI: Zondervan.

Ngewa S., M. Shaw, and T. Tienou, eds. 1998. *Issues in African Christian Theology.* Nairobi: East African Educational Publishers.

Moss Ntlha is the general secretary of the Evangelical Alliance of South Africa and is committed to seeing the evangelical movement united and speaking thoughtfully with one voice on issues confronting the nation. He also leads a local church and is involved in church planting and leadership development.

CHAPTER 21

GOSPEL AND CHURCH IN CHINA

Anonymous

There is a popular saying that whatever you say about China is probably true somewhere. This vast country is diverse in many ways: geographically, economically, culturally, and much more.

The same may be said about the church in modern China. Nobody knows how many professing Christians there actually are, though guesstimates range between 23 million and 40 million (government figures), 67 million (Pew Research figure for 2010), and 100 million (some observers both within and outside China). Chinese Christians' experiences are as varied as their country.

What is beyond question is that the Chinese church has grown hugely in the past fifty years, almost entirely through its own witness, and has equipped its people to be gospel-bearers to their countrymen. Given the historical context of official policy, played out over the decades in anything from outright persecution to reluctant tolerance, how and why has this growth happened? What lessons might there be for the church in other parts of the world?

Understanding the Context

Officially, Chinese Communism is committed to atheism and the desire to stamp out religion as something harmful, backward, and subversive. That would be as much the case in relation to Buddhism, with its long history in China, Islam, with a historic role in some minority groups especially in the north and west of China, as well as Christianity or to a host of sects.

However, Chinese are also pragmatic in many respects so in some regions of China the powers-that-be see that Christians have contributed positively to social stability and social good. Where that is the case, and where Christians do not do or say anything publicly that appears to criticize the political system, local authorities may be less inclined to crack down on groups meeting for worship. In addition, some Chinese Christians will happily affirm that under Communism many millions in China have been lifted out of dire poverty; the dismal days of endless fighting between competing warlords have long since ended; China has become powerful economically on the world stage recently; and Chinese are able to travel overseas for study, business, and tourism. For many Chinese then, life is far better than it was before Communism.

The Officially Recognized Churches

The church is divided between two streams. On the one hand, there are both Protestant and Roman Catholic churches that are officially recognized and that come under the umbrella of the China Christian Council. The ultimate control of these churches is political, and in some (but not all) cases they are theologically liberal. At the same time, many of the Three-Self Patriotic Movement "open" churches are places where people have access to the Bible and where some pastors are doctrinally orthodox. Nonetheless, there are boundaries set out by the Party, including, in the case of the Catholic Church, complete separation from the Pope and the functions usually exercised by him (e.g., the appointment of bishops). The churches are strongly discouraged (even technically forbidden) from teaching about miracles, about sin and the need for salvation through Christ, the resurrection, and Christ's return in judgment; all of these are incompatible with an atheistic, humanist view of humankind and society. Teaching is required to support the political and social agenda of the Communist Party. Not all TSPM churches observe these rules, and in some places there seems to be a growing appetite for theological reflection and emphasis on biblical teaching.

The Diversity of the House Churches

On the other hand, the majority of Christians in China are part of the house church movement. This term includes many, and often very different, strands. Some trace their origins back to the 1920s and the growing need at the time to establish indigenous churches. Many denominational mission agencies had "planted" churches that remained tied to their structures somewhere far away across the world, and these often were very foreign in ethos. In addition, many of these denominations were succumbing to the liberal developments gaining ground in many Western circles at the time. These churches were especially vulnerable when all missionary personnel were withdrawn around 1950.

By contrast, it was often the much more indigenous churches that were more flexible and able to respond to different circumstances. They had sprung up under entirely Chinese leadership, were often nationalistic, were sometimes quite informal, sometimes independent in any locality, sometimes networked, and were not in any way dependent on foreign funds. They did not depend on having a church building and focused on teaching personal piety, memorizing the Bible, prayer, and quiet sharing of their faith. When necessary they could maintain discipleship and growth through quietly meeting with one other person or in very small groups in homes or out in the fields.

The pattern of these churches—conservative in belief, committed to God's Word, simple in structure, fervent in faith—has been replicated over and over again. Their allegiance is to Jesus as Lord, with the conviction that the church should not be under state control. At the same time, they take seriously the need to be good citizens, to help maintain social stability, and to contribute to social welfare. They do not wish to be subversive, or to destabilize the state. Formal legal status, through registering with the state authorities, would bring many practical advantages, but also involve submitting to elements of control by the state. This remains a difficult and sensitive issue.

There is of course a risk element in so much independency, and China has produced many sects where influential leaders have moved away from biblical teaching. Sometimes it is quite difficult to evaluate when a group or movement has tipped over into heresy, and where people do not have access to Bibles they are especially vulnerable. Some sects have a strong emphasis on supernatural power, healing, or prosperity that deviates from what the Bible has to say about these things. Often the leader becomes the focus of loyalty, rather than the Lord. The government is especially disturbed by such groups as they are often politically subversive.

The Centrality of the Cross

"House church" is in fact a broad category, with many variations and distinctives. In general, though, they are rooted in the evangelical faith, with a strong emphasis on the cross of Christ and on the call for authentic Christians to be people of the cross: that is, willing to suffer, particularly through persecution. Many have indeed suffered, and some in certain parts of China face more difficulties than others. Perseverance and faithfulness in the face of suffering is costly but is also a mark of serious discipleship and of identification with the Lord. It is a significant reason why the church in China has both endured and grown.

Suffering does not always make unity between different streams any easier, though some evangelicals have in recent years been more concerned than in the past to bridge divides and to look for ways of working more harmoniously. Cooperation can be cautious, as the larger a congregation or network or alliance, the more visible it is likely to be, and thus the more likely to incur hostility from the authorities. Recently, several large groups have been evicted from their meeting place or have had visible signs (such as a cross on a building) torn down.

In earlier years the house churches were strongest in the countryside and among those with little education. China has experienced accelerated urbanization and also an explosion of those with higher education and professional work. This is reflected in the house church movement, which now has many groups meeting in China's huge cities and attracting those often referred to as "intellectuals." In turn this means that many leaders are well educated and take biblical and theological study seriously.

China is experiencing many social changes and the younger generation coming to adulthood face many challenges that have been unfamiliar to older people. This calls for much grace across the generations and for the church to be able to address what discipleship means in different circumstances. Also, while the government limits certain media from outside the country, more and more Chinese are exposed to ideas and values different from those of the Communist Party and its leadership. This leads to young people in particular asking many deep questions. This means that for the Chinese church, as for the church elsewhere in the world, contemporary apologetics is of high importance.

But the house churches grow most where the cross and resurrection of the Lord Jesus Christ is at the heart of teaching and life.

Four Challenges

One Chinese brother suggests that there are four particular challenges facing the church in China today. In many respects, they are challenges for the church worldwide.

First is the issue of deep-level discipleship. This is not addressed simply by implementing programs. Rather it involves the commitment of the whole body to intentional and life-long learning and growing in faith and obedience. It involves transformation at every level of personal and social life. Shallow faith is not able to withstand opposition; it also grieves and insults the Lord. In a more open China, where many Christians do not suffer for their faith in the same way as a previous generation, will believers still be able if need be to be loyal to Christ if suffering comes?

Second, reconciliation and unity. The church in China had in the past a divided and sometimes very dysfunctional history. Is there a way to bridge some of the very real (and deeply held) differences of conviction between the TSPM churches and the house churches? Is it possible for the different streams of the house churches to come together more lovingly, especially where leaders have been jealous of their own roles or have disagreed over some issue of doctrine or behavior? Reconciliation involves deep levels of forgiveness, costly and painful. But the unity of God's people is a powerful sign of the gospel to the unbelieving world.

Third, social engagement and witness. The Chinese church still reflects some of the great divides of the early twentieth century Western churches, polarizing social concern on the one hand and evangelism on the other. Historically, the TSPM churches tended to be associated with the more liberal emphasis on social concern, with less emphasis on biblical authority and evangelism. The house churches tended to be more concerned with pietistic and fundamentalist forms of faith. More Chinese Christians are realizing that this is a false dichotomy, and that authentic faith is holistic. China needs the gospel and God's truth in all its fullness; it needs Christians who worship, pray, learn Scripture, and evangelize; but it also needs them to seek the wellbeing of society, influencing it for truth and justice, love, and service, and living out their faith in all dimensions of life.

Fourth, mission and commitment. As China has opened up to the outside world, even if still to some extent on her own terms, Chinese Christians have become increasingly aware of that world, and of the challenge to cross-cultural mission. Today, millions of Chinese live and work outside China for varying lengths of time, including about two million in central and east Africa or others in parts of central Asia. Among them are many believers. Can they quietly use their employment as a context within which to engage in cross-cultural mission? How can they be better equipped to do that? Even within China, there are gospel-needy areas, and many minority cultures to be reached. There are some restrictions on moving to another region, but how can the church carry the good news to where it is most needed?

Conclusion

The story of the Chinese church is one that should lead us to thanksgiving and prayer. Today there are probably more Christians in China than in any other single country in the world. Yet in this vast populous and geographical area there remain millions who have never heard the gospel. What might the coming decades bring? Pray for China!

Questions for Reflection:

1. What can we learn from the history and development of the church in China? Give some concrete examples and reflect on how that affects the way we plant churches today.

2. According to a Chinese brother there are four specific challenges for the church in China today. How relevant are these challenges also for the church in other parts of the world?

3. How could you and your church community engage in prayer and support for the growing church in China?

About authorship: This chapter draws on the experience of several people. For security reasons, we prefer not to name them.

CHAPTER 22

EFFECTIVE PARTNERSHIP

One Successful Venture

Tom Sanchez

Recognizing that the term "partnership" has been perhaps overused during the last ten years, my desire is simply to tell the story of what happened here at Grace Covenant Church and then draw a few general conclusions from the story itself.

We at Grace Covenant Church in Austin, Texas, are privileged to have a man attend our church who, a few years back, was hired by Food For the Hungry (FFH) in an international leadership capacity. For privacy's sake, let's call him Don. Don was propelled into the world of hurt that the kingdom-oriented holistic ministry FFH is involved in. His journey through these years is a book in itself. Don is also father to two adopted children as well as three children born into the family.

On one trip to Africa, accompanied by one of the elders from our congregation, Don visited the homes of children in the Child Development Program (CDP) run by FFH in Zeway, Ethiopia. He and his traveling partner uncovered a major hole in the FFH program. The CDP is a program designed to partner with a family in need who has one or more children to provide help for the child or children to attend school on a regular basis.

However, one of the families that Don visited had children but no parents. Both parents were deceased, and a teenager was now the head of the household, responsible for younger siblings.

The painful reality that the CDP was not adequate for these child-headed households (CHH) generated a lot of concern and dialogue within FFH in Ethiopia. More than that, Don brought his discovery and pain back to Grace Covenant Church and shared it with the orphan and adoption ministry that God has raised up in the church—Bridges of Grace (Bridges).

Bridges was moved by God to dialogue with FFH in Ethiopia and ask for a ball-park figure that would allow for the special needs of the CHH's to be met. After some further consideration and dialogue, a dollar figure of $17,000 US was agreed on. Bridges developed a marketing plan to make the need known here at Grace through various means, including a silent auction of 9" x 11" framed pictures of farm animals. The plan was to slowly bring the Grace body up to speed on the needs and over time, raise the necessary $17,000 to help in Zeway.

In mid-December of 2008, God opened the hearts of the Grace body toward the CHH orphans in Zeway, Ethiopia, and $41,000 US dollars were raised. Needless to say, we were stunned into worship and thanksgiving with what God had done, and we were all—Grace, FFH, and Bridges—wondering what God had in mind.

A trip was planned. Don, some of the leaders from Bridges, and I traveled to Zeway, asking God to open our eyes to what he had for us.

In the first hour of our visit to Zeway we met with a group of political, religious, and educational leaders of the city. This included the Ethiopian Orthodox leader, the Muslim Imam, and members of the evangelical coalition. The director of FFH, a brilliant and godly man, presented to the city leaders the desire of FFH and Grace to help meet the needs of the CHH's.

Later we would meet with the leaders of the seventeen evangelical churches who form a coalition in the city in a separate venue. During that meeting, the Lord led me to share with the church leaders that our vision for the solution of the CHH's in Zeway was that the local church bodies would assume responsibility for these orphans in their community and that these children would be cared for by the churches.

In a series of letters that were exchanged over the next few months, the coalition of churches embraced this challenge as a calling from God and made it clear that, though they valued our contribution and help, they were now the front line in solving the CHH problem in their city.

Over time and with growing understanding and ownership, the Evangelical Alliance of Churches in Zeway drafted a memorandum of understanding between themselves, Food for the Hungry, and Grace Covenant Church in Austin, Texas. This was an historic event that has led to an ongoing interchange of ideas, funding, community projects, missionary sending from the evangelical churches in Zeway into the surrounding Muslim-dominated areas, and expansion of the CHH project to include children in single-parent families where the demise of the parent is imminent.

Bridges has expanded the partnership in two ways. One, it is now a multi-year project and not a one-time gift. This has also changed the dollar amount needed to go far beyond the original $17,000 US. It is enough to be a God-only thing that requires great faith. Second, Bridges is actively working to bring additional churches in the Austin area into the resourcing of both money and people for the long-term partnership that exists. We would love to see a coalition of churches in Austin that at least matches the Alliance that exists in Zeway.

Concluding Observations

When a term like "partnership" is used, a term whose primary definition comes from the business world, it is very easy to try to apply business principals to its origins and its operation. When we started with this project, we neither expected, nor envisioned the kind of partnership that God has created.

How often do you imagine that all of these variables come together in one church body? Don, an adoptive father who is also the international leader of a relief and community development NGO; an already developed orphan ministry, Bridges of Grace, with passionate, trained and amazingly capable leadership; a church in Austin, Texas, somehow prepared by the Holy Spirit for just such a time as this who would respond with such generosity? As if that were not enough, add a city in an African country that already boasts an Alliance of Evangelical Churches who would not only embrace the need when they saw it, but take full ownership of the final solution for the problem, and a gifted on-the-ground leader for FFH in Zeway, who would bring both passion and skill in implementing the first steps of action that have led to this three way-partnership?

Considering the number of variables and moving pieces, it is highly unlikely that this exact scenario will ever be repeated. It is therefore highly questionable as to whether one could extract a "reproducible ministry model" from this God-shaped reality. There could, however, be some principles that could be learned that would help others as they think about partnership endeavors on which they are embarking.

Conclusions

"A threefold cord is not easily broken" (Ecc 4:12). I have always taken that to mean God plus you plus me. I think God believes in partnership. We have been blessed and wonderful stories are being lived out by orphans in Zeway who are coming to faith and processing grief and moving into productive lives. God's fingerprints are all over this. Certainly I'm not smart enough to have thought up or created this organism.

But, partnerships that are not easily broken are woven together by God himself. Don walked in obedience, responding to the needs he observed in Zeway. Bridges walked in obedience, taking on the initial project. We stepped through a door opened by the generosity of the people of Grace as they walked in obedience in giving toward the CHH need. The churches in Zeway walked in obedience as they embraced ownership of the CHHs. FFH walked in obedience as they stepped up to the challenge of staffing and administrating the new CHH program within their CDP. None of us anticipated the dimension or the depth of the partnership that God would weave.

May God grant us the faith to walk in obedience and the courage to go where he leads.

Questions for Reflection:

1. How do we better recognize when what the world calls "coincidence" is a God-ordained calling?

2. In your own experience, have you seen examples of the Lord bringing people and circumstances together in similarly faith-stretching ways? How might testimony to this encourage others?

Tom and Brenda Sanchez served with the Navigators in Latin America for twenty-seven years. For the last eleven years, Tom has been privileged to serve as the Pastor of Global Outreach at Grace Covenant Church in Austin, Texas, USA.

Part Three

CHURCH IN MISSION:

CASE STUDIES

CHAPTER 23

GLOBALIZED CHRISTIAN YOUTH MOVEMENTS

Adriaan Adams

Rapid changes within world societies and global social structures create many challenges faced by the emerging generation today. With so many unanswered questions about financial stability and political influences as well as globalization, the emerging generation must rethink its mission and responsibility in this new world.

Jenkins states, "We are currently living through one of the transforming moments in the history of religion worldwide."[1] In no other time in history have so many different people and nations intersected in so many ways. Through the click of a mouse, we are instantly connected to the rest of the world. Traveling across continents takes only a few hours and the arrangement of global events is a common trend.

In a recent article, Aaron Fowler expresses the need for students and young adults to start raising their voices and uniting around important issues. He argues that the younger generation are perceived as loud through their actions yet silent in their opinion and reactions to daily challenges faced. He calls for the younger generation to stand up against the wrongdoings of government and reminds them that they are the innovators and problem solvers.

> Think about it, mostly everything our generation does is loud; the way we dress, the music we listen to and the pop culture we accept. However, it seems we become more vocal about the latest episode of Jersey Shore than "situations" in Frankfort, and for that I classify us as a silent generation. We cannot afford to be silent any longer.[2]

Fowler's frustration is echoed around the world by various youth leaders in many countries. In recent years the South African news has been dominated by signs of this frustration and a call for action by the African National Congress Youth League (ANCYL). Julius Malema, the suspended ANCYL president, is continuously provoking and challenging the youth of South Africa to unite for change. In a statement made at the league's centenary rally in

---

1   P. Jenkins, *The Next Christendom: The Coming of Global Christianity* (New York: Oxford University Press, 2007), 1.
2   A. Fowler, "Time for Students to Unite around Important Issues, Tuition." http://kykernel.com/2012 /02/27/time-for-students-to-unite-on-important-issues-tuition/.

Kliptown, Soweto (2012), he challenged the leadership of the African National Congress (ANC) to defend the land from other political groups, and indicated that if they do not the younger generation, the "freedom fighters," will do so. "He warned that if the leadership of the ANC was not prepared to defend the land, then the 'economic freedom fighters' would defend it.[3]

These kinds of statements have become the norm in South Africa and they speak of a much deeper frustration and challenge currently experienced by the Emerging Leadership Generation (ELG).

In the last decade another new awakening has become apparent among the younger generation. Gatherings of all kinds, of both Christian and non-Christian focus, are becoming a common phenomenon. Goll and Engle explain that;

> God is raising up an alternative government in the earth. Today, hundreds of thousands of believers worldwide are becoming part of a reformation of prayer that is unheard of in the earth."[4]

There are many examples of initiatives that support this statement. The Student Voluntary Movement assists the international network of students, leaders, churches, and organizations serving as grassroots mission movements among today's emerging generation towards the fulfillment of the Great Commission in our lifetime (www.svm2.net). The Lausanne Younger Leaders gathering in September 2006 brought together 550 younger leaders from 112 nations with the single focus of informing, inspiring, developing, and connecting younger leaders, so that the church might bring the gospel to the whole world (www.lausanneworldpulse.com). The Call2All made during the final morning of their gathering on 1 February 2008 at the Orlando Congress was a commitment, through their different networks and partnerships, to see more than one billion people reached with the gospel by 2020 (www.call2all.org). Other initiatives include MOTE, a South African coalition of students which saw over 4,300 students going on short-term mission exposure trips in the last five years (www.ftlt.org); MIA2012, which gathered and sent 461 younger leaders on short-term outreaches to over fourteen African countries south of the equator (www.movingintoaction.co.za); the Student Christian Movement of India, which has over 10,000 members from thirteen regions, united around one vision (www.scmindia.org); and Mission-net, an European network of younger leaders gathering every three years with a focus to "Transform our World" (http://mission-net.org).

All these initiatives, and many more, are committed to seeing the emerging leadership generation empowered and focused around a common mission vision—that all may have the opportunity of accepting Jesus Christ as their Lord and Savior.

---

3   SAPA, "Banning" ANCYL empowers right—Malema, 2012. <http://www.news24.com/SouthAfrica/Politics/ANCYL-banning-empowers-right-Malema-20120226>.
4   J. W. Goll and L. Engle, *The Call of the Elijah Revolution: The Passion for Radical Change* (Shippensburg, PA: Destiny Image, 2008), 30.

In July 2013 a small group of younger leaders gathered under the banner of the Movement for Africa National Initiatives (MANI) in Pretoria, South Africa. Their focus was to look at the realities the current emerging generation is facing as well as how to help others better understand who they are. With so much said during the two day conference, a few remarkable points stood out:

- The Emerging Leadership Generation (ELG) is made of creative thinking entrepreneurs that are able to create that which does not exist yet. They are not scared to take risks. They are chasers of instant rewards and prefer organic processes above structures or systems.
- The ELG generally wants to be involved rather than being mere listeners in the church. They are not monochurch based and are frequently exploring new horizons, which poses its challenges to the future of megachurch models.
- The ELG thinks differently about money, although they still have the need to be self-sustainable. They eagerly explore new possibilities and many of them are aware of the conflict between trade and aid.
- The ELG has a need for authentic interaction with the older generation; a need to have a role model and to be listened to. They are challenged with mentorship that comes with a hidden agenda of recruitment. This causes them to distance themselves from established ministries and initiatives as they feel the interest in them, as persons, is often faked.
- The ELG challenges whether existing evangelization models are still relevant and asks what should be done to stay in touch with the rapidly changing world.
- As a generation the ELG is constantly aware of the need to work more closely together. The question is not so much whether they need to do this as to how it can be done.
- The desire of the ELG is not just to learn from other global regions but to learn with them.

In the Netherlands, Eleonora Hof states that Reformed churches who consider themselves to be orthodox have a long tradition of both catechesis and youth gatherings. An elaborate structure exists in which youths during their teenage years are often obliged by their parents to participate in catechesis classes. Most denominations have established catechesis materials, youth weekends, and youth camps. However, due to factors such as secularization, involvement in these activities is not as self-evident as it was in former years. As a result, many churches are experimenting with youth services which are (partially) organized by youths themselves. In addition, national events are organized which sometimes attract large crowds of youths. The connection with Christians across the country and the festival character of these gatherings are important reasons for participating in this type of event. Recreation is also an important dimension of youth gatherings given the abundance of youth camps, sport activities, etc.

From the USA, Ken Katayama shares that in spite of growing secularism and shrinking Christianity in the West, specifically in the USA, he has seen large growth in the United States church. The majority of the growth has been reported in so called "non-denominational" churches. He believes that several members live in the "historical church" but attend the "new non-denominational church."

This is significant because most of the fastest growing churches in the USA, for example The Life Church and North Point Community Church, are reaching and engaging the younger generation who love Jesus but do not love traditional models of "how to worship and live" for Jesus. Some of the main forces driving these changes are:

- *Technology.* Some churches have high quality videos and graphics. They also utilize social media like twitter, facebook, apps, and online services to connect with their members as well as individuals interested in learning more about the church.
- *"If I can play, I will stay."* Attitudes of those that attend these churches have changed from "going to the church" to "being the church." It is no longer about attending church for an hour on Sunday morning to listen to a message and then returning home. Members who have a "being the church" attitude consider themselves followers, the body, the ministers of the church who have an active role to play.
- *Decentralized power.* No more dichotomy between secular and sacred. If we are the body then all of us are called to follow Jesus and make new followers of Jesus Christ.
- *Customer focus mentality.* Most of these churches focus their main activities and programs on Sundays to serve outsiders and not insiders, seeking to draw the outsider into the body of Christ. With this idea in mind, their members continually ask the question, "How can I add value?" and take bold steps to give back.

Some applications for the young missions movement are:

- *Flat structures within the organization.* Young believers coming from these, "next generation churches" will "smell" from far away whether they will have a place to add value to the team or just be another player fulfilling a task.
- *New ways of recruitment.* The typical "'go and raise your funds" may not be the most effective way of recruiting new workers. Not that I believe fundraising will go away, but the realities of tent-making and business as missions will be more appealing to the younger generation. The important point here is to provide options.
- *Leadership of resourcing, not authority.* The younger generation respects leadership based on authentic relationship and the resourcing that a leader can provide rather than the authority the leader carries based on his/her title.
- *Innovating as you innovate.* More than ever, fast changes and quick adjustments are non-negotiables. Technology produces culture changes in our society more than ever before. Organizations must re-work their systems and processes to allow new changes to take place at a fast pace.

In Europe, Evi Rodemann explains that there are fresh expressions of church and many innovative initiatives for rethinking church today. The 24–7 movement just celebrated their tenth anniversary in Dublin, October 2013; they have experienced an explosion of prayer and new communities all across Europe. When the riots happened in London in January 2012, 24–7 people were out on the streets cleaning. In Eastern Europe young people are eager to start indigenous mission organizations. Organizations like Operation Mobilisation and Youth with a Mission have stimulated many new organizations and mobilized thousands of young people across Europe to become more missions minded. Youth for Christ, with thousands of volunteers across Europe, has had a massive impact on youth work in churches and also outside of churches with their youth cafés. Another impact on Europe has been European-wide congresses like the IFES Student Congresses, Taize, TEMA, and Mission-Net. Under the umbrella of the European Evangelical Alliance and the European Evangelical Mission Association, young people from across Europe are called to live a missional lifestyle within the Mission-Net movement. Young people from all European nations are involved, and they seek to apply their missional lifestyle in their countries and churches. Bulgaria, for example, has experienced a prayer and fasting movement started by young leaders following a Mission-Net congress in 2010, and it has been greater than what has been seen over the past fifty years. Many youth organizations and networks have raised the rallying cry to God to once again turn our continent around.

Questions for Reflection:

1. While there might be much more to say about the Globalized Christian Youth Movement's longing for change, the question remains: what platforms are available for them to live out this change they wish to see?

2. With a need for change to come quickly and the demand for it to be visible through authentic leadership, what example is needed from existing leaders to model change in the twenty-first century?

3. How can discipleship be done without an agenda to recruit young people to fulfill a specific role within our organizations? Are we willing to disciple for the purpose of serving other organizations?

References

Goll, J.W., and L. Engle. 2008. *The Call of the Elijah Revolution: The Passion for Radical Change*. Shippensburg: Destiny Image.

Fowler, A. 2012. Time for Students to Unite around Important Issues, Tuition. <http://kykernel.com/2012/02/27/time-for-students-to-unite-on-important-issues-tuition/>.

Jenkins, P. 2007. *The Next Christendom: The Coming of Global Christianity*. New York: Oxford University Press.

SAPA. 2012. "Banning" ANCYL Empowers Right—Malema. <http://www.news24.com/SouthAfrica/Politics/ANCYL-banning-empowers-right-Malema-20120226>.

Adriaan Adams believes that Africa has the potential of becoming a global influencer and that this is possible through the empowering of the emerging generation of leaders. He serves as Executive Director at FTLT (Focus Team Leadership Training), a South African-based missional leadership development institution. From within the WEA-MC he serves as a staff member and cofacilitates the Continuum group. He is also responsible for younger leadership development within the MC. He is married and, together with his wife Lydia, has two kids, Bridget and Stephen. Two of his favorite slogans he is known by are: "God is more interested in your character than your comfort," and "Even though I may not see the results of my efforts today or even in my lifetime, I'm confident that doing the right thing—the significant thing—will produce rewards for the organization and for others far beyond what I might otherwise achieve."

Manifested through various expressions, the Globalized Christian Youth Movement is passionate to see that their spiritual transformation is tangibly visible through practical involvement in their communities.

CHAPTER 24

MEETING A POLISH ROMAN CATHOLIC

Rita Rimkiene

This is a true story—the names have been changed.

These days we are accustomed to the media's generous attention to migration. Some countries praise migration, especially if the migrants generate economic growth and create new job opportunities (for example, Spain or Greece). But there are others that would like to receive fewer migrants, like the UK.

It happened that my family and I moved to the UK in 2004. Interestingly, Lithuanians did not jump on the train heading to a "better life" to Western Europe as the Polish did in 2004. Our economy was stable and the cracks of financial difficulties only became visible in 2008. Yet, people were on the move.

We came to study at Redcliffe College. At first it was very difficult to adjust to a new culture, language, and traditions. Our daughter was only two and a half years old. People told us that children experience less culture shock than adults, but our little one had a difficult time. However, time passed and soon we felt at home.

The biggest change of all was my husband's conversion on the 7th of July, 2005. That day the whole of the UK was in deep mourning and shock as London was stunned by a series of coordinated suicide attacks. My husband was deeply touched and shaken by it and made the most important decision in his life—to follow Jesus Christ. When our lives changed, we brought changes to many homes.

For some reason, we Eastern European migrants are drawn to one another. Our body movement, always-serious facial expressions, language, and gestures are the telltale signs of our strict, Soviet regime upbringing. We know each other's past and often talk about it. This is our connection point. We even have a common language—Russian. However, Russian is used by the older generation. Generation Y has no idea what their parents and grandparents went through in order to make their lives easier and more enjoyable.

When I first met Aga she was the most joyful Polish lady I have ever met. In 2006, she left her little son to her mum and came to England. Aga is a physiotherapist, but when she came to England she had to work as a cleaner. She did not speak any English and struggled to make ends meet. The agency that she worked for moved her from one place to another, and eventually she was placed at a bed and breakfast (small hotel, B&B). The owner of the B&B noticed Aga and soon they were married.

In general Poles are open and direct people, but it takes time to build a friendship. They are suspicious of everything and everyone. They like to complain about everything and life is never good. English people start conversation with a weather update, while Poles will always start with a problem of some kind. But then it might get better and finally, you can even crack a joke.

Since our children went to the same school we set up a routine. I always stopped at her B&B for a cup of tea and then we made our way to the school. We had great chats and laughter. Aga's life is one enormous story. She always had a story to tell. After a while, I noticed that her joyful self was not built on a real joy in life.

Hardships taught her to laugh at problems rather to solve them. The truth was that their B&B business was on the edge of bankruptcy. They were in debt and Aga suffered from anxiety panic attacks. Her husband had owned the B&B for more than twenty years and was tired of just making ends meet. The big new hotels like Premier Inn were taking over the business formerly provided by small B&Bs, and many in this position had to be sold or experienced bankruptcy. They tried to sell, but could not find a buyer. So, they were stuck with a failing business.

As my visits continued, so our talks got deeper and deeper. Our families got together for meals and big celebrations like Christmas. To our surprise, Aga asked me to pray for their family and bless meals every time we dined at their B&B. As they came to our home, they experienced something very different. We prayed and we were able to move conversation topics into more serious areas of life. We played games together with our children and showed interest in their lives.

As time passed, Aga asked us what we believed and what church we went to. Aga is a devout Roman Catholic: as most Polish would say, you cannot be Polish if you are not Roman Catholic. We had a good theological discussion and I learned a lot about her faith. To my surprise she had a very good understanding of who Jesus was. She disliked the Polish Catholic Mass and began to attend an English Catholic Mass. Then, she came to every event that we ran at our Baptist church and enjoyed getting to know people and a different Christian tradition.

Often she complained about English culture and how difficult it is to make friends with locals. As our friendship grew stronger I invited her for a weekend away with another four of my English friends. These four women were strong believers and I really wanted her to make friends with them. During the weekend she noticed bits of our faith. We read the Bible and prayed, we openly talked about everything in life. Aga was the core of the group. She was a storyteller! But then there were lonely moments when we sat and talked and the sadness and worries in her eyes did not go away. After the weekend away, she had made two new friends. We began to meet regularly for meals and share our lives, pray, and rejoice in what great friends we became. Aga flourished and rested and openly acknowledged the existence of God.

And then, when I was going to the hospital to give birth to my second daughter she came along with my husband to witness a miracle. She could not stop crying. When she came to look at my baby girl, I whispered to her about God's love to her and to my family. She nodded in agreement. This story is an illustration of how we disciple people. We had a choice—do we take a person on a personal journey with us or do we sign them up for a six-week church discipleship course and never see her/him again? Is it better to tell a Roman Catholic that they have it all wrong or to take a walk of faith with her/him and show the real meaning of God's love?

Physical migration scratches only the surface of people's movement from one place to another. Spiritual migration is left unnoticed. A foreign land lifts up a shield from a migrant's eyes, her/his heart and soul tend to be more sensitive and yearn for rediscovery and re-creation of self. Aga, as with many other migrants, is very open to God's revelation in her life. What she needed was a friend to invite her on a journey of a lifetime. As a result of our friendship, Aga did not begin to go to an evangelical church, but has become more aware of her faith.

Questions for Reflection:

1. What is your experience of migration, moving yourself to a new place. or receiving migrants in your community?
2. What are some of the lessons we learn from Rita's experience coming to the UK? And what do we learn from her relationship to Aga, the woman from Poland?

Rita Rimkiene works alongside church and GARAS (Gloucestershire Action for Refugee and Asylum Seekers). This is a very new ministry not only at this church, but for the city. GARAS brings asylum seekers and Christians together once a month for meal at church. The beginning of new friendships begin at the table and expand into a family. They have seen asylum seekers coming to Christ and becoming the most amazing evangelists.

CHAPTER 25

THE DOCK CHURCH
IN BELFAST

Paul Coulter

From Bomb City to Titanic City

The city of Belfast is nestled between green hills at the mouth of the River Lagan. In recent decades it has been best known for bombs and sectarian tensions, but historically it was a vital industrial center including the world's busiest shipyards. The Northern Ireland government seeks to promote a "Shared Future" (Community Relations Unit 2005) for Protestants and Catholics who live in divided communities—95% of children attend schools segregated by religion and 80% of social housing (98% in Belfast) is segregated.[1] One of the foremost attempts to revitalise Belfast and to create a truly shared neighborhood is the ongoing regeneration of land formerly used for shipbuilding as "Titanic Quarter," named in honor of the world's most famous ship, which was built in Belfast. The people of Belfast, aware of the irony of a ship that sank on its maiden voyage becoming an emblem of urban regeneration, often comment humorously, "It was all right when it left here!"

Titanic Quarter is being developed in stages by a company, Titanic Quarter Ltd. In the shadow of two massive cranes nicknamed Samson and Goliath (an echo of the city's rich Christian heritage) are a hotel, apartments, shop units, the world-class Titanic Belfast visitor attraction, the main site for Belfast Metropolitan College, a science park, banking offices, film studios (location for filming the hugely successful HBO series Game of Thrones) and the Public Records Office. With breathtaking streetscapes integrating industrial heritage and waterfront sophistication, there is, quite simply, nowhere quite like Titanic Quarter in Northern Ireland or, arguably, elsewhere in Europe.

Another unique feature of this patch of land in a city with a "Landscape of Spires" is the absence of any church building or congregation.[2] Belfast is said to have the highest concen-

---

1   J. Hamilton, U. Hansson, J. Bell, and S. Toucas, *Segregated Lives Social Division, Sectarianism and Everyday Life in Northern Ireland* (Belfast: Institute for Conflict Research, 2008), 11; D. Schubotz, "Beyond the Orange and the Green: The Diversification of the Qualitative Social Research Landscape in Northern Ireland," *Forum: Qualitative Social Research* 6(3), Art 29 (2005), http://www.qualitative-research.net/fqs-texte/3-05/05-3-29-e.htm [7 Mar 2014]; Community Relations Unit, "A Shared Future: Policy and Strategic Framework for Good Relations in Northern Ireland," Belfast: Office of the First Minister & Deputy First Minister (2005).
2   J. D. Brewer, M. Keane, and D. N. Livingstone, *Landscape of Spires* (2006), http://abdn.ac.uk/staffpages/uploads/soc197/Landscape%20of%20Spires.doc.

tration of evangelical churches anywhere in the world.[3] In recent years, however, inner city congregations have struggled and many have closed, even as some suburban congregations in each of the main denominations have thrived. As a result, there has been a resurgent interest in church planting and the already diverse denominational landscape (a result of different national heritages and various historic revivals) has seen the addition of newer networks of churches including Vineyard and New Frontiers.

The Vision of a "Shared Medley"

The Church of Ireland, part of the worldwide Anglican Communion, is the second largest Protestant denomination in Northern Ireland. Titanic Quarter lies within the Diocese of Down and Dromore, whose bishop, Harold Miller, is an evangelical and an ardent promoter of church renewal and mission, but due to its exclusively industrial past it did not fall inside a parish. Aware of the regeneration plans, Bishop Miller hoped to see a Christian presence in Titanic Quarter, so in 2009 he appointed Chris Bennett, an ordained clergyman in his mid-thirties, to explore possibilities under the name of "Dock Church," later shortened simply to "The Dock." Chris is a dynamic individual with an infectious passion for every aspect of Titanic Quarter. He set about establishing strong links with Titanic Quarter Ltd, politicians, and other key stakeholders and, by listening to them and demonstrating his commitment to the success of the project, has met with their favor.

Chris's frustration with the fragmentation of the church in Northern Ireland—depicted over coffee in sketches on napkins of a typical village high street with multiple church buildings apparently competing with one another—resonated, for him, with the government's vision of a "Shared Future." Rather than multiple places of worship he envisioned a space in Titanic Quarter to be shared by representatives of different Christian denominations. The ideal setting, resonating with the Titanic theme, would be a boat, and Chris began to think of "chaplaincy" as a helpful term for this approach to ministry. Although this term has been questioned by some, Chris insists that the way in which chaplains operate in hospitals and universities—representing their different traditions, but sharing facilities and liaising with one another—can work in Titanic Quarter and, perhaps, further afield. He describes his concept as a "shared medley" in which diverse expressions of Christian faith—different traditions and approaches to ministry—can coexist in unity under the banner of "The Dock."

Chris's vision and personal charisma soon attracted support from others, and one-by-one chaplains and volunteers from other denominations have come "on-board." The process of gathering support has had its frustrations. Some church groups came to visit the curiosity that is The Dock, seeing the sights of Titanic Quarter in the process, but offered no financial support. The Diocese supports Chris part-time and he has worked as a tour guide at times to supplement his income. Under a scheme to fill vacant shop units, Chris was able to set up what he believes to be the world's first "honesty café"—operating entirely on the basis of a box in which people donate what they choose to rather than paying set prices. The Dock Café, now in its third incarnation, has a cool, relaxed, artistic feel to it. Other

---

3   J. Mandryk, *Operation World: The Definitive Prayer Guide to Every Nation*, 7th ed (Colorado Springs: Biblica Publishing, 2010), 859.

activities pioneered by Chris, including a book group and a social gathering called "Meet the Neighbors," share the café's value of creating a sense of community in an area that would otherwise lack it.

More recently, The Dock has held Sunday Services on the restored SS Nomadic, a boat once used to transfer passengers to the Titanic and now moored just in front of the Dock Café as a tourist attraction. Chris has made creative use of blogs and websites to promote interest in his work and has attracted considerable media interest, including global news coverage of his part in the Titanic centenary celebrations in 2012, a television documentary shown in Northern Ireland, and an episode of a UK-wide BBC television program consisting of hymns and interviews. The Dock is also recognized on the website of the Fresh Expressions movement, an initiative for new church formation that originated within the Church of England and the Methodist Church.

A Theology of Community Formation

Chris identifies as an evangelical, although he expresses some discomfort both at the way the term is sometimes perceived in Northern Irish society as a marker of fundamentalism and political Protestantism and with the attempts of some to define evangelicalism in more theologically conservative terms than he is comfortable with. Chris adheres personally to the Anglican Thirty-Nine Articles and describes the theological basis of The Dock as the Apostles' Creed. Although he feels somewhat uncomfortable with the "extremes" of sacramental Catholicism and conservative Calvinism, he also expresses his willingness for the medley of The Dock to include activities as diverse as Presbyterian Bible studies and Catholic masses so long as those who lead them can add the phrase "but that's ok" after stating their differences. Unity, he insists, must permit diversity but must also be maintained by mutual respect and acceptance. Chris's thinking also shows elements of emergent post-conservative theology, especially in a growing reluctance to think of Christian faith in strict "in or out" terms and in his experimental approach to worship through "Dock Walks" in which Scripture is read and music listened to while walking through Titanic Quarter.

Throughout his time in The Dock, often to his surprise, Chris has found the roles of entrepreneur, raiser of support, café manager, and vision-caster (not skills that featured in his ministerial training) fulfilling. He acknowledges that few of his actions would be considered openly "evangelistic" or even overtly "spiritual" (no preaching, Bible studies, Alpha Course, or literature distribution), but he has a settled conviction that his calling has been to open up the space into which others can bring the diverse elements of mission and church that will bless the people who inhabit and frequent Titanic Quarter. This was necessarily the focus in the early years, and Dock Café has become a firm favorite with college students and local residents, but Chris hopes for greater spiritual impact in future. He hopes to see varied expressions of church in Titanic Quarter, including some connected with diverse Christian traditions and others emerging from the unique context, all under the banner of The Dock.

Conclusion

Chris defines mission as: "The imperative to share the joy and love of God with people who don't know him yet," which "can (and should) take the form of deeds and not just words."

His work to date has majored on deeds, especially creating an open and inviting space within which community can develop. Some evangelicals may question this approach, as Chris himself acknowledges. Has he elevated the value of community formation above the center that makes community distinctively Christian—namely Christ and the gospel that testifies to him? Has the vision of The Dock been too influenced by the agenda of government for regeneration and reconciliation rather than a biblical vision of making Christ known? The Dock also highlights important questions about the center and limits of unity in mission, especially relating to cooperation between evangelicals and Catholics. Nevertheless, it is a unique example in the context of Belfast of church planting in a way that takes seriously the problems of the city, is defined by hopeful celebration of future possibilities, seeks to partner with the shapers of physical and social space, aims to incarnate Christian presence into a new context, and is willing to do so in a way that celebrates diversity rather than insisting on narrow uniformity.

Read more about The Dock online at www.the-dock.org.

Questions for Reflection

1. Given the unique opportunity presented by Titanic Quarter, how would you approach the task of establishing a Christian presence there?
2. How adequate do you think Chris Bennett's definition and approach to mission is?
3. Can the strengths of The Dock in terms of coordinated strategy, partnership with government and private developers, and openness to unity with diversity be reproduced on a larger scale across cities and nations?

References

Brewer, J.D., M. Keane, and D.N. Livingstone. 2006. Landscape of Spires. http://abdn. ac.uk/staffpages/uploads/soc197/Landscape%20of%20Spires.doc.

Community Relations Unit. 2005. *A Shared Future: Policy and Strategic Framework for Good Relations in Northern Ireland.* Belfast: Office of the First Minister & Deputy First Minister.

Hamilton, J., U. Hansson, J. Bell, and S. Toucas. 2008. *Segregated Lives Social Division, Sectarianism and Everyday Life in Northern Ireland.* Belfast: Institute for Conflict Research.

Mandryk, J. 2010. *Operation World: The Definitive Prayer Guide to Every Nation,* 7th ed. Colorado Springs: Biblica Publishing.

Schubotz, D. 2005. Beyond the Orange and the Green: The Diversification of the Qualitative Social Research Landscape in Northern Ireland. *Forum: Qualitative Social Research* 6(3), Art 29. http://www.qualitative-research.net/fqs-texte/3-05/05-3-29-e.htm.

Paul Coulter is a lecturer in practical theology and missiology in Belfast Bible College. He is engaged in doctoral studies on church planting by evangelicals in Northern Ireland, podcasts as the "Restless Wonderer," visits churches as a Bible teacher and trainer, and serves on the Northern Ireland Executive Committee of the Evangelical Alliance. His professional background is in medicine and he has previously worked in church-based ministry in both cross-cultural and same-culture settings. He is the husband of a Chinese Malaysian wife and father to two young children.

CHAPTER 26

IMPACTING OUR WORLD WITH HOPE

New Life Church in Stockholm

John van Dinther

New Life Church, located in the greater Stockholm area, is a regional, Swedish church with a multicultural profile including people from over fifty different nations (50% Swedish). Every weekend approximately 800 people participate in our worship services. The greater Stockholm area has over two million inhabitants and is the fastest growing city in Europe, expected to grow to two and a half million by the year 2030.

From its start in 1993, New Life Church has embraced the calling to be a church planting, multicultural church and to reflect the reality of society where it is located. Our mission is: *To Impact Our World with Hope.* In 2012, 30% of the population in the Stockholm area was born abroad or had parents who were born abroad. When New Life Stockholm was started, there were few expressions of church with a multicultural profile. We have created a bilingual (Swedish and English), multicultural environment where every participant and group is expected to participate in our main worship services. We chose English as the second language within the context of the church because many people that have moved to Sweden have a good or basic knowledge of English.

It is important to mention that throughout our history we have been challenged by individuals and groups from within the church who have wanted to divide the church into small entities so that they could celebrate their faith in a way that is more culturally comfortable to them. We know that it is important for people to hear the good news in the language of their hearts, therefore we developed the following approach based on the lessons learned from Jeremiah 29 where God tells his people that although they find themselves in captivity, that they have to embrace the city of Babylon as their own, establish themselves there, build houses and plant gardens and seek its welfare. This is a great example of enculturation. In the book of Daniel we also see how this "theology of the city" is fleshed out as he and his friends embrace the culture, the knowledge, the language, and mind-set of the Babylonian people without compromising their faith.

New Life has developed a six-step approach that gives room to relate the gospel in culturally relevant ways, but also leads to enculturation in the Swedish context:

1. & 2. *Evangelism and Discipleship.* We are focused on communicating the gospel in relevant ways and in the language of the people we are trying to reach. For example, our Mongolian ministry has developed a large network with dozens of people who have come to faith and have been baptized.

3. *Integration.* We expect every language/people group ministry to intentionally integrate new people into the overall church, its ministries and the worship services. During worship services, we provide interpretation (using head phones) into different languages, depending on the need.

4. *Multicultural lay leadership.* Key people from every group are identified, equipped, and released to be lay leaders not only in their own groups but also in ministries that benefit the whole church. In this phase, we encourage people to be involved in leadership and ministry that reach beyond their own language/people group.

5. *Multicultural staff and leadership.* As people grow in their leadership, we intentionally look for possible staff and people on eldership level among them. It is important to have role models from different cultural backgrounds for the sake of the health of the whole church. Traditional approaches to leadership, theology, and praxis are challenged through the wide diversity of people who help form the vision and direction of the church. Having this unity in diversity challenges all of our cultural and theological hang-ups!

6. *Multicultural governance.* We find the greatest challenges here. Since a good understanding of national and international legal issues is required to be able to function well, good and effective enculturation in Sweden is needed.

Circumstance or Call?

The overwhelming majority of the inhabitants of Stockholm have not really chosen to live here. The Swedes among us, oftentimes, have left their hometowns and families to pursue education or job opportunities in this the capital of Sweden. Many of the internationals have come for similar reasons. Immigrants, new Swedes, and refugees are drawn to this great city because many of their countrymen and potential natural networks can be found here. The sheer size of the city provides refuge and possibilities to the thousands of illegal immigrants as they "disappear" into the crowds.

New Life Church has identified the need to teach and disciple people with the Jeremiah 29 theology as we challenge them to see their presence in the city not as one based on circumstances but on calling! This understanding leads to a totally new perspective on their lives. People have to unpack their physical, emotional, social, and spiritual suitcases that have been in the hallway of their lives waiting for the next move. Now we call them to establish themselves here, no matter how long they might be here. We have shared tremendous seasons with people who disliked and even hated Sweden and/or Stockholm, and who learned to look at the city and nation through God's eyes. It has softened their hearts, made them commit themselves to seek the welfare of the city, and it changed their lives as they put down their roots!

As church, we see the tremendous possibilities of reaching our world with the good news of Jesus Christ as representatives of hundreds of nations and thousands of people groups and languages have flocked to our city. In our vision to be a multicultural church, we see another three-fold purpose:

1. We see the fulfillment of God's purpose and plan fleshed out in our community of faith as Swedes and people from dozens of different nations find God and celebrate true unity in Christ.
2. We see the importance of internationals and new Swedes to reevangelize our own nation and city. They are not here by circumstance but by calling! God has allowed people from all over the world to come to Sweden. Some have come to find God in a nation where there is religious freedom. Some Christians have come here because Stockholm and Sweden need them! We as a nation have fallen away from our roots and need to be taught again the ways of God. As a body of believers we don't seem to be able to reach our own nation.
3. We also see that it's possible to touch the lives of hundreds of people who are in Sweden for a season, who have found God here, or have been renewed in their faith and then return to their own nations and networks, impacting their world with hope!

There are four areas that we focus on as we try to live out our mission, *To Impact our World with Hope*:

1. *Presence.* Our authority to speak into the city, its systems, and its people is derived from our willingness to become a part of the city and be rooted. As church, we are called to help people integrate, not only into the church, but also into Swedish society. New Life Church has received The Prize of Integration from the Municipality of the Greater Stockholm Area as acknowledgment of our efforts to connect people to the city and help them feel a part of it.
2. *Prayer.* We are called to pray for our community. Jeremiah 24:7 says "Pray to the Lord for it because if it prospers, you too will prosper!" We are called to pray for the city, its leaders, its organizations, and systems. We are called to bless the city and to release God's blessings and purpose on it through our prayers.
3. *Practice.* We are called to practice our faith through action. God says that we have to work for the welfare of the city, or the shalom of the city. We are to create ministries of mercy and to serve the needs of the poor and the exposed. We are called to be advocates for the powerless, the voice of the voiceless, and the ambassadors of the marginalized. As church, we work with people who have illegal statuses, who are victims of trafficking, who abuse drugs and alcohol, who are getting out of prison, and many others. At New Life, the greatest asset is not necessarily our different ministries, but people, who gather in cell groups throughout the city and take care of each other.
4. *Proclamation.* Without proclamation people will not hear. We see the dimension of proclamation as important as the other three mentioned above.

It is the unique combination of these four aspects that fleshes out the good news from the church into our world!

Questions for Reflection:

1. The reality of many cities in the world today is a society composed by different ethnicities. What is your experience in being church in a multicultural context?

2. The New Life Church in Stockholm has developed a six-step approach for making the gospel culturally relevant to people. How applicable are these steps to your context?

3. Van Dinther mentions four "P"s as focus areas for living out their mission. How important would these be also in your ministry situation?

John van Dinther is a Stockholm, Sweden-based pastor, and church planter leading a network of churches and church plants with a predominately multicultural profile. His passion is to make disciple makers, develop reproducing leaders, and plant reproducing churches in Sweden and beyond. www.newlife.nu

CHAPTER 27

ETHIOPIAN DIASPORA MISSION

Wondimu Mathewos Game

The God of mission is also the God of history. "History is his story." Throughout history and the generations, God has been—and is—in control to accomplish his divine will through his church as well as through global trends.

This is the era of globalization. Globalization is not a threat to God and his church. On the other hand, globalization, socioeconomic factors, religious persecution, and political instability have caused extensive migration and increased the mobility of people. "Very few people today live in the geographical area where their ancestors originated. Most of us have come from somewhere else even if it was centuries ago."[1]

The effect of migration is multidimensional and wide-ranging; it inevitably creates changes in diaspora communities themselves, for their country of origin and for host countries. However, such dispersion gives ample opportunities to complete the Great Commission. As a missional church of this era, Ethiopian churches are viewing diaspora people as missionaries in the mission field. "Nonetheless, it is unfortunately true that migration has been traditionally viewed as a political and social challenge. It is only in recent years that diaspora has been taken seriously as a unique missionary gift."[2]

History of Migration and the Role of Diaspora in Cross-Cultural Mission

Since the fall of Adam, migration has been a fact of human history. "For as long as human beings have inhabited the planet, relocation, displacement, and population transfers have marked the human condition."[3] Following the division of language and dispersal of humankind, God called Abraham to go to a new country: "Go to the land that I will show you" (Gen 11:1–9). God initiated Abraham's migration and promised to give him the land, to bless him with upper level and lower level blessings, and to bless the whole family of

---

1   Lausanne Committee for World Evangelization, *The New People Next Door* (2004) www.lausanne.org/docs/ 2004forum/LOP55_IG26.pdf.
2   S. Hun Kim, *Korean Diaspora and Christian Mission* (Eugene, OR: Wipf & Stock, 2011), 1.
3   J. Jehu Hanciles, *Beyond Christendom: Globalization, African Migration and the Transformation of the West* (Maryknoll, NY: Orbis Books, 2008), 356.

the earth through him.[4] Abraham was a migrant, moving through different nations and even continents until the end of his life. Abraham's descendants—Isaac, Jacob, Joseph and all of Israel—were migrants and were scattered all over the world for a variety of different spiritual, economic, political, and social reasons. "The Old Testament patriarchs (and matriarchs) were frequently migrants. Abraham, the prototypical migrant, models the profound integration of mobility, spiritual pilgrimage, and the unfolding of divine purpose."[5]

Moreover, Daniel and his three friends glorified God while in exile. Ruth was a migrant and became an ancestor of Jesus. Naaman's Israelite servant girl witnessed to the power of the true God in a foreign land to her host family. The book of Esther also speaks of God's favor in exile. God in his mercy used the exilic situation for his glory and to bless the host land, "Seek the welfare of the city where I have sent you into exile and pray to the Lord on its behalf" (Jer 29:4–7).[6]

In the New Testament, we see how God incarnated in Jesus Christ intervened in human history, through his earthly ministry, death, and resurrection.[7] Jesus sent his disciples "unto the ends of the world" (Acts 1:8).[8]

Moreover, on the historic day of Pentecost, the church was born precisely at the time when people of the Diaspora (Jews and proselytes) were gathering from all over the world. As a consequence, those Diaspora members who converted on the day of Pentecost went back to their villages with the good news. They were the first missionaries; also the first cross-cultural church was planted through scattered disciples and Diaspora members in Samaria.[9]

Furthermore, in early church history most of the apostles were martyred in the mission field, not in Jerusalem. Peter and Paul were martyred in Rome, Thomas was martyred in India, and Matthew was martyred in Ethiopia.[10] The worldview and lifestyle of these early Christian pilgrims has been described as follows: "For them any foreign country is a motherland, and any motherland is a foreign country."[11] Thus, Christianity reached much of the world before the medieval era.

Likewise, even though the approaches used and the motives behind it were questionable, migration associated with colonialism led to church growth. "The missionary impulse intimately intertwined with the extraordinary swell of Europe migrant movement and imperial actions were equally unprecedented missionary initiatives … They were also convinced that imperial acquisitions were providentially ordained for the expansion of the gospel of salvation."[12]

---

4   Genesis 12:1–3, 10–16; 26:1–3; 28:10–15; Hebrews 11:8–11.
5   Hanciles, *Beyond Christendom*, 143.
6   Daniel 2,3,4,5:25–28; Ruth 1:11–18; Matthew 1:5–6; 1 Kings 1–7; 2 Kings 5: 1–18; Esther 7,8,9.
7   John 1:14; Philippians 2:7; John 3:16
8   Matthew 28:16–20; Mark 16:8–20; John 20:21; Acts 1:6–8.
9   Acts 2:1–13; Acts 8:1–4; 11:19, 13:1–3.
10   Patrick Johnstone, *The Future of the Global Church: History, Trends and Possibilities* (UK: Biblica, 2011), 23.
11   Andrew Louth, ed., "Letter to Diognetus," in *Early Christian Writings: The Apostolic Fathers* (New York: Penguin Books, 1987),145
12   Andrew Walls and Cathy Ross, eds., *Mission in the Twenty-first Century* (New York: Orbis, 2008), 120.

The era of globalization is "the age of migration." Migration is at an all-time high. In 2001 it was estimated that "one in thirty-five (191 million) of the world's population are registered as migrants."[13] Whatever the cause of migration, migrants travel with their religion.

> The massive migrations throughout the continent in recent decades have also stimulated an extraordinary and unprecedented expansion of the African missionary movement.[14]

> In simple terms, from both a biblical and a historical perspective, every Christian migrant is a potential missionary. Precisely because the heartlands of global Christianity are now in the south, contemporary South-North migration forms the taproot of major non-Western missionary movement.[15]

Furthermore, migrant churches are some of the fastest growing churches in Europe and America. "African churches in London are growing much more rapidly than any other."[16]

Ethiopian Diaspora Mission

Ethiopia is one of the countries in this global trend whose people migrate at a very high rate. "It has been a long time since Ethiopians started to leave their homeland and migrate to various countries due to political, economic, and social reasons."[17] And according to different sources "It is estimated that not less than two million Ethiopian diaspora are residing in North America, Europe, the Middle East, Australia, and Africa."[18]

Moreover, the local and international media has recently reported that the Saudi Arabian government expelled more than 165,000 illegal Ethiopian immigrants. This clearly indicates that an uncountable number of legal and illegal Ethiopians are living and working in the Middle East. Many Middle Eastern countries, agencies, and agents, as well as Ethiopian agencies, are recruiting Ethiopian professionals for high professional positions, as labor workers, and as house maids. Most of these migrants are Christians with a burning passion to share Christ with others.

However, the level of orientation or training for these migrants to share Christ with their words and deeds is very low. Because of the lack of proper orientation, most Ethiopian migrants are below their capacity concerning missionary responsibility. Most are more concerned with keeping their Christianity for themselves. They can easily gather within an Ethiopian Fellowship and worship in their own local language. They are often more inclined to serve their home country than their host country. Thus, most Ethiopians living abroad are living in their "ghetto," in the attitude of a refugee.

---

13   Patrick Johnstone, *The Future of the Global Church: History, Trends and Possibilities* (Colorado Springs, CO: Biblica, 2011), 4.
14   Hanciles, *Beyond Christendom*, 218.
15   Ibid, 278.
16   Lausanne Committee for World Evangelization, *The New People Next Door*, 19.
17   www.ethdiaspora.org.et.
18   www.ethdiaspora.org.et.

On the other hand, it is said that twenty-first century mission is from everywhere to everywhere. Our missionary God is raising an uncountable army from countries that were formerly themselves considered to be the mission field. "Mission fields have become mission forces and a new epoch of Christian mission has been inaugurated … Evangelical mission today goes from everywhere to everywhere and the traditional concepts of sending and receiving countries are outdated."[19]

As a result of the gravity of twenty-first century mission, most Ethiopian churches have made a policy decision to be missional churches and have officially announced their intention to become a mission force for world evangelization. Most denominations are sending missionaries: for example the Ethiopian Kale Heywet Church and the Ethiopian Evangelical Church Mekane Yesus, the two largest Ethopian denominations, have started to send missionaries. Other denominations are also preparing themselves to start missional movements.

In this era, Ethiopian Christian migrants are already in the mission field. There are lots of Ethiopian churches in Europe and North America as well as in the Middle East. Most them are well organized and are reaching many non-Christian Ethiopians and Eritreans. They have bought church buildings in different countries from mainline churches. For example, in the center of London at Kings Cross, the Ethiopian Fellowship Church in the UK bought a building from the Anglican Church and is worshiping there.

However, Ethiopian diaspora churches are often more inward looking and do not contribute significantly to world evangelization. Their main challenge relates to the attitude of leaders and ministers towards cross-cultural mission. For most Ethiopians, including church leaders and ministers, "mission is the responsibility of white people." Ethiopia has been a missionary-receiving country for decades. This has shaped the attitudes of Ethiopians to mission.

However, there are also practical barriers hindering Ethiopians' engagement in cross-cultural mission.

Language challenges: English is the second or third language of most Ethiopians. This is especially a problem when Ethiopian preachers attempt to preach in English: "this linguistic distinction is much more difficult to overcome in public preaching, which, for most African pastors, tends to be an impassioned affair."[20]

Refugee attitude/living in a ghetto: Ethiopian diaspora members are more attached to their home country than their host country. Their dream is to be a blessing to their own land. "For the diaspora church, inward-looking behavior creates barriers to reaching out to other ethnic diasporas, the host culture, and the marginalized." However, the second and third generations are better at relating to their host community and culture.

Western secularism and consumerism culture influence: For people from a Third World background, relating to the postmodern secularist worldview is one of the greatest challenges.

---

19   L. Bertil Ekström, *From "Mission Field" to "Mission Force": The Emergence of Mission Organisations in Former Mission Receiving Countries* (Ware, UK: All Nations Christian College, 2011), 325.
20   Hanciles, *Beyond Christendom*, 367.

To Ethiopian believers, the self-centered and self-worshiping tendencies of the postmodern secularist person are challenging and shocking.

To overcome these challenges and to use the Ethiopian diaspora effectively for God's mission it would be wise to focus on the following:

- Awareness-raising and attitude-changing strategies can help the Ethiopian diaspora "to live in the world for the world, but not of the world."[21] These can include capacity-building programs (including consultation and training of trainers) about diaspora in cross-cultural mission.
- Networking and engagement strategies can enhance the Ethiopian diaspora churches' impact and make them into a powerful mission force.

Conclusion

"Crucially, the interface between human mobility and divine purposes in the biblical history is unmistakable and compelling. The inextricable link between migrant movements and the *missio Dei* (the mission of God) arguably confirms the historicity of many events."[22] Whether they realize it or not, evangelical Ethiopian migrants are potential missionaries with the purpose of reaching both unreached natives and other migrants with the gospel.

In conclusion, understanding the following issues and teaching them to Ethiopian evangelical immigrants is crucial for engaging them in cross-cultural mission and maximizing opportunities:

- God is a missionary God: mission flows from him.
- The nature of the church and mission of the church: The church is missionary by her very nature. Mission is her identity and life purpose. The church exists because of and for mission. (Romans 1:14–16)
- The power of the gospel: The gospel is the power of God to transform and to redeem generations and nations.
- The life purpose of Christian disciples: God's divine agenda is more important than their wellbeing.
- Migration and the role of diaspora in the fulfillment of God's historic purposes: "The Bible's history and message would be meaningless without migration and mobility."[23]

---

21 Girma Bekele, *The In-Between People: A Reading of David Bosch Through the Lens of Mission History and Contemporary Challenges in Ethiopia* (Eugene, OR: Pickwick, 2011), 324.

22 Hanciles, *Beyond Christendom*, 141.

23 Hanciles, *Beyond Christendom*, 140.

Questions for Reflection:

1. In what ways can diaspora be seen as a unique missionary gift? What are some of the examples in history mentioned by the author that proves that affirmation? Are there other examples from your own context?

2. Wondimu Mathewos mentions several challenges that the Ethiopian diaspora face when engaging in cross-cultural mission. What are some of the other challenges that you have seen or experienced in missionary work through migration?

References

Bekele, Girma. 2011. *The In-Between People: A Reading of David Bosch Through the Lens of Mission History and Contemporary Challenges in Ethiopia.* Eugene, OR: Pickwick.

Ekström, Bertil. 2011. *From "Mission Field" to "Mission Force": The Emergence of Mission Organisations in Former Mission Receiving Countries.* Ware, UK: All Nations Christian College.

Hanciles, J. Jehu. 2008. *Beyond Christendom: Globalization, African Migration and the Transformation of the West.* Maryknoll, NY: Orbis Books.

Johnstone, Patrick. 2011. *The Future of the Global Church: History, Trends and Possibilities.* Colorado Springs, CO: Biblica.

Kim, S. Hun. 2011. *Korean Diaspora and Christian Mission.* Eugene, OR: Wipf & Stock.

Lausanne Committee for World Evangelization. 2004. *The New People Next Door.* www. lausanne.org/docs/2004forum/LOP55_IG26.pdf.

Louth, Andrew, ed. Letter to Diognetus. 1987. In *Early Christian Writings: The Apostolic Fathers.* New York: Penguin Books.

Walls, Andrew, and Cathy Ross, eds. 2008. *Mission in the 21st Century.* New York: Orbis.

Wondimu Mathewos Game belongs to the Ethiopian Evangelical Church MekaneYesus and is the International Mission Society Director/ MYIMS Director. He has a BA in Leadership and Development Study from MekaneYesus Leadership and Development College and a BA (Hons) in Biblical and Intercultural Study from Open University/All Nations Christian College.

CHAPTER 28

JAPANESE CHURCHES RESPOND TO THE EARTHQUAKE AND TSUNAMI DISASTER

Kenichi Shinagawa

On March 11, 2011 a massive earthquake (Richter scale 9.0) hit northeastern Japan (the area commonly called the Tohoku region). A sixteen-meter high tsunami followed and engulfed many towns along the Pacific coast. The Fukushima First Nuclear Power Plant was damaged by the earthquake and tsunami and radioactive substances were emitted into the atmosphere. This three-fold disaster of earthquake/tsunami/nuclear power plant accident really shook the nation of Japan: 15,883 were confirmed dead, 2,654 are registered as missing, and over 210,000 people were still in temporary housings as of September 11, 2013—two and a half years after the disaster. Despite all the efforts by the government and private sectors, the process of recovery and rebuilding has been very slow. It has been the most devastating disaster in the history of Japan after the World War II and it will take decades to rebuild the towns and villages in the disaster affected areas.

Christian churches in Japan immediately responded to this unprecedented disaster. Many churches and Christian organizations sent teams up to the disaster areas and engaged in relief work. It was quite chaotic but we felt God was leading us into the devastated communities to help the survivors with Jesus' love in our hearts. I myself was appointed as the general secretary of the Japan Evangelical Association as of April 1, 2011, right after the March 2011 disaster. On my first day as the general secretary of the national alliance, I woke up in a sleeping bag at a student dormitory of the Baptist Seminary in Sendai and I went around the disaster areas to deliver relief supplies at churches and evacuation centers. I was so overwhelmed by the tremendous devastation, but at the same time we all were assured that the Holy Spirit was working among us to bring the love and compassion of Jesus Christ to those who were suffering.

Dr. Brian Stiller, the Global Ambassador of World Evangelical Alliance, visited Japan in October 2011 and used the expression "punching above the weight" in reference to a boxer who is fighting the opponent above his weight class, to illustrate how the small churches of Japan are daringly attacking the enormous task of responding to this massive disaster. The percentage of Christians in Japan has been less than one percent for many years. There are about 8,000 Protestant churches in Japan and the average size of a church is about 30 to 40 members. In the Tohoku region, where the disaster hit, the churches are even more scarce and small—especially along the Pacific coastline where the tsunami has washed away many towns. Along the 250 kilometer stretch of the Sanriku coast line, there are only eight small churches in those fishing towns.

But after the March 2011 disaster, many churches and Christian groups from other parts of Japan, along with those who came from overseas, went into Tohoku and delivered food and relief supplies, cleaned out and fixed tsunami struck houses, and provided emotional care to survivors. In many towns, municipal governments and community leaders have thanked Christian groups for their diligent work. This good reputation through relief work has certainly contributed to earning trust from people and community leaders. In Minami-Sanriku town (one of the fishing towns along the Pacific coast where no church existed previous to the March 2011 disaster), people have asked the Christian coalition to build a Christian center in their town and have donated land. Over many years, different Christian groups have tried to plant churches in this town but they were never successful due to strong community relationships that rejected "outsiders." Rev. Tatsuo Nakazawa, the director of Minami-Sanriku Christian Center, said, "It is truly amazing how God lead us to minister to these people and opened up the door to build a Christian center here. This is the beginning of Christian presence in this town."

Tohoku region has been one of the most difficult areas to evangelize in Japan. Tohoku people have a very reserved and rather introverted nature. Their family and communal ties are very strong and traditional culture and values, which include Shinto ancestor worship (Japanese indigenous religion), remain very influential. People from other parts of Japan often have difficulties fitting in and it would take many years or even generations to become accepted members of the community. They say that Tohoku people categorize their relationships into three kinds of people—outsiders, guests, and insiders. So if a person decides to follow Christ, he/she must break away from their family and community because church and Christians are so foreign and seen as "outsiders." But through relief work in response to this disaster, churches and Christians have engaged with the local community and people in meaningful ways. A pastor who has been ministering for over twenty years in the Tohoku region said, "It seems like we Christians have finally become 'guests' now rather than 'outsiders' to this community."

Rev. Yoshiya Kondo from 3.11 Iwate Church Network shared as follows:

> We were not prepared for relief work at all, but we were plunged into it and learned by experience. Since we didn't know what to do, we started by asking people what they needed. We also decided to focus on one particular area of the town where people were left out from government support. Since we came to visit regularly, people started to trust us. In the beginning, we didn't tell them that we were Christians since we did not want to evangelize in return for relief work. But as we continued to serve them sincerely, they started asking who we were and where we came from. We told

them that we were Christians and came from church. Then some of them became interested in the Bible. So we started sharing about our faith and some of them came to believe in Jesus Christ and others wanted to learn more. Things don't happen quickly in Tohoku, but the key is our integrity in Christ. When we really live out the gospel of Jesus in our daily lives, people can see the difference and start asking questions. We don't need any 'techniques' or 'methods.' In that sense, I found that relief work and evangelism are not two separate things, but rather they are integrated in the living example of Jesus Christ. The important question is not how many tracts we handed out, but how much we lived like Christ among people. So we do not come here to help people, they help us to live more like Christ.

Rev. Masashi Moriya, the principal of the Baptist Seminary in Sendai who leads the Christian coalition in Minami-Sanriku said,

> We in the Tohoku churches, are facing the challenge of a major paradigm-shift in mission. The traditional way of our evangelism was to invite people to church and then assimilate them to church culture—in a way "tearing them off" from the community. It was a more individualistic and maybe Western style of evangelism. But through this relief work experience, we have learned to go out into the community and minister to people where they are, among their family and the community. When we engage the whole community and impact them with Christ's love, we don't need to "tear them off" from the community any more. Tohoku people are very communal and that is actually similar to the biblical context of Jewish society—they are more Asian than Western, I think. So the challenge of paradigm-shift for us is to learn from the Bible itself and go out into the local community to show the love of Christ with our actions.

In Fukushima, where the nuclear power plant accident occurred, the situation is still very difficult. The fear of radiation is dividing people. Even in the same household, the grandfather who is a farmer would be concerned about the reputation of their produce. They take pride in the vegetables they grow. But a young mother with small children in the same family would be very concerned about radiation and would not like to take risks by feeding the family vegetables from their fields. Fukushima Christian Council has started the "Fukushima Hope Project" which runs retreat camps for children over weekends as well as during summer and winter vacations. Children in Fukushima are constantly under the fear of radiation, so church networks collaborated to take children out of Fukushima for weekends and let them play freely without the fear of radiation. Pastor Keiji Kida, the chair of Fukushima Christian Council said,

> We feel very powerless here since we don't know what to do. But we are learning to depend on God and work together despite our differences. The more hopeless the situation seems, the more our hope for eternal life in Jesus shines. Please pray for us and continue to visit Fukushima. We are so encouraged by seeing people from outside of Fukushima come to visit us.

Although the reports reflected regional differences, the common factor seemed to be that God is already ministering among people in local communities and that churches need to stop looking inward. We need to go out into our communities to live out the whole gospel among the people. We are not compromising the soul-winning gospel of the Lord Jesus, but actually deepening our understanding of it and acting upon it. This kind of paradigm shift, in turn, should happen elsewhere in Japan, as many churches across Japan are suffering from a lack of engagement with their local communities. I believe God has already moved a rock. It is our turn to take up the challenge of living out the whole gospel.

> God is our refuge and strength, an ever-present help in trouble. Therefore we will not fear, though the earth give way and the mountains fall into the heart of the sea, though its waters roar and foam and the mountains quake with their surging. (Psalm 46:1–3)

Questions for Reflection:

1. Kenichi talks about a paradigm shift among churches and church leaders in Japan as a result of the relief work done after the tsunami. In what ways does he see this paradigm shift? How can that impact the Japanese society from a Christian point of view?

2. How have different catastrophes and disasters affected your own context? What was the reaction of the local and national Christian community? How can the love of God be shown in these situations?

3. What is the responsibility of the global church when disasters happen? How can your own church and ministry be prepared to help people in such situations?

Kenichi Shinagawa is the General Secretary of the Japan Evangelical Association. He has a BA in Fine Arts and Architecture from Rhode Island School of Design and a MDiv from Tokyo Uniting Christ Seminary. Kenichi has pastored a local church in Tokyo for thirteen years, where he and his wife Yumiko live together with two daughters—Megumi (means grace) and Hikari (means light of the world). He has been actively involved in disaster management as the director of the national Evangelical Alliance in Japan, executive officer of the Disaster Relief Christian Network, and Disaster Response Chaplain Committee and Tokyo Disaster Preparation Project member.

CHAPTER 29

AN URBAN CHURCH IN SÃO PAULO, BRAZIL

Edeval Campos Jr.

The reality today is that 80% of the world population lives now in cities, many in megacities with an absurd concentration of people. Some of these huge metropolitan areas are bigger than whole countries.

Our local story happens in one of them, São Paulo, with around twenty million inhabitants, the eighth largest urban agglomeration in the world.

Our community, the Filadelfia Baptist Church, is located in the neighborhood of Patriarca, in the eastern part of São Paulo. It is one of the regions with the worst social and developmental indexes but which has had big investments in infrastructure during recent years due to the World Cup games held in Brazil. A large sport stadium was built close to our church. This stadium was used for the inauguration ceremony of the World Cup and was seen by billions of people in June 2014.

São Paulo reflects the whole country with all its contradictions. It is a rich city with pockets of prosperity alongside poverty, misery, areas without a basic sanitary system, violence, distribution of illegal drugs, etc.

In this context, our church could not just keep preaching the gospel without looking at the reality around us. In 1990 we started as two young pastors in a small community of thirty members, trying to help people face the high index of unemployment caused by the economic situation in the country. Our first project was a cooperative that bought food from grocery stores and resold it to people in the neighborhood for low prices. We also started an evangelization program in the center of São Paulo with street children using typical Brazilian music (samba). Soon we realized that some of these kids would like to leave the street and the question arose where we should take them. God was preparing us for a new stage, and with the help of a Brazilian partner organization and resources from Sweden we were able to buy a house that functioned for eleven years as a place of refuge, healing, and restoration of many boys and girls. All of them are now living with families, far from the streets, and writing the rest of their story in a very different way from the path they started on.

Our local church has established a missional identity integrating the word of God into daily life and applying it to our context. We cannot any longer see a neighbor suffering and be indifferent. We must act. Today we have a well developed social project that works to prevent the social vulnerabilities in our region, offering educational activities such as extra classes for teenagers so they are not attracted to drugs and criminality on the streets. In spite of negative statistics in the city and the pessimism of social sciences regarding the recovering of young criminals, we have something to offer that goes beyond human understanding. That is the gospel as God's power to restore, release, and heal. (Isaiah 66:1). We have seen the reality of this miracle of transformation that includes both conversion and restoration.

Today we have also worked among people who are homeless. The homeless have been increasing due to the economic and social crisis and to illegal migration from Bolivia and Haiti. With some (small) resources and volunteers from the church we have been able to help several homeless people leave the street and their shelters under bridges to find their families again or to get their own housing. This makes them citizens again who can take part in society. It has also been a way of engaging new converts in the church in ministry and to help them feel that they are useful. Although it is more a kind of an emergency project that does not change social structures in the city, it has given credibility to the church and is an access for us to help many people.

We believe in an integral gospel and continue teaching and proclaiming it in all its extension. Quantitative growth is not the most important but we have been able to reach people of different social classes, including middle and upper classes, and the church has grown. The good news has come to the poor but we must not forget that it needs to be taken to all human beings, regardless of their social condition. Rich people have also their needs and the gospel message is important for them as well.

We believe that all Christians have gifts, talents, and ministries that should be used for the kingdom of God. We think that to be church is not merely to meet in a Sunday service, but to live and daily incarnate the gospel in the midst of a society that is increasingly more materialistic and egoistic but also weakened in its social structures. We do that going against the strong wave of new-Pentecostalism in Brazil with its theologies of prosperity and exploitation that force people to pay a "sacrifice" in order to be blessed, but without seeing any change in their life situation.

We believe also in a participative and shared leadership, without the centralized power of a super-leader. We are servants and as pastors we have both responsibility and authority given by God. However this authority does not mean dominion over people. The model is Jesus and it shows that to serve is revolutionary and it breaks down barriers and changes paradigms. We have opted for team leadership from the beginning and today we are four ordained pastors and a group of more than twenty leaders.

We believe also that God's calling is not just for our neighborhood and city but also for the whole world. The commission of the Lord is very clear: "Go into all the world." The local needs should not hinder us from obeying the wonderful and at the same time unexplainable order of Jesus. God calls whom he wants, when he wants and calls us to go where he wants. As a missional community we have strongly participated in cross-cultural missions, sending out people from our local church, supporting them financially and spiritually while they are working in basically all continents and in our own country. This has been a great blessing to us, knowing that in spite of being small in comparison to the challenges and few in comparison to the needs, we have been part of God's great commission and we will see in heaven men and women from every language, tribe, and nation as the fruit of our engagement.

One practical example of how we have been blessed giving priority to mission is the fact that we have been able to buy a larger property than we rented earlier as well as the neighboring house that gives us space for our teaching program. Our old building is now being used for the social projects.

In the urban context we have also planted five new churches that today have their autonomy, being also missional under their own leadership. We have also cooperated with other churches and organizations, leaving aside denominational differences and working with a kingdom mentality.

To be a "church in mission" could sound as a repetition of terms. In fact, what would be the function of a church if it were not in mission? In the postmodern context of our society, living in a globalized world that more and more follows similar patterns, it is crucial that we are churches with a New Testament DNA that repeats the words of the apostles: "We cannot help speaking about what we have seen and heard" (Acts 4:17). We need to be churches committed to the integral gospel, taking the whole gospel to all people in all places. We need to be a church that has compassion and lives in a merciful way, without discriminating against anybody.

We are in mission, a pilgrim church that knows that she is here for a limited time. Our final home is not here but while we are here we are called to proclaim the good news to all. This is a brief description of who we are, a church in an urban context, that tries to listen to God's voice and to be a godly reference for those who live in our city, showing the heavenly Father's grace and compassion.

Questions for Reflection

1. In this story, how does "one thing lead to another?" What does this tell us about how God likes to build a ministry step by step?
2. How does the gospel bring about social transformation as well as the transformation of individuals? What limits the social transformation? Are there ways of addressing that?
3. How can a church, largely built among the urban poor, still engage in world mission?

Edeval Campos Jr. is a Baptist pastor who has worked since 1991 in the megacity of São Paulo, Brazil. He is married to Sandra and they have two children, Anne Sophie and Philipe. Edeval has a BTh from the Independent Baptist Theological Seminary in Campinas and postgraduate studies (DMin in Missiology) from the South American Theological Faculty in Londrina. He teaches Integral Mission in several theological seminaries and leads a local church strongly involved in holistic mission in its neighborhood.

CHAPTER 30

REMEMBER WHEN

Bruce Huseby

You remember them—leisure suits, pet rocks, disco, pukka shell necklaces, walkmans, ska, the list of trends that come and go could go on and on. Marketers depend on it. The fashion, entertainment, and technology fields thrive because of them. It's rather intimidating that my super cool latest edition iPhone is already obsolete when this goes to press—it's so yesterday.

Trends in ministry are no different in many ways. The Christian marketers bank on it. We have seen seeker-driven, seeker-sensitive, mega church models, meta-models, purpose driven models, forty days of this, thirty days of that. A few years ago I was asked to teach and speak at a seminary in Africa. Huge banners hung across the campus for different seminars coming to the campus. The "Purpose Driven Church" conference was coming as well as "The Prayer of Jabez" conference. I couldn't help but pointing out to my African brothers and sisters that just because it comes from the West doesn't mean they should accept it because most things from the West are seldom contextualized to local cultures. I pointed out that in the West we have a Prayer of Jabez for Children, a Prayer of Jabez for Youth, a Prayer of Jabez coffee mug, computer mouse pads, and Prayer of Jabez neckties. Probably somewhere, someone made Prayer of Jabez breath mints which I am sure if you ate enough of them you truly would expand your borders. I could tell I struck a raw nerve with the administration. I have never been asked to speak at that seminary again. While this may sound overly critical of the authors of these books and seminars, please understand that I pray their original intent was noble to articulate a truth God had taught them. The problem is when placed in the hands of marketers, best intentions often go out the window. Who wouldn't want their book or seminar to go around the world?

The world of mission is not exempt. In recent years a needed focus was made on the unreached people groups of the world. Luis Bush coined the term the "10-40 Window." The 90s saw a flood of churches adopt an unreached people group and focus on the window. These were people groups that had never heard of Jesus or been exposed to the truths of the Bible. This was needed information and a needed correction for church mission programs. The problem was that many churches abandoned global servants and initiatives that were "outside the window." This caused great pain in the global body of Christ. It is still my prayer that every church will consider how they can help reach an unreached or unengaged people group. At the same time we must consider that with globalization and migration, many in that people group may live outside the "window" just as easily right next door to where you live.

"Partnerships" was the buzzword in the late 1990s and early in the 2000s. The mission world was excited about partnering with local churches, networks of organizations, and national leadership. While many partnerships that are truly interdependent do exist, by and large most "partnerships" are little more than networks of individuals and organizations sharing information that closely guard their agendas rather than a true "kingdom" agenda. Even national partnerships floundered because agreement could not be reached on basic purpose. A meeting of a national partnership was held in a former Soviet republic with nationals and global servants. They accomplished little because the "partnership" was divided over those that were there to reach the unreached people group and those who were there to reach their nation. It is interesting that today the partnership is thriving under national leadership with no global servants as part of the equation. The secret of success was the nationals wanted to be "the church" and reach all people, including special efforts to engage the unreached people group. Again, we should not stop partnering, but make partnerships truly about interdependence. This is a tall order for the Western church and for many in the global East.

Today the trend is to be "missional." This word has been used for centuries going back to people like Puritan Richard Baxter. It is used convincingly in Christopher Wright's book, "The Mission of God." Wright advocates a strong missional lifestyle based on the whole counsel of God's Word and nature of God. So, what is trendy about being missional? It seems that everybody is talking about it, but few can define it. At a recent convention held in the US I sat in a session with a group of "missional experts." The first question was to define what missional means. Most of the answers defined nothing. Finally, a clear answer I heard was, "I don't like the term."

Sharing the good news of Jesus through actions and words is the responsibility of every follower of Christ. An early problem with the missional movement in the United States was that their world was very small in which to be salt and light. The movement left out three important words in Matthew 28:19—"of all nations." The missional movement was about us, our neighborhoods, and our cities. I praise God for this focus, but it is was too small in vision and not taking into account the challenge of Jesus and the actions of the early church. As a result, many missionaries serving globally were cut off by their churches. The role of a Missions Pastor or Director seemed to be a short blip in church history. Now it became fashionable to hire people in of the cool position of "Pastor of Missional Living."

Do you remember Edgar Allen Poe's classic tale, "The Pit and the Pendulum?" In it the pendulum is razor sharp and meant to slice. If a pendulum is going to cut anything it is going to be the most effective at the center between the two extremes. Trends are like that pendulum. Often people think they want to be cutting edge, but that edge is on the fringes instead of at the center and biblically balanced. I would love to see missional in North America become a term to use, but used in the way the rest of the world uses it with proper balance of being "witnesses" in word and deed from our neighborhoods to the nations. A balance may have been struck and the term is being used in more and more everyday conversations with more of the meaning espoused by Christopher Wright. Time will tell if the missional movement is a trend that soon becomes just another blip of missions history. It may face the same pendulum shifts that the "10-40 Window" and "Partnerships" faced.

Now it seems that poverty and justice ministries have taken center stage. These are needed corrections as often mission work focused only on evangelism and church planting. At the Third Congress of World Evangelization in Cape Town, Pastor John Piper stated, "If there rises in your heart a resistance to the phrase "eternal suffering," or if there rises in your heart a resistance to the phrase "all suffering;" if resistance rises to either one of those, either we have a defective view of hell or a defective heart." Unfortunately, I am hearing of many who are sliding into doing justice without Jesus and providing for the poor without communicating the gospel. Piper went on to say, "When the gospel takes root in our souls, it impels us outward to all unjust human suffering ... when the gospel takes root in our souls, it awakens us to the horrible reality of eternal suffering in hell under the wrath of a just God. And it impels us out to rescue the perishing." The danger I am already seeing is once again churches thinking to be relevant are deserting church planting workers and replacing them with development workers. Why can't we have both in balance?

Trends often bring needed focus on areas that have long been ignored. Most of us in the world will continue to be affected by trends. Many or even most of us get caught up in the here and now without spending adequate time praying and seeing how we keep doing what Christ modeled for each believer in making disciples. We like to be cutting edge so often a tendency to strongly criticize the church for not doing what they are supposed to be doing surfaces. Let us remember to keep the primacy of the local church as God's primary means of equipping and sending of disciples to the nations. Sometimes it might be good not to be considered trendy, but known for doing the basics well.

Questions for Reflection
1. How does marketing sometimes distort mission?
2. Why do you think we move from one trend to another? Which current ones do you find most helpful, and which ones do you have reservations about? Why?
3. How do you understand the word "missional"? How might we use it more carefully?

Rev. Bruce Huseby serves as Pastor of Global Ministries at Calvary Church in Grand Rapids, Michigan. He had previously served in student ministries for twenty-five years in local churches. For the past sixteen years his focus has been on global ministries. Bruce serves in leadership for the Central Asia Consultation, the North American Central Asia Forum, the Global Leadership Council of the Mission Commission of the World Evangelical Alliance. He also serves on the Advisory Board for *Evangelical Missions Quarterly*. Bruce is married and has four children and seven grandchildren.

CHAPTER 31

THREE STORIES FROM SOUTHERN AFRICA

Willie Crew and John Scholtz

Zimbabwe: Five Hundred and Counting

Willie Crew

Pastor Simon never made a decision to become a pastor. But somehow he ended up with five hundred churches in Zimbabwe.

Simon W. Mukolo was born in 1937 to Methodist parents. Although he grew up in a religious family he only committed his life to the Lord in 1963. By the year 1994 he had planted four hundred churches, a number that has by now stretched to around five hundred—he is no longer counting.

Simon felt a conviction to tell people about Jesus Christ, so in 1965 he went to Kamativi, a small mining town in western Zimbabwe, and took up work at the tin mine there. He witnessed to the townspeople, mostly miners. They were healed and delivered and they were saved. In discipling them, Simon automatically became their pastor.

His passion for reaching the lost became contagious and his congregation joined Pastor Simon in witnessing. On the weekends he encouraged the people to go to their hometowns in the rural areas and tell people about Christ.

So the church branched out and started to bud. But there was no one to look after the plants. It was Simon's foreman, an Anglican, who suggested that he had the calling of a priest on his life and gave him leave to go look after the newborn churches.

The second church he planted was in his hometown of Hwange. His congregation started meeting in a classroom. As in Kamativi, he urged the people to go out and start more churches, and he would do the follow-up.

But the abandonment of the spirit world and even the conflict with traditional religion would not come unchallenged. The church meetings were reported to the authorities who then closed off the classrooms to them. So they met outside. And although those meetings were also protested, the church kept growing and branching out.

Pastor Simon is truly one of God's commissioned generals in Africa. Now in his seventies he is preparing to cross the border and plant churches in neighboring countries, ever thankful to God for continuously using him to reach out to people. Their salvation is evidence of God's power.

Mozambique: A Guide to Defeating Your Predators

Willie Crew

When breaking new ground in church planting there will always be predators. In the African animistic culture those predators are often concealed, and though unseen are very real.

I met Pastor Felix five months after he had been involved in a terrible car accident. Fourteen people had died and almost sixty had suffered severe injuries and amputations. And while some of the victims were still in the hospital, Pastor Felix was sitting across from me without a scratch, beaming as he ran his fingers across a hand-drawn map of the province in Mozambique where he works.

Northern Mozambique has been a mission endeavor for Pastor Felix for the past three years. Originally from Angoche, a town on the southern coast of the province, he has been planting churches in various towns and villages with his colleague, Pastor Mario. The two of them now oversee twenty-nine church plants, travelling hundreds of kilometers by bus and bicycle each month to visit them.

Being a predominantly animistic but also Muslim region there were certain conflicts to be reckoned with, but foresight could not hinder their challenges. Cholera outbreaks, cyclone attacks, break-ins, and witchcraft have cost lives, destroyed churches, and forced the pastors to flee. But setbacks like these have not caused the pastors to stagger, since ultimately they led to growth and encouragement.

One animistic superstition that Pastor Felix came across is that a person is not welcome in the community until he is greeted by the animals. And not in the way Snow White was. The first animal Pastor Felix was greeted by was a snake. Then one evening as he was taking out the dustbin, the pastor found himself approached by a hyena.

Now, African culture associates hyenas with treachery, un-cleanliness, and gluttony, most likely since their powerful jaws and digestive system allow them to eat their whole prey including skin, teeth, horns, and bones. They are scavengers and yet predators in the most primitive way.

The pastor's natural instinct nudged him to run back into the house. But he heard the Lord telling him, "Don't run." So he stopped moving. The hyena halted in turn. He didn't know what to do next, so he took three steps toward the animal. The hyena leapt a few meters to the side and stopped again to look at the pastor. So again the pastor took authority and went towards the hyena, at which point it ran off and disappeared behind the neighboring houses. The pastor went on to throw out the garbage.

Now, Pastor Felix is a wonderful storyteller and as he sat there across from me he told me one petrifying testimony after the other, but with such a pacifying smile he could have been singing lullabies. The spirit within him would not be held back by threats from religious groups or attempts on the life of the church. His vision is to plant another twenty-one churches in the province in the coming three years, predators or no predators.

Testimony of a Church in Mission

John Scholtz

When we released our local church to get on with the work of the ministry they began to significantly impact our city and our continent.

We are on the southern coast of Africa in Port Elizabeth, which means we are off the beaten track, but our people began to reach into the city, the nation, and the nations of Africa in a remarkable way.

Grant, who has an agricultural degree, started a trust called "Bountiful Grains" and got involved in "Farming God's Way." They train a minimum tillage farming method all over Africa. Increases in yields of up to ten times what rural farmers were getting before are now regular stories.

Ena started "Siya Sebenza" which means "we are working" and trains local folk how to be good employees or entrepreneurs. As their minds become renewed through the gospel many are coming to know Jesus, and she is seeing dozens of previously hopeless young people find fulfilment.

Sharron started the "Gogo Trust" which empowers grandmothers to look after AIDS orphaned children within the community and makes a way for their future.

"Bet Shekoom," started by Gary and Shelley, is a ministry to destitute women, most of whom have been prostitutes and drug addicts. The girls have found a safe home and grow vegetables. The pimps are not happy.

Maryna developed a preschool curriculum called "Action Child Mobilization" which is being used all over Africa. In one country in East Africa alone we have over nine hundred Muslim children attending these preschools.

Ingrid collects some Christian friends on a Saturday morning and takes them to needy people to make a difference. She calls it "Hands On."

Daniel is an architect, and after he went on a weekend mission with his Zone Pastor and some friends he got so inspired that he came back and started building a house for a refugee couple. He plans to build more.

One of our small groups goes every year to a school in a rural area some distance from the city. Every year they have done something to improve the community's life there and it is beginning to show.

Elmarie's heart was broken by abandoned babies. After years of making her home a place of refuge and arranging adoptions, the Bangaliso Trust came into existence.

Kobus and Lynette left the business world and opened a boarding house for the homeless and now look after between four and five hundred people, many of them destitute.

Richard and Kemi have five aftercare facilities looking after over five hundred underprivileged children in a ministry they call "House of Wells."

Gavin was the headmaster of our school, but is now involved in Christian education across the continent. In the DRC alone he has had direct input into the curriculum of 17,000 schools through training in biblical worldview. It involves some eighteen million children.

It does not end there, and the exciting thing is that most of what has happened has had nothing to do with us as the leaders of the church.

Questions for Reflection:

1. These three short stories tells us about local initiatives of both church planting and care for people in society. What are the similar stories from your own church and ministry context?

2. How do you see the role of "lay people" in your church community? How can church and mission leaders encourage and prepare local Christians for initiatives like the ones mentioned in this chapter?

Willie Crew and his wife Lydia are founders and directors of the World Mission Centre, based in South Africa. The WMC was established in 1989 with the purpose of awakening a deeper understanding of missions and to mobilize Christians at a local level.

John Scholtz is senior pastor of the Harvest Christian Church in Port Elizabeth, South Africa, and one of the directors of the World Mission Centre.

CHAPTER 32

CHURCH-BASED TRAINING

Paul Ng

Training in missions has been carried out by mission organizations for a considerable period of time. Not only are they well organized and well researched, the trainers are also well trained. In the light of this, has the church anything to add to the training that is available today? The answer is a resounding yes.

First there is something only the church can do. It is to act as a model to other churches as to how a church should function. Until one actually goes through the challenges and the joys and heartaches of running a church, he is only able to impart knowledge and maybe even skill. The ability to cope with grief, to react with compassion and passion, to handle the many lessons arising out of crisis points in the church life are all picked up in the course of running the church. These are the key points that will make a difference when churches do training in church planting.

Another factor to bear in mind is that mission organizations tend to specialize in some area or other. A new church plant, and even a church that is growing, quickly raises the need to address many different issues. These include bringing together people of different generations, for instance, and integrating a broad spectrum of ministries, such as Sunday School, youth work, small groups, worship, etc. Most churches would include all of these and not just one or two specific ministries. Churches are thus best placed to conduct generalized training. Mission organizations are usually better at more specialized training.

Second is the cost factor. Many of the training functions carried out in churches are by volunteers. These are people who have the requisite skills and who are doing training without being paid for it. Often these volunteers are highly capable individuals who would have to be paid considerable sums of money to conduct training. As part of their contribution towards the work of God, they are prepared to do it without charge.

In some cases, these volunteers even join short-term mission teams to do training in the mission field at their own costs. If members take up this challenge and not rely upon the church to pay for their travelling costs, much resource can be released to sow into the mission field itself. Thus in the church where I worship, teams of people go regularly at their own expense to do equipping in churches, amongst undergraduates and even with pastors and workers.

Third is the fact that members of churches are working in the marketplace. While we are used to thinking of the mission field as nations and even people groups, the fact remains that the marketplace is the largest mission field in the world. Full time ministers and those working in mission organizations have little access to the marketplace. It is those working in the marketplace who have access to it. Johnson and Rundle see "Marketplace Ministry," "Business As Mission," "Tentmaking," and "Enterprise Development" as part of a broader movement which could be termed the first great missions movement of the twenty-first century.[1]

If we examine who does the training for the people involved in this movement, it is clear that many are from parachurch organizations. Churches have yet to grasp this paradigm change that the marketplace is a mission field. Consequently there is little support for this ministry in churches and those interested have to seek their equipping largely from para-church organizations who have been swift to see the paradigm change. However the training resources continue to reside in the church. If there was more support in the church, more equipping could be done for ministry in the marketplace. Similarly as regards business as missions, it is easier to train business people to do evangelism, discipleship, and coaching than it is to train pastors, missionaries, and ministry workers to become business people. Yet many strategies regarding unreached people groups center on sending people who have no business skills to run a business as a means to gain access to restricted access nations. The church can through its training process equip people who can disciple, teach, and even minister. When their members are released into the mission field they can function well not only in their secular jobs but in ministry areas as well.

While there is still a need for parachurch organizations to do training, there is a need to encourage churches to see that they can do training themselves. In fact they have much to offer.

Questions for Reflection:

1. Is the church-based training Paul Ng suggests possible in all churches, or mostly only in larger churches?
2. In your own church, which areas of training are intentionally and effectively carried out? How? What more could be done?
3. What are some of the particular opportunities and particular challenges for those engaged in "business as mission"?

Reference

Neal Johnson and Steve Rundle. 2006. Distinctives and Challenges of Business as Mission. In *Business as Mission*. Ed., Johnson and Rundle. Pasadena, CA: William Carey Library.

---

1   Neal Johnson and Steve Rundle, *Distinctives and Challenges of Business as Mission*, http://www.faith-at-work.net/Docs/DistinctivesAndChallengesOfBusinessAsMission.pdf, 23–24.

Paul Ng has had more than twenty years experience in equipping pastors, church planters, and marketplace ministers in Asia, Russia, Australia, South Africa, and the Middle East. He graduated with a Doctor of Ministry from Singapore Bible College.

CHAPTER 33

UNREACHED PEOPLE PARTNERSHIP IN CENTRAL ASIA

A Christian Brother

It all started in 1992. Freedom had come to the former Soviet Union. Throngs of Westerners poured into Eastern Europe, Russia, and Ukraine. To the eastern newly established countries, few went. During this time, our church went with the throngs into the region, but we were also concerned about others who had never heard of Jesus to the east. We began to pray that God would show us how to reach an unreached people group. It was during this time a church staff member introduced us to Olga.[1] She told us of her new country, and the millions of ethnic people who had never heard of Jesus. As a church, we knew God had spoken and we began "adopting" Olga's people.

In 1992 there were an estimated five known local believers among the millions within the borders of Olga's country. Pioneering work began. Community development, radio, libraries, computer labs began to spring up. Soon, more and more workers began to go to reach these wonderful people with the good news of Jesus.

We asked, what do we do as a church? The obvious decision was to help resource new ministries, but giving money alone wasn't really going to engage our people. During these early years, an organization called Interdev began a partnership meeting focused on Central Asia. Connecting with that meeting as well as a North American Partnership for that nation helped us as a church understand the spiritual climate, challenges, and needs of the area. We began to partner with organizations, workers, and other churches to pray, strategize, and begin new initiatives. More and more local people started coming to Christ and a holistic wave of ministries was in full force. We began to mobilize short-termers and career workers in the region. Pastoral training, youth training, leadership training, church planting, and many other efforts began.

I will never forget meeting Almuz. She was a local believer who had come to Jesus about a year before I met her. Shortly after she trusted Christ, she longed to tell her family. Many told her not to because her family may not just disown her, but also harm her. She boldly

---

1   All names are changed for security reasons.

was willing to die for her faith; she had to share the gospel with her family. The day I met Almuz I also met her brother and sister. I then met friends who the brother and sister had seen come to Jesus. Those friends introduced me to friends they saw accept Christ. Their friends introduced me to ... well, you get the point. In that room were five reproducing generations of disciples that resulted from one woman's willingness to stand for Jesus. Almuz became an inspiration for me to do whatever it took for us as a church to be involved. Instead of just attending partnership meetings, we looked for ways to engage. This resulted in training venues and wonderful models of business as mission.

In 2006 the progress we had seen came to an abrupt halt. Almost every foreign worker was kicked out of the country. Churches were forced underground. Most of the projects we had funded were closed. Olga's country is now listed in the top ten of most persecuted countries. The North American Partnership was rocked as many churches withdrew. It became apparent that some had been committed to the workers, not the people group.

As we sought the Lord, it became apparent that he wasn't finished reaching the nation. The national believers rose to the task of leading their young church in this land. We also became more keenly aware of the millions from this nation who lived in neighboring lands. This helped us move beyond geographical borders and helped us more fully engage with the entire region of Central Asia. We are now twenty years into our quest to reach an unreached people group, and the estimate of local believers varies; most put it around 5,000. Out of twenty-eight million, that means the vast majority still has not heard of Jesus.

What has this taught us that may help you as you consider engaging with an unreached people group?

1. Seek the Lord—pray for his guidance.
2. Research—the "Joshua Project" website is a great resource: http://www.joshuaproject.net.
3. Adopt an unreached people group (UPG) that is connected to a partnership (most UPGs fall into this category—because of security reasons, we are not publishing those; if God calls you to a particular group, contact the publisher and we will seek to connect you with a partnership).
4. After connections are made, schedule a trip to visit this people group.
5. Commit to this people group for the long haul. This will require total buy-in from church leadership.
6. Creatively communicate with your church about the UPG.
7. Form a team committed to pray for this group, and think through how God could use your church to engage.

I am convinced that we would not still be part of ministry to this area of the world if it were not for the strong relationship we have built through the partnership formed in this region. These entities can be messy at times, but they are worth it. I have often heard a partnership mantra that uses that great African proverb, may we never lose sight of its importance: "If you want to go quickly, go alone—if you want to go far, go together."

Questions for Reflection:

1. God is sovereign, and the Holy Spirit is not bound by the political changes seen in this narrative. How should we respond to events like these, as doors appear to open and then shut?

2. What can we learn from prayers in the Bible to help us pray for the spread of the gospel where the authorities suppress it?

POSTSCRIPT

Bertil Ekström

The "trialogue" between biblical and historical theology, ecclesiology, and missiology is at the same time an exciting and a challenging exercise. When our current study group under the Global Missiology Task Force of the WEA Mission Commission met for the first time in Glasgow in April 2013, there was a clear sense that we should try to engage in this triad: gospel, church, and mission. Not because we lacked resources on each of these areas, but more because we wanted to discover further how they interrelate and what voices from different cultural contexts have to say about it.

The majority of the texts in this book discuss the relationship between gospel, church, and mission from a missiological perspective. That is the context in which the WEA Mission Commission operates. As reflective practitioners it would also be natural to look at it from both theoretical and practical angles. Much more could be said, of course, and we believe these rich chapters play a role in that broader conversation that must continue. Ours is certainly not a "final word" of the discussion around the role of the church in God's mission, but it does offer some new and important insights and perspectives. We have avoided any idea of writing a "manual" for the church in mission or suggesting easy steps to success in church planting or in mission enterprise. It is a sincere and honest discussion that critically reveals both the strengths and the weaknesses of our common effort to be faithful to the Great Commission and the Great Commandment.

My hope as editor is that you as reader have also discovered the Trinitarian emphasis in this book. Not equally in each chapter but as a whole. The gospel is about God's salvation plan through his Logos, the incarnated Word, Jesus Christ, a Word made alive and understandable by the Spirit; the church is the body of Christ, formed by God's chosen people and transformed by the regeneration of the Spirit; the mission is God's mission, exemplified and commanded by Jesus and led and empowered by the Holy Spirit.

A missional (or mission-shaped) church, sensitive to the guidance of the Spirit, is an urgent necessity in the chaotic world we live in. More than discussing the right use of terms or the hegemony of certain models of church planting and church engagement in society, it is time for a collaborative effort in order to make a genuine difference in each place where God has established and is establishing Christian communities. Our credibility as followers of Jesus does not depend on well-formulated strategies but on concrete actions that demonstrate God's love. And it is the whole church that needs to be involved, which includes the local congregations, the national and global Church bodies, the mission organizations, and all the Christian entities that promote kingdom values.

Church in Mission: Foundations and Global Case Studies contributes to this conversation and therefore to transformative and creative initiatives which advance the kingdom of God worldwide.

Throughout the production of this resource, our prayer has been that the study of this book would stimulate a deeper reflection on the nature and role of the church today and in the coming years; but also that we all take more seriously the transformational task given to us by our Lord Jesus Christ to "make disciples." After rereading the chapters several times that prayer is even more relevant for me now, realizing the challenges of being "church in mission" today. At the same time we can all celebrate the many good things God is doing through his church around the globe.

Bertil Ekström, Sweden-Brazil

APPENDIX

Mission Commission Books
World Evangelical Alliance

In Chronological Order of Production

Williams, Theodore, ed. 1979. *World Missions: Building Bridges or Barriers*. Bangalore, India: Evangelical Literature Service Press.

———. 1983. *Together in Mission*. Bangalore, India: Diocesan Press.

Jaffarian, Michael, Loh Hoe Peng, Phyllis Howard, Marnie Toh, eds. 1989. *World Directory of Missions Research and Information Centres*. Singapore, SCEM.

Lane, Denis. 1990. *Tuning God's New Instruments: A Handbook for Missions from the Two-Thirds World*. World Evangelical Fellowship Missions Commission in partnership with Overseas Missionary Fellowship. Littleton, CO: OMF Books.

Windsor, Raymond. 1990. *World Directory of Missionary Training Centers*. Singapore: World Evangelical Fellowship Mission Commission.

Bush, Luis. 1990. *Funding Third World Missions: The Pursuit of True Christian Partnership*. Singapore: World Evangelical Fellowship Missions Commission. Title change in 1991 to *Funding Two-Thirds World Missions: The Pursuit of True Christian Partnership*.

Taylor, William D., ed. 1991. *Internationalising Missionary Training: A Global Perspective*. Milton Keynes, UK: Paternoster Press; Grand Rapids, MI: Baker Book House. Translated into Portuguese and Spanish.

———, ed. 1994. *Kingdom Partners for Synergy in Missions*. Pasadena, CA: William Carey Library.

Ferris, Robert W., ed. 1995. *Establishing Missionary Training: A Manual for Programme Developers*. Pasadena, CA: William Carey Library.

Harley, David. 1995. *Preparing to Serve: Training for Cross-Cultural Mission*. Pasadena, CA: William Carey Library. Translated into Spanish and Portuguese.

Windsor, Raymond. 1995. *World Directory of Missionary Training Programmes*. Pasadena, CA: William Carey Library.

Brynjolfson, Rob, and Jonathan Lewis, eds. 1995. *Becoming an Intentionally Intercultural Church: A Manual to Facilitate Transition*. Pasadena, CA: William Carey Library.

Lewis, Jonathan, ed. 1996. *Working Your Way to the Nations: A Guide to Effective Tentmaking*. Downers Grove: IVP. Translated into Portuguese, Spanish, French, Chinese, Arabic.

Taylor, William D., ed. 1997. *Too Valuable to Lose: Exploring the Causes and Cures of Missionary Attrition*. Pasadena, CA: William Carey Library. Translated into Portuguese, Spanish, Korean.

Hoke, Steve, and William Taylor. 1999. *Send Me! Your Journey to the Nations.* Pasadena, CA: William Carey Library.

Taylor, William D., ed. 2000. *Global Missiology for the 21st Century: The Iguassu Dialogue.* Grand Rapids, MI: Baker Academic. Translated into Portuguese, Spanish, Korean.

Mission Commission Staff Team. 2001. *Starting and Strengthening National Mission Movements.* Belleville, ON, Canada: World Evangelical Fellowship Missions Commission.

O'Donnell, Kelly, ed. 2002. *Doing Member Care Well: Perspectives and Practices from Around the World.* Pasadena, CA: William Carey Library. Translated into Portuguese, Spanish.

Tiplady, Richard, ed. 2003. *One World or Many: The Impact of Globalisation on Mission.* Pasadena, CA: William Carey Library. Translated into Spanish.

Brynjolfson, Rob, and Jonathan Lewis, eds., 2006. *Integral Ministry Training: Design and Evaluation.* Pasadena, CA: William Carey Library. Translated into Portuguese, Spanish, Korean.

Hay, Rob, Valerie Lim, Detlef Blöcher, Japp Ketelaar, and Sarah Hay, eds. 2007. *Worth Keeping: Global Perspectives on Best Practice in Missionary Retention.* Pasadena, CA: William Carey Library. Translated into Portuguese, Spanish.

Dowsett, Rose, ed. 2011. *Global Mission: Reflections and Case Studies in Contextualization for the Whole Church.* Pasadena, CA: William Carey Library. Translated into Portuguese.

Taylor, William, Tonica van der Meer, and Reg Reimer, eds. 2012. *Sorrow and Blood: Christian Mission in Contexts of Suffering, Persecution, and Martyrdom.* Pasadena, CA: William Carey Library. Translated into Portuguese and Spanish.

INDEX

World Evangelical Alliance

The Mission Commission of the World Evangelical Alliance

The WEA Mission Commission is an international and inter-generational community of global mission leaders proactively reflecting on shared issues in order to advance God's mission. As disciples of Jesus we stand with national and regional mission movements and global networks as instruments to assist churches to engage in mission. When the WEA MC gathers reflective practitioners in dependence upon the Spirit, a platform and space is created to address crucial mission issues and apply them to concrete ministry contexts. For more information go to mc.worldea.org